The International Monetary System

The International Monetary System

Beyond the First Stage of Reform

J. Carter Murphy

American Enterprise Institute for Public Policy Research
Washington, D.C.

J. Carter Murphy is professor of economics at Southern Methodist University and was senior staff economist for the President's Council of Economic Advisers in 1971–1972.

Library of Congress Cataloging in Publication Data

Murphy, John Carter, 1921-
The international monetary system.

(Studies in economic policy) (AEI studies ; 259)
1. International finance. 2. Foreign exchange.
I. Title. II. Series. III. Series: American
Enterprise Institute for Public Policy Research.
AEI studies ; 259.
HG3881.M88 332.4'5 79-23483
ISBN 0-8447-3362-8

AEI Studies 259

Printed in the United States of America

CONTENTS

PREFACE

Five years of experience with managed floating exchange rates and ratification of the comprehensive second amendment to the charter of the International Monetary Fund provide an appropriate opportunity for stock-taking in international monetary affairs. In this study I have attempted to gain perspective on the experience with floating rates and on the meaning of the International Monetary Fund's amendments so as to identify problems and policy options that lie ahead of us.

As I complete the writing, commentators in many quarters are still deploring the decline in value of the dollar during 1977–1978 and are calling for a return to fixed or quasi-fixed exchange rates. But this is nostalgia. Fixed rates are no more a viable alternative for the 1980s than they were for the 1970s, since the maintenance of fixed exchange rates requires a greater degree of international coordination of countries' economic policies than present political institutions can achieve, or even should achieve. In my view, the goal of fixed exchange rates, despite its superficial appeal, should be set aside for the foreseeable future.

This is not to say that governments ought never to intervene to provide depth and tone to the markets for foreign exchange or that all countries should treat their exchange rates in the same way. In general, however, governments' exchange market interventions should be brief.

While flexible exchange rates can provide each government some leeway to follow internal financial policies of its choice, the choice is not unconstrained. Economists agree that the present high international mobility of capital limits the form that a nation's demand management can take if the management is to succeed while creating minimal disturbances abroad. Indeed, I conclude on this matter that monetary and fiscal policies must meet domestic needs without affecting real interest rates if the exchange rates are to vary without improperly disrupting other countries' competitive trading positions. Policy makers have yet to face up to this constraint on their choices, and they have yet to be realistic about what demand inflation can achieve. Their misapprehensions about the nature of the system have resulted in policy choices in the 1970s that have seriously impaired world economic performance.

Remaining at the hub of a dollar-centered international economy, the United States faces unparalleled opportunities and risks. With a sufficiently restrained monetary policy this country can provide the world with a currency serving international monetary needs on an ever widening scale and can create a focus for political and economic integration. With an unrestrained monetary policy, on the other hand, the United States stands to encounter inflation much more severe than the country might have expected with similar policies in the 1960s, and our actions will contribute to sustained world economic disorder.

I am indebted to Thomas F. Johnson, of the American Enterprise Institute, for suggesting this study, but I fear that its completion has taken longer than either he or I expected. In preparing it, I have amassed debts to many other people, only a small number of whom can be mentioned here. Marina von Neumann Whitman of the University of Pittsburgh provided helpful comments and much needed encouragement after reading drafts of the first few chapters. Frank Southard of Kearns International and Thomas Willett of Claremont Men's College kindly read the entire manuscript and improved the argument at numerous points, without necessarily agreeing with all that they read. Jacques Polak of the International Monetary Fund and Paul Volcker of the Federal Reserve Bank of New York, caused the author to rethink, and rewrite, particular points in the manuscript. Mr. Volcker thoughtfully forwarded notes from Federal Reserve Bank of New York staff members which contributed to the reduction of factual errors. To a very special degree I am indebted to Gottfried Haberler of the American Enterprise Institute for reading large parts of the manuscript more than once and for offering, in his own gracious way, advice that was invariably wise. Patricia Cantrell, Takao Itagaki, and A. Wahhab Khandker went far beyond what can be expected from research assistants as they carried out the sometimes laborious statistical calculations. And above all, Gloria Jones, with extraordinary cheerfulness, willingness, and efficiency, saw the typescript of each chapter through its various stages to final form. The International Monetary Fund, the Organization for Economic Cooperation and Development, and the Morgan Guaranty Trust Company kindly provided useful unpublished data.

Behind most books there are people who tolerate with understanding the author's absentmindedness while he or she is writing. Their patience is a *sine qua non* of the undertaking. In my case, those persons have been most of all my mother and my wife, and to them with love and gratitude I dedicate the outcome of the work.

The literature of international economics is enormous, and the statistical base available for empirical analysis extensive. I have made free use of both while remaining incapable of fully exploiting either. In particular, new theoretical and empirical work appeared in 1977 and 1978 which I have not assimilated and which finds no place in the picture I have painted. Furthermore, the statistical series presented end for the most part in the spring and summer of 1978. With some effort, I might have incorporated further materials and might have extended the statistical time series a few more months. But I am convinced that, given the volume of useful materials currently being published, the time I might take to exploit the present backlog would only give rise to a new one. Hence I have gone to press with what there is. Only my readers can tell me if that decision was right. In an epilogue I have reviewed policy developments of the fall and winter of 1978–1979.

The appraisals and assessments in the study are mine. So also are the errors of fact and judgment. I hope that the appraisals may prove to be right, or at least provocative, and that the errors may prove to be few and at worst forgivable. I cannot assure the reader easy reading, for the issues considered are complex. But I can give assurance that the matters are of enormous importance and that some lessons seem, at least to me, to be written in rather bold relief. I have tried in every chapter to keep the lessons in the spotlight. If what I understand from the experience is even partially correct, it mandates a reconsideration of what we are doing, especially here in the United States.

J. Carter Murphy
Southern Methodist University
March 1979

1
Prologue

With the ratification in 1978 of a comprehensive amendment to the charter of the International Monetary Fund (IMF), the 133 member countries of that organization changed in a significant way the rules that govern international monetary relationships. This book is about the monetary system evolving out of the new practices and the new understandings.

The amendment to the charter proceeded from a set of historic compromises reached in Kingston, Jamaica, in January 1975 by the finance ministers who constituted the IMF's Interim Coordinating Committee—compromises that were described at that time as the monetary system's "first stage of reform." To the dismay of some observers, the Jamaica accord was markedly at odds with an *Outline of Reform* which had appeared in 1974 and which was itself the product of two and a half years of negotiations. One prompt and critical appraisal of the 1976 agreement was entitled "Between Outline and Outcome the Reform Was Lost,"[1] and Robert Triffin, whose 1960 book, *Gold and the Dollar Crisis,* had heralded for many the beginning of the search for strengthened international monetary arrangements, said the Jamaica accord was a "fiasco."[2] A scholarly executive director of the IMF suggested it be called a "non-reform."[3]

In fact, however, the reform is fundamental. For the core of the structure of an international monetary system is in the nature

---

[1] Fritz Machlup, in E. M. Bernstein and others, *Reflections on Jamaica,* Essays in International Finance, no. 115 (International Finance Section, Princeton University, April 1976), pp. 30-38.

[2] "Jamaica: 'Major Revision' or Fiasco," in Bernstein, *Reflections on Jamaica,* pp. 45–53.

[3] Tom de Vries, "Jamaica, or the Non-Reform of the International Monetary System," *Foreign Affairs,* vol. 54 (April 1976), pp. 577-605.

of the exchange rate regime, and between *Outline* and "outcome" a number of governments came to accept the necessity of a more permanent status for the regime of managed floating exchange rates. Early in the negotiations which led to the *Outline* a cautious preliminary agreement had called for exchange rates to be based on "stable but adjustable par values" with floating authorized in "special circumstances." The ambiguity of these words was of course intentional in order to leave room for vast differences in fundamental objectives. To many, however, the words put high priority on stability in the exchange rates and seemed to define a world of international finance little different from that which had collapsed during the 1971–1973 period. In the weeks prior to the Jamaica meeting, heads of state of Britain, France, Germany, Japan, and the United States at last acknowledged floating as a normal policy, at least for the time being, and agreed to terms that in fact make a return to mandatory par values for exchange rates remote. In the monetary system that has since been developing, the emphasis has been on exchange rate flexibility—albeit managed flexibility among blocs of countries—with market forces predominating in the determination of exchange rate levels. It is a far cry from the regime left behind, in which markets were expected, as much as possible, to adapt to officially selected and maintained exchange rates. The changes have profound implications for private traders and investors, for governments making national policies, for potential international conflicts of interest, for opportunities for international cooperation and institution building, and for the efficiency and equity with which the world's resources are employed. They also expose the world, and especially the United States, to some peril. Although it cannot penetrate the subject deeply, this book attempts to pull together a substantial body of evidence about the functioning of contemporary arrangements and seeks to identify problems left behind and some that lie ahead.

Why Bretton Woods Failed

To be clear about the strengths and weaknesses of contemporary arrangements it is necessary to turn to the recent past. What happened to the dreams of only three decades ago? Are statesmen's goals for institution building constrained in previously unrecognized ways? Or did policy makers blunder in the execution of otherwise well-laid plans? A review of the experiences under monetary rules designed at the 1943 Bretton Woods conference reveals that there were blunders, but it also suggests that constraints limit the forms that international monetary cooperation can take in the present and the years immediately ahead. While a review of the past does not need to lead to pessimism, it provides a reminder that attention must be given to foundations before dependable superstructures can be built.

A fundamental reason for failure in the Bretton Woods design is that the divergent monetary and fiscal policies of member governments made prompt exchange rate adjustments more necessary than the rules had anticipated. The IMF charter was drafted at a time of hopeful expectation that policies in industrialized countries aimed at full employment and stable prices would keep international payments imbalances small and transitory even in a world of liberalized trade and investment. Official "par values" for the exchange rates might be changed in cases of "fundamental disequilibrium," but for any country such an action was to be a policy of last resort. The IMF's resources and other reserves would finance temporary disturbances. Early successes in implementing this perception of proper financial arrangements, together with the increasing extent to which the dollar became the numeraire and vehicle currency of world commerce, prompted some writers and political leaders in the 1950s and 1960s to point expectantly to the advantages of globally integrated financial markets based on fixed exchange rates among national currencies and to dream of the day when a common international currency would be used within as well as among many nations.

Such hopes, as well as the more limited but still optimistic expectations of the architects of Bretton Woods, have not been realized. Those who want the simplicity of genuinely fixed exchange rates in this last quarter of the twentieth century are asking for the fruits of an international civilized society before the tree has grown. International monetary arrangements in the 1970s and 1980s, despite support from electronic gadgetry, a high level of professional expertise, and improving market organization, remain primitive because the political infrastructure of the world is primitive, resting as it does on ideas of sovereignty inherited from a distant past. Governments which assume major responsibility for the performance of their national economies and which are ultimately responsible to national electorates follow, when their constituents demand it, policies aimed at strictly domestic goals, even when the policies are sharply divergent from those of their neighbors. In these circumstances fixed exchange rates are incompatible with liberal trading conditions.[4]

[4] Charles Kindleberger in 1976 expressed this thought by saying that the "optimum economic area for many purposes . . . is the world. At the same

As an historical parallel to recent events, it is interesting to recall payments arrangements within the United States little more than a hundred years ago. The history of that period illustrates the fact that conditions that make possible a common currency are very demanding and can usually evolve only with time and with the integration of political institutions. Financial intermediation in the mid-nineteenth century was for the United States, as it is now for much of the world, concentrated in the country's eastern cities. Because of the relatively undeveloped state of intermediation there was substantial latitude for differences in monetary and fiscal policies among regions of the country. In these circumstances, some state legislatures spawned banks and bank credit with little restraint in order to finance their development plans. As a result, while the currency of the land had a common name, it was by no means a common currency. Notes issued by banks in the East, where credit creation was generally more restrained, were exchanged against notes from banks in the West, where credit was often more liberally extended, in markets in Baltimore, Philadelphia, and New York at premiums and discounts reflecting the relative abundance of the notes of the various regions as well as the creditworthiness of particular issuing institutions. The movements of the rates in turn influenced in some degree the course of trade and investment. Much is to be learned from this "disorderly" period of American financial history because it illustrates how market-determined exchange rates between the different regions made possible a period of rapid economic growth while monetary and fiscal policies were dominated more by local decisions than by national policies. It is probably fair to say that not until after World War I, when the nation had a much stronger sense of common purpose, when it had a central bank, and when the personal income tax had opened the way to federal, rather than state and local, domination of fiscal matters, did this nation develop a genuinely common currency.

Recent efforts in Europe to achieve a monetary union among members of the Common Market are similarly instructive. Even in this geographically compact and intensely interdependent region,

---

time the optimum social area remains relatively small, one in which the individual can find a sense of participation." Kindleberger, who has for many years argued for global integration of financial markets, still believed in 1976 that the economic forces would predominate, although he added at that time that perhaps this would be only in the long run. See his essay, "The Exchange-Stability Issue at Rambouillet and Jamaica," in Bernstein, *Reflections on Jamaica*, pp. 25-56.

the preconditions for sustained progress toward monetary union have so far been lacking.[5]

The original plan for the International Monetary Fund did not envision wholly inflexible exchange rates, although it was hoped that the need for exchange rate changes would be infrequent. In fact, however, pressures accumulated to make the rates increasingly rigid. Few par value changes were made among currencies of the twenty-two industrialized member countries of the Organization for Economic Cooperation and Development (OECD) between 1958 and 1964 and fewer between January 1964 and May 1971. Reluctance of governments to make exchange rate changes stemmed in part from the political consequences of doing so. In countries with a balance of payments surplus, an increase in the exchange value of the currency was unpopular with powerful groups involved in exporting or in competing with imports, even though it was popular—when understood—with consumers of these goods. Capital gains and losses in terms of domestic currency for those with net assets or liabilities in foreign currencies were also involved. At the very least, a decision by the government to allow a jump in the value of a currency could upset the political balance in a not entirely foreseeable way and had consequently to be regarded as a politically risky course. For deficit countries there were parallel considerations—users of internationally traded goods and debtors in foreign currencies stood to be losers, while producers of tradable goods and claimants on foreign currency stood to be gainers as a result of a depreciation. In addition, a government unable to maintain the foreign currency value of its money was vulnerable to accusations that its policies had failed. Governments initiating an exchange rate change had to take responsibility for its consequences, and some constituents would unavoidably be injured. Conrad Oort, in his 1974 lecture for the Per Jacobsson Foundation, pointed out in connection with a discussion of possibilities for small but frequent exchange rate changes that it is unrealistic to assume that governments will take responsibility for rate changes unless the need is great, which is to say that the rate change must be substantial.[6]

---

[5] The European experience has been carefully documented and assessed by Polly Reynolds Allen, *Organization and Administration of a Monetary Union*, Studies in International Finance, no. 38 (International Finance Section, Princeton University, 1976). The 1978 agreement among European governments to move toward a payments union with target zones for exchange rates is briefly discussed in Chapter 9 and the Epilogue below.

[6] *Steps to International Monetary Order* (Washington, D.C.: Per Jacobsson Foundation, 1974).

The exchange rates also became rigid because private capital movements accompanying the decisions on the changes were highly disturbing. Business firms and also governments and central banks that anticipated a change in par values of currencies naturally shifted assets from currencies expected to depreciate to those expected to appreciate. But such "prudent" shifts of funds, often amounting to hundreds of millions, even billions, of dollars on critical days, constituted disruptive shocks to the sensitive financial structure. Outside the United States, the shifts corresponded to rapid redistributions of reserve assets among countries and to disruptions in central bank efforts to maintain balanced domestic monetary policies. Flights of funds from the United States were not disruptive to U.S. markets in quite the same way as in other countries so long as foreign central banks which received the funds placed them once again in U.S. commercial bank deposits or money-market instruments. But flights from the dollar destroyed international reserves to the degree that foreign authorities requested gold for their new deposits, and in any case the flights undermined confidence in the dollar as a reserve asset. They also imposed disturbances on U.S. securities markets as a result of the shifting of holdings from the pattern preferred by those who gave up their dollar assets to the pattern preferred by those who acquired them.

It is sometimes contended that the exchange rate system of adjustable pegs failed because capital became increasingly mobile among countries in the 1960s with the multinationalization of the activities of large American and British banks and corporations.[7] It should be remembered, however, that the gold-exchange standard of the late 1920s also foundered on disruptive capital movements, without Eurocurrency markets and the multinational corporations of the 1960s, and that the framers of the IMF charter sought but found no solution to this problem other than to dictate that international capital flows should be subject to national controls. It is ironical that the institutions which contributed much to the internationalization of the money and capital markets in the 1960s—multinational firms and Eurocurrency banks—were themselves hastened into existence by the misalignment of exchange rates resulting from the system of par values and by the national controls on capital movements established by the United States and the United Kingdom to defend the misalignment. In short, market forces, feebly contained by national controls, generated new institutions which in

[7] John Williamson, "The Benefits and Costs of an International Monetary Nonsystem," in Bernstein, *Reflections on Jamaica*, p. 55.

the end swept away the barriers that governments had sought to establish around capital markets.

This review of the Bretton Woods experience suggests the unlikelihood that a fixed exchange rate regime can be sustained in a world in which disturbances have different effects in different countries and in which government policies are made in response to the will of national electorates.

Still the system might have functioned passably for a few more years had not the key currency of the system, the dollar, become overvalued. Strong forces were arrayed against any change in the dollar's par value, and imbalance in the system's payments flows resulting from dollar overvaluation finally undermined the ability of that currency to serve the functions in the system that it was uniquely qualified to serve.

The history of the attrition of the dollar's value relative to gold and other currencies in the just over two decades under the original IMF charter is helpful in understanding both why the system succeeded so well for a time and why it then became increasingly crisis prone.[8] The early years of the International Monetary Fund were characterized by the liberalization of international payments arrangements within Europe and then, in the late 1950s, by progress toward general convertibility of the currencies of the industrialized countries. Under the aegis of the General Agreement on Tariffs and Trade (GATT), commercial policies were successively liberalized. Expanding world production in these circumstances was accompanied by unusually rapid growth in trade and investment, and governments everywhere welcomed a more balanced distribution of international reserves. These favorable trends, however, took place in a world in which the dollar's undervaluation was steadily disappearing and in which the trade and payments controls sustaining a disequilibrium set of exchange rates were becoming less necessary. As the 1960s progressed and the United States became embroiled for the second time in fifteen years in overseas military operations, the broad economic equilibrium of the world deteriorated once again, and the dollar this time became overvalued. Central to the experience, in hindsight, was a change in U.S. monetary policy in the early 1960s that significantly raised the average annual growth rate of Federal

[8] H. Peter Gray has said, "The three main sources of the system's strength were the slow release of suppressed disequilibria, the key currency status of the main deficit nation, and, very important, the willingness of the United States to see its liquidity position worsen through gold sales and through increases in its short-term liabilities to foreigners." *An Aggregate Theory of International Payments Adjustment* (Lexington, Mass.: D. C. Heath, 1974), p. 16.

Reserve credit. Protectionist sentiments intensified in the United States while capital controls proliferated abroad. A global misallocation of resources was developing as trade and investment were misdirected by the nonequilibrium exchange rates and prices. Speculative flights of capital became more frequent and larger, and the suspicion grew that the dollar's convertibility into gold could not be maintained. U.S. policy makers chafed at the constraints the balance of payments imposed on foreign policy initiatives that otherwise seemed imperative for building and defending a free and democratic international community.

As the country whose currency was a numeraire of the par values of the Bretton Woods system, the United States could adjust its exchange rate only by changing the value of the dollar against the other chief reserve money, gold. Such a change seemed so fraught with risks, economic and political, that it was generally abhorred, although perhaps more so in the United States than abroad. But this abhorrence, together with the natural concern other countries felt for their dollar exchange rates, placed the initiative for par value change in the hands of other countries which increasingly became creditors of the United States. In deficit to the United States they devalued in due course. But with surpluses in their trade, they were less willing to make politically distasteful decisions to eliminate an exchange rate problem. This strengthened the tendency toward dollar overvaluation and toward exchange rate rigidity in the late 1960s. Europeans maintained it was the responsibility of the profligate United States to slow its spending and creation of money, or to devalue; the United States, in turn, thought it would be appropriate for the Europeans and the Japanese to revalue. Critics of the U.S. capital export restraint program urged on this country a policy of "benign neglect" of the balance of payments;[9] later many foreign observers erroneously felt that such a policy had indeed been adopted. As the problem matured, it became more intractable because the general undervaluation of currencies in relation to the dollar was accompanied by varying degrees of disequilibrium *among* the foreign currencies. Revaluation relative to the dollar of any but the most undervalued currency would worsen the disequilibrium of the revaluing country in certain directions even though improving it in others. A simultaneous adjustment toward a

---

[9] Gottfried Haberler and Thomas D. Willett, *A Strategy for U.S. Balance of Payments Policy* (Washington, D.C.: American Enterprise Institute, 1971), Special Analysis No. 1; and Lawrence B. Krause, "A Passive Balance of Payments Strategy for the United States," *Brookings Papers on Economic Activity*, vol. 3 (1970), pp. 339-68.

pattern of equilibrium exchange rates was necessary, but this was not easily accomplished in the par value structure. The Germans, accompanied by the Dutch, made a small revaluation of their currency in 1961, but in the end that effort proved little more than a gesture. The unleashing of speculative forces began with a flight from the French franc in 1969, led to the breakdown of German resistance to a second and third revaluation of the mark, and then culminated in the run on the dollar in 1971 that brought the Bretton Woods rules to an end.

An additional aspect of the Bretton Woods experience suggests that the creation of a more durable fixed exchange rate regime may have to await the evolution of a supranational political base. A fixed exchange rate system with a reserve currency elevates the monetary authority of the reserve currency country in a substantial degree to the position of monetary authority for the world. Monetary expansion in the United States under the Bretton Woods system spilled over into foreign hands where the dollars were acquired by foreign monetary authorities against their own currencies; this set the stage for credit multiplication abroad. In the early history of that system, mildly expansive U.S. monetary policies were compatible with efforts in other major countries to spur reconstruction and to add to their foreign currency reserves. But in the later more expansive period, especially after high domestic wage costs began to drive U.S. firms abroad—President de Gaulle said Americans were trying to buy up France—and after U.S. participation in the Vietnam conflict, other countries found U.S. monetary leadership unacceptable. There followed a tragic heightening of tensions among members of the North Atlantic Treaty Organization (NATO) over commercial policy, investment policies, foreign aid policies, the sharing of the defense burden, and whatever else impinged on the balance of payments. To be tough and durable a fixed exchange rate regime needs a monetary base under the control of an authority which gives all participants a voice and which can alleviate the difficult adjustment burdens experienced from time to time by all countries and regions. On the other hand, if the United States should follow in the years ahead so moderate a monetary policy that other countries again find advantages in a loose association with a North American "island of stability," an extensive dollar area of unilaterally pegged exchange rates without formally declared par values might be a spontaneous result.

The Bretton Woods international monetary system was faulty in that the IMF was made too small and was designed as much to limit creditor countries' exposure as to finance payments imbalances. The original quotas of the IMF's member countries totaled only $9.2 billion, and only about half that sum corresponded to subscriptions in currencies that became usable for international settlements after 1957. Meanwhile, the imbalance in trade across only the North Atlantic in the early postwar years, financed largely by the United States Marshall Plan, amounted to $3–5 billion *per annum*. The IMF's usable resources would have been dissipated in a few months had they been employed at that time for their stated purpose. Nor have the resources ever become large relative to the task of financing the global imbalances that can arise under fixed exchange rates. Even after the enlargement of total IMF quotas to $39 billion in conjunction with the 1978 amendment to its charter, the IMF's resources constituted a smaller proportion of world trade than they did in 1946. Furthermore, demands on it by a single country, such as the British standby credit of $3.8 billion in early 1977, could send the IMF scurrying to its larger members for additional funds. It is no wonder that the dollar exchange standard reemerged in the two decades following World War II in spite of the intent at the Bretton Woods conference to banish such arrangements forever, and that the IMF's role in discussions of international policy remains more that of mediator than of decision taker.

A final characteristic of the system deserves mention. The system was based on multiple reserve media, particularly gold and dollars, although the position that dollars would come to occupy was certainly not clearly foreseen in the original plan. Sterling and other European currencies, as well as the IMF's special drawing right (SDR), also played some reserve role. Since the Bretton Woods plan was necessarily superimposed on an existing structure of monetary institutions, some ancient and some modern, it could not constitute an ideal design. The incentive, however, the system created for both private and official speculation in currencies and gold when one or more of these seemed to be coming into excess demand or supply, finally proved the arrangement's nemesis. Clearly the catalyst in terminating the regime was the impending inability of the United States to continue its pledge of gold convertibility. Barbara Henneberry and the late James Witte have likened the Bretton Woods experience to a vast demonstration of Gresham's Law, in which holders of gold moved the metal to the United States in exchange for dollars for a time but then sought to reverse the flow and convert dollars back to gold when the dollar came into excess supply.[10] Recognition of the instability inher-

[10] Barbara Henneberry and James Witte, "The IMF Gold Auction: More Bitter Fruit from Bretton Woods?" paper presented at the meetings of the Allied

ent in a system based on several monetary media prompted the reform negotiators to work on plans that could lead to unification of the world's reserves, perhaps in the form of the IMF's special drawing right. As we shall see in Chapter 2, however, the negotiations toward this end failed. The problems of maintaining interconvertibility between the reserve assets gold and dollars also explains the determination of the United States to reduce the monetary role of gold through the sale on the open market of gold held by the IMF and other official agencies.

The System That Emerged

While the Bretton Woods regime may be said to have ended with the U.S. suspension of gold convertibility for the dollar in August 1971, the new regime must be dated from the decision by Common Market countries to float their currencies against the dollar in March 1973. The interim period saw a fruitless effort to revitalize a fixed exchange rate system based on realigned rates.

The system that has evolved since 1973 is neither based on par values nor free floating. It can be characterized as one of managed floating among blocs in which countries exercise their own discretion in the election of their exchange rate regulations.

Table 1 and Figure 1 give an indication of the arrangements that were in effect at the end of April 1978. It will be seen that a number of countries in Latin America, Africa, the Middle East, and Southeast Asia maintain margins for their exchange rates against the U.S. dollar, although sixteen of the group of forty-two countries that maintained such margins in 1978 had in fact dual or multiple exchange rate systems, and several of them followed a practice of frequently adjusting their exchange rates. Five small countries where British influence has been strong maintained exchange rates against sterling, and a group of fourteen African former French colonies pegged their currencies on the French franc in 1978. The SDR, a form of credit money allocated from time to time by the IMF to its members and itself a composite of sixteen national currencies, was the peg for

---

Social Science Association, Atlantic City, N.J., December 1976. Thomas D. Willett, however, has emphasized that the problem of the 1960s was not necessarily marked by U.S. balance of payments overall deficits; deficits no greater than the growth in foreign demand for dollars would not have imperiled the system. Deficits larger than that amount did bring the system of fixed exchange rates to an end. See Thomas D. Willett, *Floating Exchange Rates and International Monetary Reform* (Washington, D.C.: American Enterprise Institute, 1977), pp. 85-91.

TABLE 1

EXCHANGE RATES AND EXCHANGE RATE REGIMES, APRIL 28, 1978

		Exchange Rate Maintained Against							
Member	*Currency*	U.S. dollar[a]	Pound sterling[a]	French franc[a]	Other single currency[a]	Special drawing right[a]	Currency composite other than SDR[b]	Other curren-cies in group[c]	*Exchange Rates Other-wise Deter-mined*[b,d]
Afghanistan[e]	afghani	—	—	—	—	—	—	—	45.0
Algeria[e]	dinar	—	—	—	—	—	4.009	—	—
Argentina[e]	peso	—	—	—	—	—	—	—	7.61[f]
Australia	dollar	—	—	—	—	—	—	—	0.880126
Austria	schilling	—	—	—	—	—	14.8825	—	—
*Bahamas[e]	dollar	1.00	—	—	—	—	—	—	—
*Bahrain	dinar	—	—	—	—	0.476190	—	—	0.3878
*Bangladesh[e]	taka	—	27.025	—	—	—	—	—	—
*Barbados	dollar	2.00	—	—	—	—	—	—	—
*Belgium[e]	franc	—	—	—	—	—	—	48.6573	32.2775
Benin	franc	—	—	50.00	—	—	—	—	—
*Bolivia	peso	20.0	—	—	—	—	—	—	—
Botswana	pula	0.828157	—	—	—	—	—	—	—
Brazil[e]	cruzeiro	—	—	—	—	—	—	—	17.165[f]
*Burma	kyat	—	—	—	—	8.50847	—	—	6.9683
*Burundi	franc	90.00	—	—	—	—	—	—	—
Cambodia[g]		—	—	—	—	—	—	—	—

Cameroon	franc	—	—	50.00	—	—	—	—	—
Canada	dollar	—	—	—	—	—	—	—	1.1339
Central African Empire	franc	—	—	50.00	—	—	—	—	—
Chad	franc	—	—	50.00	—	—	—	—	—
Chile	peso	—	—	—	—	—	—	—	30.94[f]
*China, Republic of	new Taiwan dollar	38.00	—	—	—	—	—	—	—
Colombia[e]	peso	—	—	—	—	—	—	—	38.58[f]
Comoros	franc	—	—	50.00	—	—	—	—	—
Congo, People's Republic of the	franc	—	—	50.00	—	—	—	—	—
Costa Rica	colon	8.57	—	—	—	—	—	—	—
Cyprus	pound	—	—	—	—	—	0.387672	—	—
*Denmark	krone	—	—	—	—	—	—	8.56656	5.6625
Dominican Republic[e]	peso	1.00	—	—	—	—	—	—	—
Ecuador[e]	sucre	25.00	—	—	—	—	—	—	—
Egypt[e]	pound	0.391305	—	—	—	—	—	—	—
El Salvador	colon	2.50	—	—	—	—	—	—	—
Equatorial Guinea[e]	ekuele	—	—	—	1.00[h]	—	—	—	—
*Ethiopia[e]	birr	2.07	—	—	—	—	—	—	—

(Table continues on next page)

TABLE 1 (continued)

Member	Currency	*Exchange Rate Maintained Against* U.S. dollar[a]	Pound sterling[a]	French franc[a]	Other single currency[a]	Special drawing right[a]	Currency composite other than SDR[b]	Other currencies in group[c]	*Exchange Rates Otherwise Determined*[b,d]
Fiji	dollar	—	—	—	—	—	0.871156	—	—
Finland	markka	—	—	—	—	—	4.23	—	—
France	franc	—	—	—	—	—	—	—	4.606
Gabon	franc	—	—	50.00	—	—	—	—	—
Gambia, The	dalasi	—	4.00	—	—	—	—	—	—
*Germany, Federal Republic of	deutsche mark	—	—	—	—	—	—	3.15665	2.0709
Ghana[e]	cedi	1.15385	—	—	—	—	—	—	—
Greece	drachma	—	—	—	—	—	—	—	37.571
Grenada	East Caribbean dollar	2.70	—	—	—	—	—	—	—
Guatemala	quetzal	1.00	—	—	—	—	—	—	—
Guinea[e]	syll	—	—	—	—	24.6853	—	—	20.1665
Guinea-Bissau	peso	—	—	—	0.85[h]	—	—	—	—
*Guyana	dollar	2.55	—	—	—	—	—	—	—

Haiti	gourde	5.00	—	—	—	—	—	—	—
Honduras	lempira	2.00	—	—	—	—	—	—	—
Iceland	krona	—	—	—	—	—	—	—	256.50
India	rupee	—	—	—	—	—	8.60045	—	—
Indonesia[e]	rupiah	415.00	—	—	—	—	—	—	—
*Iran[e]	rial	—	—	—	82.2425	—	—	—	70.475
*Iraq	dinar	0.296051	—	—	—	—	—	—	—
Ireland[e]	pound	—	1.00	—	—	—	—	—	—
*Israel	pound	—	—	—	—	—	—	—	16.7307
Italy	lira	—	—	—	—	—	—	—	867.65
Ivory Coast	franc	—	—	50.00	—	—	—	—	—
*Jamaica[e]	dollar	1.05	—	—	—	—	—	—	—
Japan	yen	—	—	—	—	—	—	—	223.60
Jordan	dinar	—	—	—	—	0.387755	—	—	0.313
*Kenya	shilling	—	—	—	9.66	—	—	—	7.886
Korea	won	485.00	—	—	—	—	—	—	—
Kuwait	dinar	—	—	—	—	—	0.27715	—	—
Lao People's Democratic Republic	kip	200.00	—	—	—	—	—	—	—
Lebanon	pound	—	—	—	—	—	—	—	2.9315
Lesotho	rand	—	—	—	1.00[j]	—	—	—	—
Liberia	dollar	1.00	—	—	—	—	—	—	—
*Libya	dinar	0.296053	—	—	—	—	—	—	—
*Luxembourg[e]	franc	—	—	—	—	—	—	48.6573	32.2775
Madagascar	franc	—	—	50.00	—	—	—	—	—
Malawi	kwacha	—	—	—	—	1.05407	—	—	0.861116

(*Table continued on next page*)

TABLE 1 (continued)

		Exchange Rate Maintained Against							
Member	*Currency*	U.S. dollar[a]	Pound sterling[a]	French franc[a]	Other single currency[a]	Special drawing right[a]	Currency composite other than SDR[b]	Other currencies in group[c]	*Exchange Rates Otherwise Determined*[b,d]
Malaysia	ringgit	—	—	—	—	—	2.4014	—	—
Maldives[e]	rupee	3.93	—	—	—	—	—	—	—
Mali	franc	—	—	100.00	—	—	—	—	—
Malta	pound	—	—	—	—	—	0.398247	—	—
Mauritania	ouguiya	—	—	—	—	—	46.26	—	—
Mauritius[e]	rupee	—	—	—	—	7.713759	—	—	6.30171
Mexico	peso	—	—	—	—	—	—	—	22.7426
Morocco[e]	dirham	—	—	—	—	—	4.2789	—	—
*Nepal[e]	rupee	12.00	—	—	—	—	—	—	—
*Netherlands	guilder	—	—	—	—	—	—	3.35507	2.2115
New Zealand	dollar	—	—	—	—	—	0.984833	—	—
Nicaragua	cordoba	7.00	—	—	—	—	—	—	—
Niger	franc	—	—	50.00	—	—	—	—	—
Nigeria	naira	—	—	—	—	—	—	—	0.622548
*Norway	krone	—	—	—	—	—	—	8.18706	5.4150
*Oman	rial Omani	0.345395	—	—	—	—	—	—	—
*Pakistan	rupee	9.90	—	—	—	—	—	—	—
Panama	balboa	1.00	—	—	—	—	—	—	—

Papua New Guinea	kina	—	—	—	—	—	—	—	0.720980
Paraguay[e]	guarani	126.00	—	—	—	—	—	—	—
Peru[e]	sol	—	—	—	—	—	—	—	130.322
Philippines	peso	—	—	—	—	—	—	—	7.365
Portugal	escudo	—	—	—	—	—	—	—	41.956[f]
Qatar	riyal	—	—	—	—	—	—	—	3.8785
Romania[e]	leu	12.00[k]	—	—	—	—	—	—	—
*Rwanda	franc	92.84	—	—	—	—	—	—	—
Sao Tome and Principe	dobra	—	—	—	—	45.25	—	—	36.9667
Saudi Arabia	riyal	—	—	—	—	—	—	—	3.445
Senegal	franc	—	—	50.00	—	—	—	—	—
Seychelles	rupee	—	13.3333	—	—	—	—	—	—
Sierra Leone	leone	—	2.00	—	—	—	—	—	—
Singapore	dollar	—	—	—	—	—	2.3302	—	—
*Somalia[e]	shilling	6.23270	—	—	—	—	—	—	—
South Africa[e]	rand	0.869565	—	—	—	—	—	—	—
Spain	peseta	—	—	—	—	—	—	—	80.909
Sri Lanka	rupee	—	—	—	—	—	—	—	15.90
Sudan[e]	pound	0.348242	—	—	—	—	—	—	—
Swaziland	lilangeni	—	—	—	1.00[j]	—	—	—	—
*Sweden	krona	—	—	—	—	—	4.6430	—	—
Syrian Arab Republic	pound	3.925	—	—	—	—	—	—	—
*Tanzania	shilling	—	—	—	—	9.66	—	—	7.87869
*Thailand	baht	—	—	—	—	—	20.40	—	—
Togo	franc	—	—	50.00	—	—	—	—	—

(Table continues on next page)

TABLE 1 (continued)

Member	Currency	*Exchange Rate Maintained Against* U.S. dollar[a]	Pound sterling[a]	French franc[a]	Other single currency[a]	Special drawing right[a]	Currency composite other than SDR[b]	Other currencies in group[c]	*Exchange Rates Otherwise Determined*[b,d]
Trinidad and Tobago	dollar	2.40	—	—	—	—	—	—	—
Tunisia	dinar	—	—	—	—	—	0.423360	—	—
Turkey[e]	lira	—	—	—	—	—	—	—	25.25
*Uganda	shilling	—	—	—	—	9.66	—	—	7.87869
*United Arab Emirates	dirham	—	—	—	—	4.7619	—	—	3.878
United Kingdom[e]	pound	—	—	—	—	—	—	—	0.549178
United States	dollar	—	—	—	—	—	—	—	1.00
Upper Volta	franc	—	—	50.00	—	—	—	—	—
Uruguay[e]	new peso	—	—	—	—	—	—	—	5.61
Venezuela	bolivar	4.2925	—	—	—	—	—	—	—
Vietnam[e]	South Vietnamese dong	—	—	—	—	2.13087	—	—	1.74080
Western Samoa	tala	—	—	—	—	—	0.7485	—	—
Yemen Arab Republic	riyal	4.5625	—	—	—	—	—	—	—

*Yemen, People's Democratic Republic of[e]	dinar	0.345395	—	—	—	—	—	—	—
Yugoslavia[e]	dinar	—	—	—	—	—	—	—	18.5339
*Zaire	zaire	—	—	—	—	1.00	—	—	0.816944
*Zambia	kwacha	—	—	—	—	0.976311	—	—	0.836766

* The member avails itself of wider margins of up to ± 2.25 percent.

[a] Rates as notified to the IMF and in terms of national currency units per unit listed.

[b] Market rates in currency units per U.S. dollar.

[c] Belgium, Denmark, the Federal Republic of Germany, Luxembourg, Netherlands, and Norway maintained maximum margins of 2.25 percent for exchange rates in transactions in the official markets between their currencies and those of the other countries in this group. No announced margins were observed for other countries. Rates shown are central rates expressed in terms of SDRs as valued in accordance with Article XXI, Section 2, of the IMF's Articles of Agreement. The European common margins arrangement was succeeded by the European Monetary System in April 1979. See Epilogue.

[d] Under this heading are listed those members who described their exchange rate regime as floating independently, those who adjusted their exchange rates according to a set of indicators (see note f), and certain other members whose regimes are not otherwise described in this table. In addition, U.S. dollar quotations are given for the currencies which were pegged to the SDR and for those which participated in the European common margins arrangement.

[e] Member maintained multiple currency practice and/or dual exchange market. A description of the member's exchange system as of December 31, 1977, is given in the *29th Annual Report on Exchange Restrictions* (Washington, D.C.: IMF, 1978).

[f] Exchange rates adjusted according to a set of indicators.

[g] Information not available.

[h] Per Spanish peseta.

[i] Per Portuguese escudo.

[j] Per South African rand.

[k] Rate for noncommercial transactions.

SOURCE: International Monetary Fund, *IMF Survey*, May 22, 1978, pp. 156–57.

fifteen currencies in Africa, the Middle East, and Asia because of the attractiveness of the SDR as a "halfway house" in the movements of the currencies of the major trading countries.[11] In northern Europe six countries maintained narrow margins for the movement of their exchange rates against one another in the arrangement commonly called "the snake"; these currencies with their satellites jointly floated against the world's other currencies.[12] Seventeen widely scattered countries chose in 1978 to peg their currencies to a currency composite other than the SDR, usually a weighted average of the currencies of their major trading partners. And, finally, fifty countries notified the IMF that their currencies were not being maintained within specified margins in terms of any other currency. (The United States, from the point of view of its undertakings, was in this category.) Areas in white on the map (Figure 1) are political entities whose currencies are floating against the other blocs, entities whose exchange rates are adjusted according to selected sets of economic indicators, or entities which are not members of the IMF.[13] All in all, the picture is one of a substantial dollar bloc floating against most other currencies, including the snake, the French franc area, the remainder of the once significant sterling area, and the now significant SDR area.

Within blocs, international trade still moves, of course, in a context of fixed exchange rates except insofar as the pegs within the group are changed or the trade is subjected by national regulation to special rate requirements.[14] But across the bloc lines, trade moves at rates that are not maintained. The distinction here can be easily overdrawn. For within blocs some rates have been changed frequently, and between blocs heavy intervention by monetary authorities has limited short-term movements of the rates and resisted some broader movements. Still, the tendency of the currencies to associate into blocs is

[11] For the makeup of the SDR currency basket see Table 2, below.

[12] Until the agreement to limit rate movements against the dollar to ± 2.25 percent was abrogated in March 1973, the European narrow margins arrangement was whimsically labeled the "snake in the tunnel" after a description in those words by the deputy director of the Bundesbank. When the boundaries against the dollar disappeared, references to the snake continued. A still narrower exchange rate constraint among currencies of the Benelux nations was sometimes called "the worm in the snake." The snake was succeeded by the European Monetary System (EMS) in April 1979. For a description of the EMS, see the Epilogue.

[13] Equatorial Guinea pegs to the Spanish peseta; Guinea-Bissau pegs to the Portuguese escudo; and Lesotho pegs to the South African rand.

[14] Some of the pegs are also rather loose. Two Arab countries linked to the SDR, for example, permit variation within a band that is ± 7.5 percent wide.

FIGURE 1

THE WORLD'S CURRENCY BLOCS, APRIL 1978

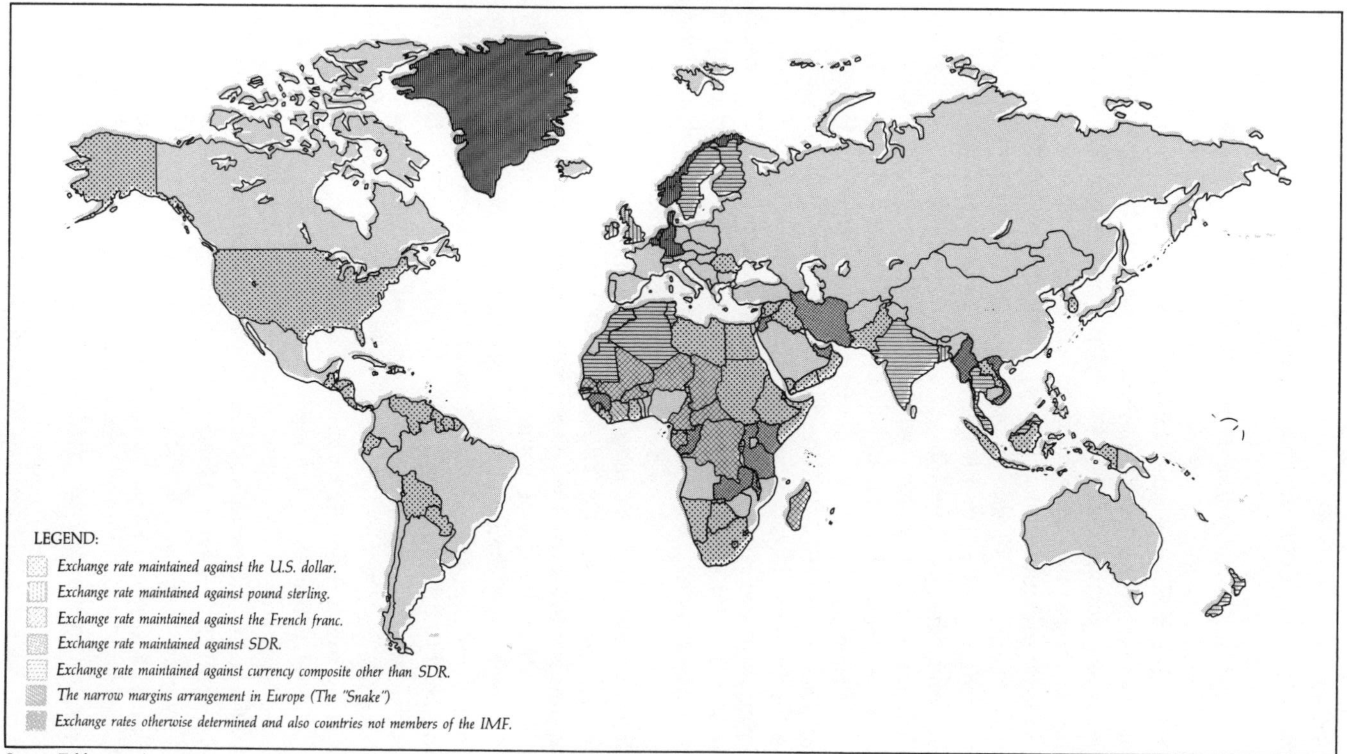

Source: Table 1.

sufficiently significant to warrant assessment of the shares of world trade that move within and across the bloc boundaries.

Comparison of a matrix of merchandise trade for 1975 with the bloc definitions of Table 1 indicates that more than six-sevenths of world trade moved in 1975 in paths which in 1978 implied the use of flexible exchange rates (rates for which the movements were not maintained within preannounced margins by governments). The remaining portion consisted of transactions within the areas in which the exchange rates were more or less aligned on a common numeraire. Trade within the dollar bloc and within the European snake group constituted most of this amount. This situation, in which world trade is predominantly conducted under exchange rates which are not officially supported within preannounced margins may be contrasted with one as recent as 1970 when only Canada among the industrialized countries had a unified and flexible exchange rate.

Probably all governments have intervened in their exchange markets since 1973 in one way or another to influence the rates. In the industrialized countries the direct interventions have taken the form of official purchases and sales of foreign currencies out of owned or borrowed reserves, and a number of developing countries have continued their customary use of exchange controls. Nevertheless, market forces have everywhere played a more important role in determining the rates than they did for short- to intermediate-term periods prior to 1971, and the rates have undergone broad swings. In January 1974 the snake currencies of northern Europe, for example, fell against the dollar some 8 percent below the March 1973 level at which they had been set free, and in March 1975 they were 16 percent above, a swing amounting to nearly 25 percent of the March 1973 levels (see Figure 3 in Chapter 4). Furthermore, the pound sterling and the Italian lira had both lost some 30 percent of their March 1973 dollar values by mid-1976, while the Swiss franc had by the end of 1977 gained 50 percent.

Interventions in the exchange markets by monetary authorities have been large. Total monthly changes in reserves (excluding use of IMF credit and with reserves partially adjusted for exchange rate changes), for France, March 1973–June 1978, were $16.4 billion; for Italy, the total was $29.2 billion; for Japan, $33.1 billion; for the United Kingdom, $33.3 billion; for Switzerland, $45.0 billion; and for Germany, $48.2 billion.[15] In addition to using owned reserves, monetary authorities have relied on bilateral swap arrangements, have

[15] See Table 2, Chapter 4, and its accompanying text.

borrowed from other governments outside the swap lines, have drawn from Eurobanks and from long-term capital markets, have directed state agencies to use external rather than internal financing, and have employed various inducements to persuade private banks and other firms to lend or borrow abroad in accordance with the official appraisal of the needs of the foreign exchange market.[16] Data concerning these interventions are reviewed in Chapter 4.

The familiar "crisis of the foreign exchange market" that captured headlines in the late 1960s has appeared less often and, when seen, has taken a less ominous form. It has recurred for countries defending fixed rates within blocs—especially for the countries associated with the European snake—and it has appeared in altered guise in concern that particular exchange rates were moving too far or too fast, especially in connection with rates on the dollar. The system of flexible rates has nonetheless weathered rather successfully the storm of violent shifts in trade and investment associated with the oil crisis, strenuous inflation and recession, famines, droughts, political scandals, and apprehensions about political upheavals. The rates have in many cases also broadly maintained the competitive positions of countries which have otherwise experienced quite unequal changes in money supply, prices, and costs. The rates have moved with frightening quickness, however, during periods of uncertainty, demonstrating that stabilizing speculation cannot materialize unless an intermediate-term equilibrium rate can be reasonably estimated. These matters are further considered in Chapters 3 and 4.

Tariffs, payments restrictions, and other restraints on trade did not markedly worsen in industrialized countries after 1973 despite worldwide recession and extensive unemployment, although there was some resurgence of protectionism in 1977–1978. Progress continued toward trade liberalization through several avenues, including the Tokyo Round of negotiations on tariff and nontariff trade barriers, the reduction of tariffs between the older and newer members of the European Economic Community (EEC) and between the EEC and the European Free Trade Association (EFTA). Several unilateral reductions by industrialized countries of tariffs on exports of developing countries were made through the introduction or extension of generalized preferences and through the Lomé Convention among the EEC

[16] The Italian loan of $2 billion from Germany in 1974 and the package loans to the United Kingdom of $2.5 billion in 1974, $5.3 billion in 1976, and $6.9 billion in 1977 were the largest and best publicized of the direct government borrowings.

and forty-six Asian, Caribbean, and Pacific countries.[17] The restrictions on international capital movements, which intensified during the troubled period 1971–1973, continued to be relaxed after 1973, although Swiss restrictions on inward capital movements and Italian restrictions on outward movements were notable exceptions.

To a surprising degree, the dollar has retained the roles it played during the Bretton Woods period. Although no longer redeemable in gold at a fixed price, in 1977–1978 the dollar continued to be the leading medium chosen by governments for their international reserves. IMF estimates indicate that 81.2 percent of the $173 billion of foreign exchange reserves reported by seventy-six countries at the end of 1977 was dollar denominated. This compares with 80.9 percent for the end of 1970. While a number of countries moved to diversify their foreign exchange holdings after 1972, the aggregates show that at least up until 1978 this was largely a substitution of deutsche marks for sterling, leaving the share of reserves in dollars little changed.[18] Furthermore, other data indicate that the dollar's role in foreign exchange reserves was greater in 1970 than in 1968 and 1969.[19] It now appears that the crisis of confidence in the dollar on the part of governments in 1971 concerned chiefly confidence about convertibility of dollars into gold at a fixed price—an option many governments wanted. But with that option removed, and with only a second-best option in the form of convertibility into other reserve assets at fluctuating market prices available, many governments, including those of the Organization of Petroleum Exporting Countries (OPEC) into whose hands a portion of the dollars subsequently moved, saw dollars as the best alternative available for a reserve medium. This occurred no doubt partially because the rate of increase of the U.S. money supply and prices appeared moderate in 1974–1976 by international standards. Accelerating growth of the money supply in the United States in 1977–1978 once again revived awareness that a dollar-centered system, for all its internal reinforcements, could not survive a chronic decline in the dollar's foreign exchange value. This matter returns to haunt the discussion in Chapter 9 of the longer-range outlook.

The dollar has continued to serve as the chief intervention currency for authorities buying or selling in their foreign exchange

---

[17] Discussions expected to lead to a second Lomé convention opened in July 1978.

[18] See the report by Robert Heller and Malcolm Knight in *IMF Survey*, May 22, 1978, pp. 154-56.

[19] IMF, *Annual Report*, 1975, table 15, p. 39.

markets to influence the course of their currency's value, except within the French franc and the sterling blocs. Arrangements for EEC countries announced in 1978, however, suggest that a renewed effort may be made to reduce the use of dollars as an intervention medium to preserve the intra-European exchange rate structure. While the IMF has made its SDR the numeraire for par value and central exchange rates of record, the dollar remains the numeraire of the system of exchange rates in a vital and operational sense.

Although statistical data are lacking, there is no reason to believe that the dollar's role as the vehicle for a large share of the world's private commerce was reduced by the advent of widespread floating, at least before 1978. Certainly nonbank, private holdings of dollars, in U.S. and foreign banks, continued to grow. And generalized floating doubtless increased the attractiveness of pricing and invoicing in a single currency recognized worldwide. While fear of dollar depreciation relative to other currencies has led some groups to price their wares in terms of SDRs—the Suez Canal Authority is among these agencies, and the International Air Transport Authority and OPEC continue to consider it—actual payments and receipts must of course take place in a traded currency, and the dollar's popularity in this role was well sustained into 1978. In the few actual data available on invoicing and settlement practices, Sven Grassman, extrapolating from data for Sweden, West Germany, and Denmark, estimated that some 25 percent of world trade in 1968 may have been denominated in dollars, while the U.S. share in world trade was only 15.4 percent. In a subsequent (1973) analysis of invoicing practices for Swedish trade he concluded that the dollar's role as a vehicle currency had grown a bit at the expense of sterling but that the general patterns had not changed.[20]

Certain problems and technical developments in the 1960s led to the development of institutions that greatly increased the international mobility of short- and long-term capital. Among these institutions are Eurobanks, which effect the rapid redistribution of funds in wholesale lots from points of the globe where interest rates are lower to points where they are higher. While such institutional changes cannot help but increase the productivity of the world's scarce savings, in providing balance of payments financing they have also exacerbated the problem of containing inflationary forces in areas

[20] Sven Grassman, "A Fundamental Symmetry in Payments Patterns," *Journal of International Economics*, vol. 3 (May 1973), pp. 105-16, and "Currency Distribution and Forward Cover in Foreign Trade: Sweden Revisited, 1973," *Journal of International Economics*, vol. 6 (May 1976), pp. 215-21.

where the inflation is generated. In view of the irreversibility of institutional developments, the accelerated mobility of capital, which was partly induced by misaligned exchange rates and by national efforts to suppress older capital markets, will not disappear. Eurocurrency banking and multinational corporations are permanent elements in the emerging monetary system. The implications of the enhanced capital mobility they make possible are further considered in Chapters 5 and 7 along with some problems of the safety of international banks and bank consortia.

Problems at Least Temporarily Behind Us

Some problems that seemed critical for the international monetary system in the 1960s are now behind us, at least for the time being. One is the fear that supplies of international reserve money will be inadequate. Concern with this problem in the mid-1960s led to the protracted negotiations which produced the special drawing right in the International Monetary Fund as a new fiduciary money for intergovernmental settlements. The fears which motivated those negotiations stemmed from the inability of governments to increase monetary gold stocks while world output and prices of other goods were climbing. Economists argued that government efforts to hold on to a share of this primary reserve money as supplies became relatively more scarce would lead to excessively deflationary monetary and fiscal policies and to beggar-my-neighbor commercial policies. In the United States concern was voiced that without adequate backing in the form of other reserves, the dollar could not continue to play its role as a reserve money in the heterogeneous reserve stock. As mentioned earlier in this chapter, fears about the attractiveness of the dollar as a reserve asset in fact disappeared with the termination of the promise to make dollars convertible into the other assets at a fixed price. The dollars held by monetary authorities outside the United States have multiplied several times since 1971—before March 1973 chiefly as a result of exchange market interventions by governments to slow the appreciation of their currencies, and after the oil crisis of 1973 as a result both of further exchange market interventions and of the decision of petroleum-exporting countries to accumulate liquid assets in dollars. In addition, governments have discovered that private capital markets are significant adjuncts to their reserve holdings. Therefore, while the distribution of external liquid assets and credit potential among countries is a matter for some concern, the alarm expressed a decade ago about prospective deficiencies in the aggregate of international reserve money has been transformed by events into a fear that international reserve multiplication may be excessive and even out of control.

It cannot be assumed, nonetheless, that the problem of reserve adequacy is any more than dormant. The problem could be quickened by irresponsible monetary policy in the United States which could lead to the destruction of reserves and the disruption of exchange rate patterns through repatriation of official funds. Such events, if allowed to worsen, could seriously increase inflation in the United States and engender economic deterioration abroad. This ominous possibility is considered again in Chapter 9.

Even when the problem of reserve adequacy was disappearing from view, the matter of an "overhang" of what were said to be excessive official dollar holdings by European countries and Japan was also fading. Devaluation of the dollar in terms of other currencies and worldwide inflation of prices in dollar terms, by reducing the purchasing power value of earlier holdings, converted a part of many countries' undesired dollar holdings to desired holdings. Another major element in the reduction of the overhang was the current account deficits that followed the rise in oil prices in 1973 and seemed to require official financing. Currency depreciation was understood by governments of oil-importing countries to be no solution to this trade imbalance because the deficits were worldwide, focusing on a few countries as suppliers, and because oil-importing countries faced the political necessity of moderating the inflation and unemployment potentials of the disturbance. Most oil importers therefore sought additional dollar loans and held on to existing dollar balances in this period. Meanwhile, governments of oil-exporting countries saw the dollar as the best currency alternative for denominating their accumulating earnings until those earnings could be put to more permanent use. In addition, a few countries added to their official dollar stocks at a great rate in order to influence the dollar exchange rates of their own currencies.

A number of the pressures acting to reduce unwanted dollar holdings are stable and irreversible so that an overhang of excess supply of dollars in official balances will not easily return. Nevertheless, since the desired dollars necessarily depend on changing events, including expectations about the dollar's future exchange value, an overhang can never be deemed permanently eliminated.

Economists in the mid-1960s regarded the adjustment problem as the central source of difficulty in the monetary system. In its broad form the problem was the inability or unwillingness of governments to adopt policies to end the growing payments imbalance between the United States and the United Kingdom, on the one hand, and the rest of the world, on the other. Events since 1971 have also significantly changed all this. Of course the initial devaluation of the dollar, negotiated as part of a multilateral realignment of exchange rates at the Smithsonian Institution in December 1971, was traumatic, and the subsequent effort to perpetuate a fixed exchange rate regime proved that financial diplomacy is no substitute for a working price system. The events of 1972 and early 1973, nevertheless, paved the way for acquiescence in more prompt adjustments to changing economic circumstances with exchange rates providing the needed element of flexibility. Under flexible exchange rates the volume of world trade probably grew twice as fast as did real output in 1973, it grew five times as fast in 1974, it contracted less than output in 1975, and it continued its growth relative to output in 1976 and 1977. While a number of countries turned to external financing in order to continue consumption and investment programs in 1974–1976, and some countries have engaged in implicit protectionism in resisting appreciation of their currencies, there can be no doubt that there have been international economic adjustment forces at work which were absent or suppressed in the 1960s.

An element in the absence of adjustment a decade ago was the reticence of governments to take the initiative in an exchange rate change. A perennial debate centered on whether a surplus or a deficit country should initiate a needed change. In the post-1973 milieu, the burden of responsibility for such changes has shifted from governments to the market, and this welcome solution to the problem is, in a way, the source of the progress that has been made. New questions have risen, however, about who may resist—or anticipate or accelerate—market developments and when. These questions are among those yet to be answered.

Remaining Problems

Critics of the IMF amendment, which condones floating and permits governments to intervene in the exchange markets almost at will, express several concerns. Some feel that since 1973 the exchange rates have often moved too rapidly and too far. Others disagree on the purpose that exchange rate changes are to serve. Toward what ends are they to be managed? Should the exchange rates respond to seasonal disturbances? To longer cyclical disturbances? To any disturbances that may be expected to be reversed and whose buffering by official reserves might yield an appropriate social return? Is it appropriate for governments to retard, by the accumulation or reduction of reserves, exchange rate movements that are not expected to be reversed? What are disorderly markets? Is it appropriate for the reserve currency country to take a passive role in the exchange market? These matters are given some attention later in this book.

Another concern about the emerging exchange rate system focuses on the absence of rules. While admitting the necessity of exchange flexibility, some critics abhor the absence of explicit restraints on foreign exchange rate manipulation by governments. The Bretton Woods framework was at least a rule of law, and the 1978 revision of the IMF charter is considered by these critics to be a step backward, although the IMF is charged in the amendment with developing policies and techniques for surveillance of governments' exchange rate policies and the working of the international monetary system. Chapter 3 will consider some alternative rules for exchange market intervention and the question whether a general rule can be designed that is superior to ad hoc negotiation among governments about disagreements as they arise. It must be asked whether any rule dealing with exchange market interventions alone can do all that one might want it to do.

A third criticism of the performance of the exchange markets under floating suggests that the exchange regime is actually unimportant, since the present regime is performing very much like the one it replaced. Weir Brown, for example, has noted that inflation, reserve accumulation, and exchange market intervention have, under floating exchange rates, continued trends which began under fixed rates.[21] It may be inferred from this that, to change the system, one must change more than the exchange rate regime; governments must, perhaps, change the way they view their policy role. This is important, for it will become clear that for any international policy rules to be significant, they must cover more than the exchange rate. Nonetheless, the exchange rate is important, if for no other reason than that the choices faced by governments are different under flexible or under fixed exchange rates.

Among problems of the emerging monetary system that go far beyond the exchange markets are unresolved theoretical questions concerning the interaction among national policies aimed at managing inflation and unemployment. Do flexible exchange rates, for example,

---

21 *World Afloat: National Policies Ruling the Waves*, Essays in International Finance, no. 116 (International Finance Section, Princeton University, May 1976).

exacerbate inflation as a result of a ratchet effect when wages and prices are inflexible downward but flexible upward? Has fiscal stimulus by a single government become largely ineffective as a means of reducing unemployment because international capital is mobile and exchange rates are flexible? Are relative price changes essential or essentially unimportant in the adjustment of international disturbances? One small irony in a system of floating currencies has been its emergence just when the once fashionable set of arguments in its favor began to be seriously questioned by economic theorists who earlier advocated the arrangement. The older arguments maintained that flexible exchange rates would give governments the autonomy they desired in domestic monetary and fiscal policies while national economies were substantially isolated from external disturbances. Newer views emphasize that disturbances may be internationally transmitted through the capital as well as through the money accounts of the balance of payments and that a flexible exchange rate that does no more than reduce the flow of reserve money among countries may not, therefore, ensure the previously expected degree of isolation. Growing international economic interdependence and the shift in the exchange rate regime increase the importance of understanding the mechanism by which economic pressure is transmitted throughout the system and the consequent implications for one government's problems of another government's policy shifts. Not only actual market changes, but expectations of changes in wages and prices, interest rates, and exchange rates, for example, have shown themselves to be very important. Chapter 5 returns to these various matters.

The explosion of liquidity, national and international in both private and public hands, that began under the par value exchange rate regime has continued in the flexible exchange rate period and has supported a worldwide inflation of exceptional intensity. Increasingly governments of developing and developed countries alike have agreed to the importance of bringing the inflation to a halt. Older views focused on the stock of international reserves as a means of controlling global inflation. But in a world where currencies are not convertible into reserve assets on demand, reserve gains by countries resisting currency appreciation do not imply reserve losses—with consequent inducements to deflate—for countries experiencing above average rates of inflation. In any case, with flexible exchange rates, a country's ability to inflate is not constrained by its reserves. Hence the significance of the aggregate reserve stock in relation to global inflation can now be called into question. At the level of money in circulation, inflation depends on financial policies pursued by governments and their monetary authorities and perhaps on the extranational role of banks insofar as Eurobanks extend credit outside the usual framework of national monetary controls and monetary surveillance. We return to further considerations of the problems in this domain in Chapters 5, 6, 7, and 9 where the importance of monetary policy in the United States again comes to the fore.

Inflation and the expansion of bank credit almost everywhere in the first half of the 1970s reduced the ratio of commercial bank equity and subordinated debt to bank assets, a ratio which represents the cushion of safety provided by bank owners and their longer-term creditors to depositors. The increased international lending by banks, as opposed to more traditional domestic lending, together with the growing debt burden of foreign borrowers also raised questions about the risk to which bank asset portfolios have become exposed. In addition, there has been concern that many bank loans denominated in external currencies and undertaken through participation in international syndicates may be multiplying without adequate central bank surveillance and without clear-cut lines of responsibility among central banks for the protection of depositors in the event that some banks get into difficulty. These matters involve the safety and stability of the international financial structure and the dependability of capital flows to developing areas. Is there danger of a domino effect in which one bank's failure may lead to failure or dramatic credit contractions by other banks in an international panic reminiscent of 1931? Some of the available evidence for evaluating these problems is presented in Chapter 7.

Many developing countries have voiced concern with exchange rate flexibility and have expressed preference for a return to par values, although others have adapted well. In any case, developing countries constitute one among many groupings of countries which feel that they have common, special interests in the monetary system. Pleas voiced by Robert Triffin and others for an enlargement and consolidation of a European monetary bloc have added stimulus to discussions of regional clearing associations and monetary unions in many parts of the world. Africa, South and Southeast Asia, and the Middle East are alive with diplomatic activity aimed at creating regional arrangements to rationalize financial flows. Can such arrangements accelerate economic growth? Are they natural complements to regional preferential trading arrangements? Some of the problems of concern to special groups of countries and the ramifications of solutions being proposed are taken up in Chapter 8.

Finally, some questions concerning the extent to which the emerging monetary system can contribute to broader international economic policy goals are raised in Chapter 9. Among the matters considered these are ways in which the monetary regime can affect the resolution of conflicts between developing and developed nations—what has sometimes been called the North-South axis of confrontation—and ways in which the monetary regime may affect the relationships within and between military and economic alliances, East and West. Can flexible exchange rates facilitate progress toward freer international trade and investment, or will misalignment of the rates and new forms of uncertainty exert irresistible pressures for protectionism? Are there opportunities for the SDR to play a more significant role? Can a dollar-centered system survive chronic dollar depreciation? Speculations on such questions come at the end of this book, but now it is time to look more carefully at the evidence.

2
The First Stage of Reform

The international monetary arrangements that took form in 1946 with the IMF at their center were from their beginning in a process of planned and unplanned evolution. Among the unplanned changes prior to 1971 were the degree to which the dollar emerged as the elastic source of reserves for the system, the degree of growth in the size and number of multinational enterprises, the growth of Eurocurrency banking, and developments in the gold market. Among the products of diplomacy were the IMF's General Arrangements to Borrow, the provision for SDRs, the flexible employment of bilateral lines of credit among central banks, enlargement of the IMF's resources and improvement of access to them, and an unprecedented level of central banker consultation. Just as many of the unplanned changes seemed to threaten the financial relationships based on par value exchange rates, the planned ones had as their purpose the defense of the system. The changes embodied in the second amendment to the IMF Articles of Agreement have now relaxed the previous commitment to par value exchange rates, and in that sense the amendment ushers in a new set of diplomatic assignments.[1]

[1] An insightful and personal history of monetary events and negotiations has been provided by Robert Solomon in *The International Monetary System 1945-1976: An Insider's View* (New York: Harper and Row, 1977). A revealing view of events from the perspective of the New York Federal Reserve Bank has been written by Charles A. Coombs, for many years special manager of the Federal Open Market Committee, in *The Arena of International Finance* (New York: John Wiley, 1976). Other literate assessments of recent developments by official participants are Thomas D. Willett, *Floating Exchange Rates and International Monetary Reform* (Washington, D.C.: American Enterprise Institute, 1977); and John Williamson, *The Failure of World Monetary Reform: 1971-1974* (New York: New York University Press, 1977). The nearest thing to an "official" history is found in two excellent reference works prepared at the International Monetary Fund: J. Keith Horsefield, ed., *The International Monetary Fund,*

The events that led to this change of direction began with President Nixon's dramatic announcement August 15, 1971, suspending the conversion of officially held dollar balances into gold and stating that the United States sought reform of the monetary system. Since dollar holdings were a substantial part of the international reserves of a number of countries and the dollar's gold convertibility at an official price was the system's prime link to the traditional monetary metal, the President's unilateral decision by itself modified the "rules of the game." It precipitated negotiations aimed at solving simultaneously a number of the system's problems.

The negotiations that began in 1971, however, proved especially difficult. Four and a half years passed before a comprehensive amendment to the IMF's articles could be drafted. This chapter summarizes the issues around which differences of views emerged in those talks as well as the agreements that finally constituted the compromise package.

The Negotiating Forum

The 1971 annual combined meeting of the IMF and the World Bank opened only six weeks after the U.S. policy break. It took place in an atmosphere of charges and countercharges and achieved little toward monetary reform beyond an instruction to the IMF's executive directors to begin without delay a study of "all aspects of the international monetary system." The report that subsequently emerged from that first mandate, reflecting in considerable degree the efforts of the IMF's distinguished economic counselor, Jacques Polack, was a sober consideration of a number of issues and provided intellectual guidance to the discussions of the following months. Beyond that, however, its significance was limited. Governments in 1971–1972 were still considering their positions, and the serious discussions in the spring and summer of 1972 were concerned more with the forum in which the issues would be negotiated than with their substance.

The international forum in which the first amendment to the IMF charter—that providing for SDRs—had been hammered out in 1967–1969 was the Group of Ten (G-10), the large industrialized countries that had in the General Arrangements to Borrow made their currencies available in special circumstances to the Fund. Since these countries together commanded an overwhelming majority of IMF votes, their

1945-1965, 3 vols. (Washington, D.C.: IMF, 1969); and Margaret Garretsen de Vries, *The International Monetary Fund*, 1966-1971, 2 vols. (Washington, D.C.: IMF, 1976).

decisions, once taken in the privacy of G-10 meetings, were virtually assured of favorable action under IMF procedures. Remembering the difficulty of the SDR negotiations, however, the United States in 1972 did not consider the G-10 an ideal forum for broader reform talks. It furthermore did not want the IMF staff to dominate the discussions, feeling that the staff would be biased in favor of the status quo. At the same time, the IMF's managing director, Pierre-Paul Schweitzer, sought a role in the negotiations for representatives of the 113 Fund member countries which did not belong to the Group of Ten.

In the end, it was agreed to constitute a special committee on reform of the international monetary system and related issues. The committee, created by the Fund's board of governors in July 1972, had twenty members and alternates, echoing the constituencies which cast votes in decisions taken by the Fund's executive directors, hence giving some representation to all Fund members. Unlike the decision process in the Fund, however, decisions in the Committee of Twenty, or C-20, as it came to be called, were to be taken by consensus with all points of view reported. The C-20 had a parallel committee of deputies. The forum was unfortunately large and unwieldy; there were some 200 participants in the ministerial level meetings, with sixty entitled to speak, and equal numbers in the committee of deputies. The G-10 continued to provide a convenient caucus from time to time for an exchange of views among the larger countries, and as a counterweight to this group the developing countries instituted their own caucus, the Intergovernmental Group of Twenty-four (G-24).

The environment of monetary developments in which the Committee of Twenty had to execute its work was turbulent. The realignment of exchange rates, which had been implemented in late 1971 in association with a widened band for permissible movements of the rates,[2] was tested by heavy speculation early in 1972 and again in the late spring and summer of the same year when the deutsche mark was realigned and the pound sterling floated. The negotiated structure of rates then broke apart into further realignments and generalized floating early in 1973. Inflation, measured by the IMF's international average of monthly consumer price changes, advanced to an annual 9.6 percent rate in 1973 and to 15.1 percent in 1974 without eliminating high levels of unemployment in many countries. The

[2] The new rates were designated "central rates" as opposed to "par values" to permit fluctuations to be broadened from the ± 1.0 percent called for in the IMF charter to ± 2.25 percent. In practice the intervention boundaries of most countries around the older par values had been ± 0.75 percent.

action by OPEC countries in embargoing oil shipments in late 1973 and then, in subsequent months, in raising prices approximately fourfold constituted a massive shock to world trade and finance.

The uncertainties engendered by these vast disturbances contributed to the decision to wind up the work of the Committee of Twenty in June 1974, although only limited progress had been made. Also contributing to the decision was the apparent intractability of a number of the central issues. Early in 1974, governments acknowledged that change in the system would have to be evolutionary. In June, therefore, the Committee of Twenty terminated its work with a report and an *Outline of Reform.* The *Outline* provided the basis for some of the changes subsequently incorporated in the second amendment to the IMF articles. But it was marred by having been drawn up under the directive that exchange rates were to be based on stable but adjustable par values with floating only in particular situations. Had the committee been able to focus its negotiations directly on the needs of a world of managed floating exchange rates, its *Outline* would doubtless have been different.

Matters at Issue

Convertibility and Asset Settlement. Some European countries, especially the French, went to the C-20 negotiations hoping to obtain a return to the convertibility of national currencies, especially the dollar, into other international reserve assets, preferably gold, at fixed prices. These governments wanted such convertibility for several reasons. First, they coveted the privilege of balancing at will their portfolios of reserve assets among several monetary instruments, including gold, dollars, SDRs, and nondollar national currencies. The rebalancing of existing portfolios seemed especially important in view of the dollar's weakness in the years that had just passed and in view of the large dollar accumulations that had come into the hands of some governments. There was perhaps even more interest in the convertibility of future dollar accumulations. The United States' step of closing the gold window had emphasized the degree to which the international financial system had become dollar centered and dominated by U.S. policies, and the demand that the dollar be made once again convertible into other assets was an expression of protest against this state of affairs. It should be noted that the U.S. action did not interfere with convertibility of dollar balances held by foreign official agencies, or anyone else, into any other asset at market prices. The European approach, calling for unfettered official convertibility among reserve assets at fixed prices was, therefore, associated by implication with a desire to return to officially fixed foreign exchange rates.

A second reason for wanting dollar convertibility at officially set prices went beyond the mere desire of some countries to have unlimited transferability among reserve assets. Representatives of France articulated most vigorously the view that the United States and all other countries should be denied the special privileges that came to countries whose currencies were used as reserves by other countries, namely the privilege of paying for balance of payments deficits with an asset that did not have to be earned. The attack here was on what some writers have called the "seigniorage" privilege of the reserve currency country by which that country could enjoy consumption and investment which it paid for with a money created at little or no cost to itself. The French demanded for all countries asset settlement of payments imbalances, as opposed to payment with bank liabilities. The French preference was for settlements in gold, a monetary medium no country could costlessly create; but the French were prepared to consider alternative international assets, including SDRs.

Consolidation and Management of Currency Reserves. Of interest especially to those concerned with systemic performance was a desire to reduce the variety of forms in which international reserves were held, and thereby remove one source of chronic instability from the system. To the extent this consolidation could be achieved, better opportunities for controlling the supply of reserve assets and hence new opportunities for limiting global monetary disturbances might be created. In particular, it seemed necessary to resolve the dilemma which had arisen in connection with the dollar's reserve role. That dilemma lay in the need of countries other than the United States for U.S. balance of payments deficits to provide them with desired growth in reserves, while at the same time prolonged growth in such external dollar liabilities undermined confidence in the dollar's convertibility into other reserve media.

Toward these ends, then, at least lip service was paid by many governments to the idea of increasing the role of the IMF's new reserve asset, the special drawing right, and somehow to making the SDR the center of the system. There were, nonetheless, misgivings about this. Many countries probably had little intention of abandoning the privilege of holding gold among their reserve assets, and the attractiveness of gold was heightened during the negotiations by its high price on the private market as compared with the official price.

Many countries also wanted the privilege of earning the best possible return on assets held as reserves, and SDR holdings in excess of allocations at that time were earning only 1.5 percent interest while the rate obtainable on U.S. Treasury bills was 6 to 7 percent. Although many countries subscribed to the desirability of controlling international liquidity in general, they wanted no heavy hand on their own privilege of borrowing or otherwise acquiring needed reserves. For its part, the United States was not interested in the promotion of any nondollar reserve asset unless the step was associated with arrangements which would provide an improved adjustment process. The United States wanted maximum assurance it would not again be pressured, in the degree it was during the several years prior to 1971, by demands to tailor its domestic and foreign policies to meet the needs of other participants in the international monetary system. In any case, since it was an asset which could not be held by private parties, the SDR could not be used by governments as an exchange market intervention medium, so that working balances in dollars or some other asset would have to be retained. In the end, these several reservations about substituting SDRs for other reserve assets proved too much for the negotiators to overcome.

Adjustment. Reform of the monetary system clearly meant something different to each of those who approached the C-20 negotiations. The positions taken by the governments of France and of the United States contrasted most sharply. The French wanted stabilized exchange rates—reserving the privilege of countries like themselves to change the peg—while the United States wanted an improved adjustment process, which from the U.S. perspective meant an increase in exchange rate flexibility, as compared with experience in the late 1960s. The United States especially wanted assurance that countries in surplus would allow their currencies to appreciate against the dollar as readily as countries in deficit allowed their currencies to depreciate, for U.S. authorities believed asymmetry in such rate adjustments had in the past been a key factor weakening the U.S. balance of payments. Leitmotifs in the U.S. position, therefore, were flexibility, symmetry in the adjustment responsibilities of surplus and deficit countries, and objective indicators to remove any doubt about the existence of a disequilibrium requiring policy changes. "Symmetry," indeed, became a popular word with the negotiators although the word was employed differently by its various users. The French, for example, wanted symmetry in convertibility requirements while the United States wanted symmetry in adjustment requirements.

The only reasonably comprehensive proposal for reform made public during the C-20 negotiations was distributed to the C-20 deputies by the United States in November 1972. The core of that proposal was a mandate that would require countries in a surplus or deficit position to adopt policies suitable for reestablishing international balance. The presence of the imbalance would be indicated by the accumulation or decumulation of reserve assets by those countries. The proposal called for adjustment action by any country when its reserves reached a warning point; international sanctions could be applied to it when its reserves diverged enough from preestablished norms to reach outer limits. The U.S. proposal did not attempt to specify the degree to which reserves should be held in the form of prime reserve assets—gold, SDRs, or reserve positions in the IMF—on the one hand, or foreign exchange assets, on the other, but made the assumption that at least some of the reserves of most nations would be in the form of foreign exchange, with safeguards provided to the reserve currency countries against excessive conversion demands.[3]

The American proposals were received with skepticism by the European negotiators. To begin with, the proposals raised technical problems, such as the definition of reserves, the criteria for establishing and updating base reserve levels, the matter of how to appraise balance of payments implications of adjustment policies undertaken by countries in response to the mandate to limit reserve changes, and the problem of avoiding disturbances caused by private capital movements which would seek to anticipate policy changes called for by the reserve indicators. More fundamentally, however, the Europeans saw in the proposal the American expectation that the United States would continue to be the chief reserve currency country and an American effort to compel them to adjust their balances of payments no matter what the U.S. economic policies might be. Under the U.S. proposals, if the United States were profligate in its monetary and fiscal policies, as Europeans were prone to feel this country had been in the late 1960s, the Europeans would have to appreciate their currencies or join in the profligacy. They wanted other alternatives, even the right to accumulate dollars.

In short, many Europeans sought arrangements for asset settlement in the negotiations to force internal policy adjustments on the United States. The United States sought acceptance of reserve changes as an objective indicator of the need for policy changes by others.

[3] The U.S. proposals were published in the *Economic Report of the President* (Washington, D.C., January 1973), pp. 160-74.

It seems certain that each side might have taken a different position had the recent experiences involved chronic U.S. balance of payments surpluses instead of deficits. In the background of the debate lay disagreement over the wisdom of financial policies of the reserve center country in the recent past and mutual suspicions about policy decisions that might be taken in the future.

Assistance to Developing Countries. Finally, some issues that led to increasingly acrimonious discussions concerned amounts and forms of assistance to developing countries. At the outset of the negotiations consideration of these matters focused on whether and in what way the allocation of SDRs should be linked to development assistance. Developing countries pointed out that the more developed countries were favored in the 1969 compromise in which an aggregate SDR allocation is apportioned among participating countries in proportion to their IMF quotas. Developing countries saw, in a restructuring of the allocation formula, a means of increasing their command on the world's output without being recurrently subject to the lash of political processes in donor countries. Invoking, therefore, a moral claim for greater equality in the international distribution of wealth, they sought a sympathetic review of the SDR allocation process. The proposal for a link between SDR allocation and development assistance was resisted by a number of developed countries, including the United States, not only on the ground that it sanctioned gifts which might or might not have the approval of the givers, but on the ground that it tied the important but politically sensitive matter of foreign aid to a matter that was itself too important to be so burdened, namely the management of the supply of the world's first fiduciary international reserve asset. It was clear that SDR allocations were potentially an engine of inflation, and equally clear that few guidelines existed for the management of this money. To put the experiment under pressure by countries whose needs for external financing would be insatiable for the foreseeable future seemed to some governments unwise.

As it happened, the debate on the matter of the link became largely academic because the enormous reserve accumulation between 1971 and 1974 by some countries and the accompanying inflation made further substantial, near-term SDR allocations seem unlikely. Meanwhile, the immediate needs of many countries for assistance to finance oil-induced current account deficits after 1973 became paramount. In the end, in the 1975–1976 reforms the developing countries gained increased voting strength and credit facilities in the IMF, a trust fund initially financed with profits from sale of a portion of the IMF's gold, an enlargement of the facility for financing temporary shortfalls in export earnings, and a new facility for financing intermediate-term balance of payments deficits. The added resources were not large relative to developing countries' hopes, but some of the changes were structural and hence will probably be durable in character.

The Report of the Committee of Twenty

The C-20's *Outline of Reform* had three substantive parts.[4] The first, subtitled "The Reformed System," reflected the degree of agreement that could be obtained on the general form the system might take. The second, subtitled "Immediate Steps," suggested the creation of an Interim Coordinating Committee to carry forward the reform discussions and also recommended several measures to help finance foreseeable trade imbalances, to improve the functioning of the SDR, and to limit the risk of near-term resort by members to restrictive trade and payments practices. The third substantive part of the *Outline* comprised a set of annexes in which the chairman and the vice-chairmen of the deputies undertook to record the state of the discussion concerning a number of matters on which the agreement of the entire committee was not obtainable. Each substantive part was significant. In addition, the Committee of Twenty produced valuable reports from seven technical groups.

Part I of the *Outline* recorded the outcome of the committee's discussion of international monetary reform and indicated the general direction in which the committee believed that the system could evolve. In the committee's own words, the main features of the emerging international monetary reform would include:

(a) an effective and symmetrical adjustment process, including better functioning of the exchange rate mechanism, with the exchange rate regime based on stable but adjustable par values and with floating rates recognized as providing a useful technique in particular situations;
(b) cooperation in dealing with disequilibrating capital flows;
(c) the introduction of an appropriate form of convertibility for the settlement of imbalances, with symmetrical obligations on all countries;

[4] International Monetary Fund, Committee on Reform of the International Monetary System and Related Issues, *International Monetary Reform: Documents of the Committee of Twenty* (Washington, D.C., 1974).

(d) better international management of global liquidity, with the SDR becoming the principal reserve asset and the role of gold and of reserve currencies being reduced;
(e) consistency between arrangements for adjustment, convertibility, and global liquidity; and
(f) the promotion of the net flow of real resources to developing countries.[5]

Key words in the agreement, however, such as "effective," "particular situations," "cooperation," "appropriate," "better," and "promotion," were not given operational content.

In discussing adjustment, the *Outline* called for surveillance of the continuing operation of the adjustment process by the IMF executive board and by a permanent high-level council, to be established. It called on countries to keep their official reserves within limits which would be internationally agreed on from time to time. No agreement was reached, however, on the nature of suitable reserve indicators or on sanctions or pressures that might be applied by the Fund to countries failing to take appropriate adjustment action. Consideration of these matters was relegated to the annexes. Also relegated to the annexes were discussions of intervention systems that would allow all currencies, including the dollar, equal and symmetrical degrees of flexibility around their par values or central rates and the sensitive matter of the conditions under which a country would be authorized to float its currency, together with guidelines for such floating.

The *Outline* announced agreement that "the SDR will become the principal reserve asset, and the role of gold and of reserve currencies will be reduced."[6] But methods for assessing global reserve needs, permanent techniques for determining the value of the SDR, consideration of ways to relax existing constraints on SDR use, the subject of future arrangements for gold in the system, and operational provisions of a substitution account in which foreign exchange reserves might be exchanged for SDRs were among many points on which there was no agreement.

The reformed monetary system was to "contain arrangements to promote an increasing net flow of real resources to developing countries."[7] But again possibilities for such arrangements could be explored only in an annex. Agreement was reached and subsequently effected to create a new facility in the Fund under which developing

[5] Ibid., p. 8.
[6] Ibid., p. 15.
[7] Ibid., p. 17.

countries could receive balance of payments financing for more extended periods than those usually allowed.

One of the immediate steps recommended in Part II of the *Outline* was the creation of an interim committee of the Board of Governors of the Fund to supervise the management and adaptation of the monetary system, to oversee the continuing operation of the adjustment process, and to deal with sudden disturbances. This committee, structured like the reform committee on the twenty constituencies of the Fund and expected to be the antecedent of a permanent council, would bring figures of higher political rank than the Fund's executive directors into the regular procedures for decision making about the Fund and the evolution of the monetary system. The interim committee would advise the Board of Governors until the committee could be succeeded by the council, which would have delegated powers in the reformed system. The final annex to the *Outline* also recommended appointment of a joint ministerial committee of the Fund and the World Bank to carry forward the study of broad questions relating to economic development and the transfer of resources to developing countries. That recommendation was subsequently executed, in tandem with the appointment of the interim committee, by the creation of a joint Fund and Bank Development Committee.

Besides creation of these committees, Part II of the *Outline* mentioned a number of other measures that might be taken immediately. These included:

- establishment of a facility in the Fund to assist member countries in meeting the initial impact of the increase in oil import costs
- immediate establishment of an extended Fund facility, mentioned earlier, to provide longer-term balance of payments finance to developing countries
- valuation "in present circumstances" of the SDR in terms of a "basket" of currencies, "without prejudice to the method of valuation to be adopted in a reformed system" and periodic determination of the SDR rate of interest by the executive board.

In the interim before reform could be consolidated, the *Outline* called on countries to pledge themselves to various principles and practices mentioned in the document that were aimed at preserving liberal trading and investment conditions. Among these was a call for countries to follow guidelines concerning exchange market intervention that were prescribed in an annex. The guidelines were "designed to promote exchange market stability and the international consistency of policies affecting exchange rates and reserves."[8] Countries were invited to pledge themselves for two years on a voluntary basis "not to introduce or intensify trade or other current account measures for balance of payments purposes without a finding by the Fund that there is balance of payments justification for such measures."[9] It was expected that in seeking adjustment to international imbalances countries would take prompt and adequate adjustment action, taking into account repercussions on other countries as well as internal considerations. They would aim to keep official reserves within limits which would be internationally agreed on from time to time. They were to "apply adjustment measures in a manner designed to protect the net flow of real resources to developing countries."[10] In addition, they were asked to cooperate to limit disequilibrating capital flows and, in so doing, to avoid the use of capital controls for the purpose of maintaining inappropriate exchange rates or avoiding appropriate adjustment action.[11]

The Fund was called on to exercise surveillance of the adjustment process, seeking to "gain further experience in the use of objective indicators, including reserve indicators, on an experimental basis" but not using such indicators "to establish any presumptive or automatic application of pressures." The Fund was asked also to give consideration to substitution arrangements for consolidating international reserve assets and to give further study to arrangements for gold. The executive board was specifically asked to begin work on draft amendments for possible recommendation to the Board of Governors at an appropriate time.[12]

In the work of the Committee of Twenty, events overwhelmed the reform rather than the reform molding the events. The few details the committee was able to enunciate in its *Outline* aimed more at salvaging a semblance of order from the chaos that seemed to be threatening than at defining a monetary system. A central element in the committee's failure was its focus on problems associated with a par value exchange rate system. The committee was seeking means to make such a system workable and at the same time to maintain safeguards against illiberal trade and payments practices by national governments under great pressure to serve national ends. In particular, the United States and European countries demanded freedom from

[8] Ibid., p. 35.
[9] Ibid., p. 20.
[10] Ibid., pp. 8-9.
[11] Ibid., pp. 12-13.
[12] Ibid., pp. 19-22.

obligations that would subject domestic policy options to external constraints, and they also wanted to sustain progress toward limiting beggar-my-neighbor trade and payments practices. In disturbed times, these objectives were incompatible with stabilized exchange rates unless there were facilities for massive support for countries that lived beyond their means by countries that did not, and no government had an appetite for *carte blanche* commitments of that sort. Meanwhile, the ingredients of a reform had to be integrated and made mutually supporting; nothing critical could be decided until all the main decisions were visible. Reform waited on the resolution of fundamental issues.

Negotiating Basic Issues

Specific immediate steps called for by the Committee of Twenty were promptly implemented. An interim committee was recommended in June 1974 by the executive directors and approved by the Board of Governors in October; a parallel Joint International Monetary Fund–World Bank Development Committee was created; an oil facility in the Fund was established in July and an extended Fund facility was established in September; the SDR's valuation was changed as of July 1 from that of a fixed weight of gold to the value of a basket of specified amounts of each of sixteen currencies (see Table 2); and guidelines for the management of floating currencies were adopted in June by the Fund's executive directors. Members of the Fund were invited at the end of June to sign a two-year pledge to eschew intensifying trade or current account measures for balance of payments purposes in their individual efforts to deal with the world's large payments disequilibrium, and by June 1975 fourteen members, having 40.66 percent of the voting power, had done so.[13]

But basic issues remained. Most large members of the Fund were in violation of the articles in failing to maintain exchange transactions at rates conforming to prescribed limits about stated par values, rancor among governments was growing because no agreement had cleared the way for gold reserves to be used in financing payments imbalances, the volume of foreign exchange reserves was growing enormously as oil-importing countries borrowed to gain time for economic adjustment, and the need of some developing countries for financing assistance was acute.

[13] Technically, the acceptances were never binding since the declaration was to become effective only upon acceptance by countries having 65 perent of the Fund's voting power. See International Monetary Fund, *Annual Report, 1975*, p. 58.

TABLE 2

DEFINITION OF SPECIAL DRAWING RIGHTS IN TERMS OF A BASKET OF NATIONAL CURRENCIES

	Number of Units of Currency Included	
Currency	July 1, 1974–June 30, 1978	Beginning July 1, 1978
U.S. dollar	0.40	0.40
Deutsche mark	0.38	0.32
Pound sterling	0.045	0.050
French franc	0.44	0.42
Japanese yen	26.00	21.00
Canadian dollar	0.071	0.070
Italian lira	47.00	52.00
Netherlands guilder	0.14	0.14
Belgian franc	1.6	1.6
Swedish krona	0.13	0.11
Australian dollar	0.012	0.017
Danish krone	0.11	—
Norwegian krone	0.099	0.10
Spanish peseta	1.1	1.5
Austrian schilling	0.22	0.28
South African rand	0.0082	—
Saudi Arabian riyal	—	0.13
Iranian rial	—	1.7

NOTE: One SDR was originally defined as the sum of the market values of the currency amounts listed in the first column above. As of July 1, 1978, the currency amounts were adjusted to reflect economic data of the 1972-1976 period.

At this juncture the sixth general review of IMF quotas fell due, and pressures materialized for the quotas to be increased and redistributed to reflect better the economic realities of the later 1970s. The subject of quotas was inextricably tied to other matters central to the negotiations, for example, to the arrangements that might be made for gold. Under existing rules 25 percent of the subscription corresponding to any new or enlarged Fund quota was normally payable by the member in gold, but if the role of gold in the system were to be reduced, the gold subscription might not be necessary. Indeed, in the Fund's 1974 fiscal year, at the recommendation of the executive directors the Bahamas had become a member without paying any of its subscription in gold, Nepal was permitted to postpone the final installments of payments for its previous quota increase because of uncertainty about the future role of gold, and four countries had similarly been permitted postponements of obligations to repurchase Fund holdings of their currencies with gold. Furthermore, disproportionate quota increases affect control of the IMF since voting power on Fund decisions is proportionate to quotas. Many countries, among them developing countries, were eager to have larger quotas at the Fund, especially if the gold payment in the subscription were avoided, because they wanted larger drawing rights and a greater voice in control. Control, however, was a matter different from credit in the eyes of developed countries, perhaps especially in the eyes of U.S. officials, and this complicated the subject.

Progress in the negotiation of the several issues was slow but on some fronts steady after the October 1974 meetings of the Fund and the World Bank, and it took place in various forums. In general, material shifted back and forth between the Fund's executive directors and staff, where drafting was undertaken and options prepared, and the interim committee where advisory decisions were reached and further instructions issued. The broad debate on monetary arrangements also intruded into conversations wherever officials of different countries met: in the joint Fund and World Bank Development Committee, where there was special interest in a trust fund for the benefit of developing countries; in the United Nations Conference on Trade and Development (UNCTAD), in the OECD, in the G-10 and the G-24, in regional and commodity-oriented organizations, and in the United Nations General Assembly, which devoted a special session to the world economy in September 1975. The agreements that emerged were influenced by the North-South dialogue that began with the dramatic change in the economic position of the oil-producing nations. They were, needless to say, affected also by the apparent need for continued financing of large imbalances in the pattern of world trade.

At its second, third, and fourth meetings in January, June, and September 1975, respectively, the interim committee considered progress reports from the executive directors concerning a number of draft amendments to the IMF articles and also matters related to the Fund's oil facility and the sixth general review of quotas. A wide range of problems was represented in these deliberations. By September some decisions had emerged.

The Council. It was agreed that the council, called for by the Committee of Twenty, should be authorized by an appropriate amendment, although it would come into being only on the vote of an 85 percent majority of weighted Fund voting power. All authority of the Board of Governors of the Fund should be delegable either to the council or to the executive directors, or both concurrently, by decisions of the Board of Governors. Under the amended articles, each member of the council, representing one of the Fund's twenty constituencies, would be able to cast the votes of the constituency countries separately, rather than as a bloc as executive directors must do.

Gold. It was agreed that the role of gold in the monetary system would be reduced as a counterpart to the decision to enhance the role of the SDR as the central asset in the system. In furtherance of this goal, the official price of gold would be abolished, and all obligations to use gold in payments between the Fund and its members would be abrogated. Furthermore, a portion of the Fund's gold would be sold at market prices for the benefit of developing members, particularly those with low incomes, and another portion would be returned to members in exchange for their own currencies at the present official gold price. While both the U.S. and the French negotiators had previously insisted that any agreement on gold be linked to an agreement on exchange rates, first the French and then the Americans agreed, at the September 1975 meeting of the committee, to allow a separation of the issues. Accordingly it was decided that 25 million ounces (approximately one-sixth of the Fund's gold) would be sold for developing countries and another 25 million ounces would be returned to members. Enabling authority would be provided for disposition of still more of the Fund's gold, but it would be exercisable only with an 85 percent majority. Some commentators felt that the restitution of 25 million ounces to all members in proportion to their quotas was a regrettable compromise of the principle that the Fund's gold profits would be distributed to the Fund's poorest members. But it was an unavoidable concession to hard-pressed countries that would be ineligible for trust fund assistance.

In June the committee said a reasonable formula should be found for understandings among monetary authorities, and between them and the Fund, to prevent the reestablishment of an official price and to regulate the volume of gold held by monetary authorities. The Group of Ten countries made a two-year agreement in August that none would take any action to peg the price of gold, that the total stock of gold in the hands of the Fund and the monetary authorities of the G-10 would not be increased, and that parties to the arrangement would notify the Fund and the Bank for International Settlements semiannually of gold purchases and sales. The

United States had sought a ban on individual government purchases of gold for an indefinite period, but it abandoned this goal in the negotiations, settling for a collective ceiling during a two-year renewable period. That agreement subsequently lapsed in 1978.

There was continuing discussion but no consensus about a substitution account through which members would be able to exchange part of or all their gold holdings for SDRs issued for the purpose.

The Special Drawing Account. The executive directors were asked by the interim committee to continue their work toward improving the SDR so as to move toward making it the principal reserve asset of the monetary system. At its inception, the SDR had been hedged about by a number of constraints, partly because of disagreement about whether the asset was to represent generalized purchasing power—money—or an instrument of credit. Among the constraints are limitations on each member's obligation to accept and hold SDRs; obligations on members to reconstitute their SDR holdings so that their average holdings during each moving five-year period are at least 30 percent of their cumulative allocations; payment of interest, by members whose SDR holdings are less than their allocations, to members whose holdings are greater than their allocations; a requirement that a country demonstrate balance of payments "need" before it spends SDRs in its account; and a requirement that the IMF designate members eligible to receive SDRs and that it approve SDR transfers. In its final form, the second amendment to the articles only slightly modifies these constraints. It permits transactions in SDRs between members whenever the transaction is mutually agreeable, and it enables the executive directors to take decisions relating to other SDR usage with smaller majorities than before. Meanwhile, the Bank for International Settlements in Basel has been authorized to hold SDRs, and the rates of interest and charges on SDRs have been linked to the market interest rates in a group of international financial centers. As mentioned above and detailed in Table 2, the SDR's value was divorced from gold and tied to a sixteen-currency basket beginning in 1974.

The General Account. Several amendments to the way the Fund's general account might function were accepted. The most important of these probably was the provision in the amended articles of terms designed to ensure that all the Fund's currency holdings are made usable. Since a large part of Fund resources have from the beginning been in currencies rarely used in international settlements and since prior to the second amendment currencies sold to members were those elected by the member, the utility of much of the Fund's stock of assets was impaired. The amended articles allow the Fund to specify the currencies in which any member's purchase, or any member's repurchase of its own currency, will be executed. If a country's currency is sold by the Fund but is not "freely usable" money, the country is then under obligation to exchange the currency for one that is freely usable. The step substantially enlarges the Fund's capabilities.

The pressing needs of developing countries, together with the improbability that the Fund's oil facility would continue indefinitely, raised issues about further means of providing external financing to such countries. While the New International Economic Order called for by the U.N. General Assembly in 1974 emphasized stabilizing world prices of primary products through international commodity agreements, falling prices of such products in 1975 sharpened the calls for action along these lines. The interim committee requested that the executive directors consider modifications to the Fund's facilities for compensatory financing of fluctuations in export earnings and also consider assistance to members in connection with their contributions to international buffer stocks. In particular, it was agreed that a member using the Fund's buffer stock facility would not have that credit charged against its position in the general accounts of the Fund; a similar provision already applied to drawings under the Fund's compensatory financing facility.

Quotas of Members. It was agreed in the winter and spring of 1975 that there would be a general enlargement of quotas, but implementation was made subject to agreement on a satisfactory set of amendments to the articles. Subject to that condition, the total of existing quotas would be increased by 32.5 percent and rounded up to approximately SDR39 billion. The quotas of the major oil exporters as a group were increased to approximately 10 percent of the total from 5 percent, and the collective share of all other developing countries was held at its present level. By implication, proportionate shares in the Fund and the voting power of developed countries had to be reduced. The U.S. share at that time was 21.87 percent, and the share of the original six members of the Common Market was 18.11 percent. Various important questions in the Fund, including amendment, required an affirmative 80 percent vote. To protect its position, the United States demanded and won acceptance of the principle that certain decisions previously taken by an 80 percent majority would henceforth require an 85 percent vote, the majority already specified for approval of allocations of SDRs. Surprisingly little concern seems to have been expressed that this very high majority permits small clusters of countries easily to put together vetoes. The 25 percent share of the increases in quotas previously payable in gold would, after amendment of the articles, be paid in SDRs, in the currencies of certain members subject to their concurrence, or in the member's own currency. This slice of the quotas would be referred to as the "reserve tranche." The period within which the next general review of quotas would take place was reduced from five to three years.

Exchange Rate Arrangements. Notwithstanding progress in negotiating certain issues, the interim committee had made no headway on the central issue of the adjustment process by the summer of 1975. In its press communiqué following the June meeting, the committee "reiterated its agreement that provision should be made for stable but adjustable par values and the floating of currencies in particular situations, subject to appropriate rules and surveillance of the Fund in accordance with the Outline of Reform."[14] Insofar as the currencies of most industrialized countries had by then been floating for more than two years, these words had a hollow ring. At its September meeting the committee acknowledged that "acceptable solutions must be found on the subject of the exchange rate system under the amended Articles, so that these agreed solutions can be combined with those on quotas and gold."[15]

Some straws were in the wind. Before leaving Paris for the September meetings in Washington, the French finance minister acknowledged in an interview that a return to fixed but adjustable exchange rates was perhaps two to four years away and that "a better system of floating" was of high priority.[16] And in his address to the annual Fund meeting, the IMF's managing director expressed in measured words the views of the Fund's staff.

> In light of these considerations, it seems to me that we would be wise to adopt an amendment of our Articles of Agreement that would allow the exchange system to develop in the manner best suited to evolving circumstances.

[14] International Monetary Fund, *Annual Report, 1975*, p. 100.

[15] Ibid., p. 121.

[16] *Wall Street Journal*, August 22, 1975.

When the existing inflationary climate recedes, when the magnitude of payments disequilibria is reduced, and when the effects of recent shocks to the system are absorbed, greater stability in the pattern of exchange rates by more coordinated management should be a realistic possibility. If at some time a sufficient number of Fund members wish to return to some form of par value system, the amended Articles should permit this; equally, scope must be left for countries to adopt floating or some other arrangement, provided they observe the relevant guidelines. All members, floating and nonfloating alike, should adhere to rules of the game, which will need to be worked out more specifically than has been possible so far. In this way, we will have a system which responds to the needs of individual countries, while continuing to assert the primacy of the general interest in a matter which concerns the welfare of all.[17]

Rambouillet and Jamaica

The breakthrough in the negotiations finally came at talks among the heads of state and heads of government of France, the Federal Republic of Germany, Italy, Japan, the United Kingdom, and the United States. The meeting convened at the invitation of France at the Chateau de Rambouillet, November 15–17, 1975. Bilateral talks at that time between the U.S. and French presidents, preceded by critical negotiations at the ministerial and subministerial level, produced an agreement that led directly to a draft of an amended Article IV, on exchange arrangements, of the IMF articles.

While this amended article specified some general obligations of members, it leaves countries for the most part free to implement the exchange rate arrangements of their choice. General obligations require each country to collaborate with the Fund and other members to assure orderly exchange arrangements and to promote a stable system of exchange rates. In particular, each member shall:

(i) endeavor to direct its economic and financial policies toward the objective of fostering orderly economic growth with reasonable price stability, with due regard to its circumstances;

(ii) seek to promote stability by fostering orderly underlying economic and financial conditions and a monetary system that does not tend to produce erratic disruptions;

[17] H. Johannes Witteveen, *IMF Survey*, September 15, 1975, p. 262.

(iii) avoid manipulating exchange rates or the international monetary system in order to prevent effective balance of payments adjustment or to gain an unfair advantage over other members; and
(iv) follow exchange policies compatible with the undertakings under this Section.[18]

Beyond these very general responsibilities, however, members are free. The article specified that exchange rate arrangements may include:

(i) the maintenance by a member of a value for its currency in terms of the special drawing right or another denominator, other than gold, selected by the member, or
(ii) cooperative arrangements by which members maintain the value of their currencies in relation to the value of the currency or currencies of other members, or
(iii) other exchange arrangements of a member's choice.[19]

The Fund may, by an 85 percent majority of the total voting power, make provision for general exchange arrangements (this is what the French took home from the negotiations), but these may not limit the right of members to make exchange arrangements of their choice consistent with the general obligations. In particular, an 85 percent majority of the Fund may determine that conditions permit the introduction of a widespread system of exchange arrangements based on stable but adjustable par values in terms of the SDR or another common denominator (which, however, may not be gold or a currency). Any member not wishing to establish a par value for its currency in these circumstances may, nonetheless, opt out, and it may terminate an initially established par value, although the Fund by an 85 percent majority may object to the termination. A country that has terminated a par value may, at any time, propose a new par value. The Fund is to exercise firm surveillance over the exchange rate policies of members and adopt specific principles for the guidance of members.

Following the agreement on exchange rate arrangements, the Group of Ten, meeting in December, agreed on closer consultation on exchange market conditions and interventions, in particular by extending to the United States, Canada, Japan, and Switzerland the

[18] *Proposed Second Amendment to the Articles of Agreement of the International Monetary Fund,* A Report by the Executive Directors to the Board of Governors, International Monetary Fund (Washington, D.C., March 1976), p. 288.
[19] Ibid., p. 6.

European Economic Community's practice of daily telephonic exchanges and by providing for periodic consultations among finance ministers and among their deputies.

The agreement on freedom of choice for members in their exchange rate arrangements—that is, their freedom to float whenever they choose—paved the way for acceptance of the previously negotiated package of reforms. The package was sealed at the fifth meeting of the interim committee in January 1976 at Kingston, Jamaica. There most reforms previously accepted fell into place, except that developing countries now pressed for an enlargement of the unconditional credit tranche in the IMF. The previous December the executive directors of the Fund had already enlarged the drawings a member suffering a temporary shortfall of export earnings could make on the Fund. This compensatory financing facility was especially valuable to primary product exporters who had experienced declining prices for their products on world markets in 1975. Permissible drawings under the compensatory facility were in December increased to 75 percent from 50 percent of quota, with the provision that as much as 50 percent of a member's quota (up from 25 percent) could be drawn in one year. But developing countries now sought, in addition, unconditional access to 75 percent of their normal quotas in the Fund, in lieu of the 25 percent available in the past. Most developed countries and the IMF staff opposed wholesale abrogation of the principle that extensive credit should be subject to careful stipulation of performance conditions for the borrower. In the end, there was again compromise.

The total package of enlarged access to resources obtained by developing countries in the negotiations emerged as follows. Quotas were enlarged 33.6 percent for the Fund as a whole. It was agreed, however, that these quotas would not be available until ratification of the amendment to the articles. For the period prior to ratification, the size of each of the three IMF credit tranches—in which credit conditions became progressively more stringent—was increased by 45 percent. Although the credit liberalization was less than developing countries had sought, the increase was substantial and retained the principal of conditionality. In addition to the quota enlargements and the interim credit expansion, the credit facility for compensatory financing was enlarged from 50 to 75 percent of quota, as mentioned above. Furthermore, drawings under the facility to finance buffer stocks were made fully additional to drawings under the gold and credit tranches, like drawings under the compensatory facility. And finally agreement was reached concerning gold and the establishment of a trust fund. Under the gold agreement, 25 million ounces of gold would be returned to members, in proportion to their gold subscriptions, at the official price of gold which was SDR 35 or $42.22 an ounce. The IMF was also to dispose of another 25 million ounces at market prices, with profits dedicated to a trust fund for the benefit of developing countries. The share of each developing country in the latter 25 million ounces was made equal to its respective share in total IMF quotas; only profits on the remainder, about two-thirds of gold sales for the trust fund, would become available for use as balance of payments assistance to the countries with lowest per capita incomes. The cutoff, in terms of per capita incomes, for countries eligible to share in trust fund loans was set at SDR300 in the Jamaica agreement, and the executive directors have subsequently certified that sixty-one countries are eligible to receive such loans, in proportion to their respective Fund quotas, for periods up to sixteen years and at an interest rate of 0.5 percent per annum. Loans from the trust began in February 1977, and the trust distributions in which all developing countries share began in July of the same year.

The managing director of the Fund in January estimated that the total value of these several sources of financing amounted perhaps to $3.0 billion for 1976. Representatives of developing countries noted, however, that the new facilities coincided with the termination of the oil facility, an arrangement under which some $2.3 billion had been made available to developing countries in 1974 and 1975.

The Reforms Appraised

As a whole, the comprehensive agreement may be considered in three parts, which concern the exchange rates, gold, and IMF resources. The amendment of the IMF Articles achieved nothing toward consolidating the reserve assets of the system, and nothing was achieved to ensure greater international control over the multiplication of reserves in the form of foreign exchange.

The monetary system now ordained can hardly be characterized as a dollar standard, for it has no standard money—or else it has multiple standards, one or more in each of the currency blocs which have emerged. Nevertheless, it is very much a dollar-centered system, for the dollar is the transactions currency for a large share of international commerce, it is the intervention currency used by most monetary authorities for managing their foreign exchange rates, and it is the currency in which more than four-fifths of the world's official foreign exchange reserves are denominated.

Although the U.S. representatives won in the negotiations the legitimation of flexibility in the exchange rates that they sought, they have only a general assurance that countries will "avoid manipulating exchange rates or the international monetary system in order to prevent effective balance of payments adjustment or to gain an unfair competitive advantage over other members" to protect them from the results of other countries' exchange rate policies.

The intent to phase gold out of the system has been only partially realized. With the termination in February 1978 of their two-year agreement, the Group of Ten countries regained the right to purchase and sell gold on open markets in any amount. They are also free to revalue gold in their accounts and to use it in settlements among themselves in any way they choose. Meanwhile, all IMF members are in the process of receiving back from the Fund one-sixth of their gold subscriptions.

The abrogation of gold as a money medium acceptable in IMF transactions and the mild market-depressing effects of IMF gold sales over a four-year period have tended to reduce the utility of gold as a prime form of international money. Unwillingness by the U.S. government to purchase gold or to sell it at a fixed price may in the end be more important. Although nothing in the new international monetary arrangements prevents gold's reviving as a means of international settlement, U.S. unwillingness to participate in such a system will limit the likelihood of that event and limit as well its economic importance if it occurs. Furthermore, and most important, gold is disarmed in the system in the sense that no government is obligated to provide it at a price that is fixed over time.

The SDR has won little more than praise. It is the numeraire for the Fund's accounts; it is valued in terms of a basket of currencies, rather than in gold; the interest paid to authorities who hold it and the charge on authorities who use it has been raised and linked to market interest rates; transactions with the Fund which formerly required gold payments now generally require SDR payments; countries can now freely use SDRs in international settlements when the transfer of SDRs is mutually agreeable between the countries involved; and voting majorities required for future liberalization in the use of SDRs are generally reduced. But the quantity of SDRs in circulation remains small; they constituted only about 3.1 percent of reserve assets held by countries in mid-1978, and they will remain proportionately small after the 1979–1981 allocations. There is no substitution facility in the Fund for replacing other reserve assets with SDRs, and the use of this asset remains encumbered with restrictions. *De facto,* the amendment acquiesces in the dollar's role at the center of the system and leaves the SDR at the periphery, although the way is open to change in the light of further experience.

The International Monetary Fund proved a flexible instrument in assisting the financing of an enormous disequilibrium in international payments in the mid-1970s. Some observers feel its potential for development finance has not yet been fully exploited. In fact, however, the Fund has moved perilously close to long-term financing functions for which it was not designed and which would jeopardize its central role. I return to this matter in Chapter 7.

The Fund is no doubt a weaker organization now than in earlier years. Prior to 1971, explicit rules and sanctions determined the relationship of members to the Fund. The Fund's present mandate to exercise surveillance over not only exchange rate policies but also the international monetary system as a whole is broader but much less specific. The authors of the 1976 *Annual Report* of the Bank for International Settlements have pointed out that in the IMF as previously constituted stability was supposed to flow from the exchange rates back to the national economies; in the new design, stability in national economies will, to the degree it is achieved, bring stability to the international exchange rates.[20]

The Fund's resources are smaller, even following the sixth general increase in quotas, relative to world trade and relative to total international reserves, than they were at the Fund's inception; in relation to world trade they are much smaller. But though the world has stepped back from its effort to fix the exchange rates, it has not rejected the idea that nations must face up to international responsibility for the economic policies they individually elect, an idea cultivated throughout the Fund's early years. The new basis for building an international economic community places the responsibility where the decision-making capability has always been, in the hands of national governments. The Fund can continue as a catalyst for stability; the international community is hardly ready for it to be more.

The second amendment became effective April 1, 1978, following its acceptance by three-fifths of the Fund's members wielding four-fifths of the Fund's votes.

---

[20] *IMF Survey,* June 21, 1976, p. 189.

3
Principles of Exchange Rate Policy

The monetary arrangements that emerged in the mid-1970s are a major improvement over the former commitment to fixed but adjustable exchange rates in that they have helped to depoliticize the process of adjusting international disequilibria. Since under the par value system each government was held responsible by its constituents for exchange rate changes it initiated, but not for changes initiated by others, individual governments pressured each other to take exchange rate actions. The system consequently fostered conflict between as well as within nations. All too often these conflicts produced policies aimed at avoiding rather than accommodating adjustment. With emphasis now on market forces, governments are better able to avoid censure by their electorates for facing up to international adjustment responsibilities while they remain nonetheless accountable for the results of their overall economic policies. Since they are not committed to a fixed exchange rate, governments have new options for exchange market intervention and opportunities for resisting or yielding to the market and for testing and sensing the strength of market pressures. Consultation among governments meanwhile provides a degree of international coordination, although the inflation since 1973 suggests that more coordination is needed.

The current scheme has advantages over the system of adjustable par values, as well as over other proposals put forward and seriously discussed in recent years. Nevertheless, important problems remain. This chapter considers some of those problems as well as proposals for their solution that have received serious attention in recent years.

A system of managed but market-dominated floating is not yet universally accepted. The ink was scarcely dry on the IMF second amendment before the French minister of the economy and finance stated, "As soon as the conditions of the world economy allow us to do so we shall unceasingly insist on the adoption of a system of stable and adjustable rates."[1] At the 1976 meetings of the International Monetary Fund and World Bank, the spokesman for the African governors reiterated the view held by governments of many developing countries that, "while the developed countries are better prepared to absorb without risk the effects of erratic exchange rate fluctuations, the same is not true of the developing countries."[2] Even many who would not return to fixed par values feel that exchange rate swings since 1973 have been excessive, sometimes described as so large "they can have little to do with comparative advantage and the efficient allocation of resources."[3]

The tangled controversy over proper exchange rate policy has many strands. New emphasis in recent years has been given to maximizing the utility of money to its individual users. It is clear that money's usefulness as a medium of exchange, as a conveyor of price information, and as a liquid store of value is enhanced as the market area in which the money is employed grows larger. Kindleberger has pointed out in this regard that money is like a language, and Mundell, among others, has argued for the formation of supranational currency areas.[4] A regime of fixed exchange rates between countries and perhaps even a common currency among nations has thus found wide support.

Chapter 1 demonstrated, however, the difficulties encountered when governments want to exchange national money units at fixed

---

1 Statement by Jean-Pierre Fourcade at the fourth session of UNCTAD, Nairobi, May 6, 1976 (New York: Ambassade de France, Service de Presse et d'Information).

2 Statement of Marie-Christiane Gbokou, finance minister of the Central African Republic, *IMF Survey*, November 1, 1976.

3 Paul A. Volcker, president, Federal Reserve Bank of New York, "Remarks before the National Foreign Trade Council in New York City on Monday, November 17, 1975," Federal Reserve Bank of New York *Monthly Review*, January 1976.

4 Charles Kindleberger, *The Politics of International Money and World Language*, Essays in International Finance, no. 61 (International Finance Section, Princeton University, August 1967); and Robert A. Mundell, "Uncommon Arguments for Common Currencies," in H. G. Johnson and A. K. Swoboda, eds., *The Economics of Common Currencies* (London: Allen and Unwin, 1973), pp. 114-32.

rates but pursue disparate monetary policies. Furthermore, disparate policies are justified by differences in the preferences of national electorates and when short-run price rigidity and low labor mobility between national markets create different national rates of unemployment. The social utility of money (nationally and internationally) is clearly not a simple aggregation of money's utility to private individuals, and the search for optimal international monetary arrangements must consider factors beyond maximizing money's usefulness as a private unit of account and a store of value. Another way of putting the matter is to say that institutional constraints require a second-best solution to the exchange rate problem insofar as maximizing the utility of money to a typical individual is concerned. In the final chapter of this study it is argued that a dollar-centered system without fixed exchange rates can constitute such a second-best arrangement; in this system private balances held by non-U.S. residents to accommodate international transactions could take a dollar form while balances to accommodate domestic transactions would be held in domestic currencies. But discussion of this matter lies far ahead.

Market responses to a supply or demand disturbance are different under fixed and flexible exchange rates (1) because changes in relative product prices seem to be obtainable more easily with exchange rate changes than with national aggregate demand changes; (2) because price level changes (and hence effects on the holders of money balances and money claims) accompanying adjustment are not the same under the two arrangements; and (3) because surplus areas are more directly involved in the adjustment under flexible exchange rates than they are under fixed rates. Each of these differences will be explored further.

In doing so, it is useful to divide the discussion into two parts. The first considers the adjustment process itself—an unavoidable process so long as markets encounter disturbances—and the second considers uncertainty and how best to deal with it. Untypically, the discussion under each of these headings is divided into matters of equity (who bears burdens) and matters of *efficiency* (how costs may be minimized).

Adjustment. Both equity and efficiency differences exist in the adjustment process under fixed and flexible exchange rates because relative price changes seem to occur more readily under flexible than under fixed exchange rates and because of differences in the direction of price level changes among countries under the two systems. To eliminate problems of uncertainty from the discussion at this point, assume that every day's exchange rate is expected to be permanent and that decisions are made as if that were the case. Adjustment under the two systems may then be contrasted as follows.

Under flexible exchange rates, excess supply of a nation's currency causes the currency to depreciate in the foreign exchange market with a consequent rise in the domestic prices of exportable and importable goods. These price rises are relative to the prices of nontraded goods, including the price of labor, and also relative to the nominal value of the stock of money. The shift in internal relative prices causes consumption to shift away from exports and imports and causes production to shift toward them, thereby helping remove the excess supply of the currency from the foreign exchange markets. The rise in internal prices relative to the stock of money, by raising the demand for money, then contributes to removing the remaining currency excess. Since exchange rates are merely relative prices, depreciation of one country's currency implies appreciation of another's. In the country whose currency appreciates, changes in the relative and average price level are opposite in direction to those of the depreciator, with opposite effects. The price of tradable goods falls relative to the price of nontradable goods and labor, and prices on the average fall in terms of domestic money. Cash balance effects and production and consumption adjustments in the appreciating country interact with those in the depreciating country to restore world markets to equilibrium, and they are capable of doing so without any changes in countries' nominal money supplies or their levels of aggregate demand for factors of production.

Under fixed exchange rates, an adjustment typically works out differently. Here the stimulus for a change in relative prices within a country has to come from a change in overall demand. This change is associated with a transfer of spending and money balances from one country to another as a result of an initial disturbance. If the price level should promptly fall in the deficit country under the stimulus of a fall in demand there, the prices of that country's nontraded goods would tend to be affected more than prices of its traded goods—the latter being sustained by conditions in external markets—and this would achieve the desired change in the ratio of prices. But where domestic prices (and wages) are sticky in the face of falling money demand, the relative price change is slow to materialize, and unemployment of resources appears as a result of the decline in demand. Without an adequate change in relative and average prices, demand and output continue to decline in the deficit country until a loss in real income holds spending on foreign goods in check and curbs further money losses. Countries with balance of payments surpluses under fixed exchange rates may, but need not, contribute to an overall adjustment. They will contribute if their money supplies and their demands for goods and services are permitted to expand as a result of the surplus, especially if prices are flexible. Relative price changes in countries with surpluses will induce greater consumption and smaller production of imports and exportable goods, but sticky prices will inhibit this adjustment. If, in addition, governments of surplus countries seek to maintain price level stability by neutralizing the effects of money inflows—for instance, by borrowing at home to acquire foreign exchange—little adjustment stimulus may originate there. The difference in price flexibility that gives rise to a large part of the distinction between adjustment processes under flexible and fixed exchange rates is an institutional matter well documented by experience. Its implications for equity and efficiency are considered below.

Equity. Under flexible exchange rates, depreciation of a country's currency worsens the well-being of that country's users of internationally traded goods while it improves the well-being of producers of such goods. In the longer run, when resources tend to be recombined in production after a relative price change, depreciation may favor the owners of factors of production used intensively in exports and import-substitutes relative to factors used intensively in non-traded goods. Correspondingly, in a country where the currency is appreciating, declining prices of imports and exports cause the internal welfare transfer to go the other way; users of traded goods gain and producers lose. As discussed later, the loss imposed on politically powerful producers in countries with appreciating or overvalued currencies has become a new stimulus to protectionist policies in the regime of flexible exchange rates, with protection often taking the form of government interventions in the exchange market to resist appreciation. In addition to real income changes enforced by relative price movements, wealth will be redistributed as a result of the change in relative values of the two currencies. The purchasing power of privately held money, and claims to money, declines in the country whose currency depreciates, benefiting debtors and penalizing money holders and creditors, and the purchasing power of money and money claims in the country whose currency appreciates rises, penalizing debtors and benefiting money claimants. There may be, but need not be, a change in relative prices between countries (a change in the terms of trade) further redistributing income and wealth.

The permanence of relative price changes within and between countries depends on the nature of the original disturbance to equilibrium. Proponents of the monetary approach to international adjustment emphasize a dichotomy between real and monetary phenomena in which relative prices among goods and services are in the long run independent of monetary changes, including exchange rate adjustments. In this view, relative price changes are permanent—under flexible or fixed exchange rates—only when the initiating disturbance is a change in the "real" system of tastes, technology, or supply of resources. Whether or not the dichotomy thesis is completely valid, a currency depreciation gives rise to relative price changes of the sort described here for at least a transitional period and therefore causes at least a transitional change in real incomes and hence a permanent change in relative wealth holdings. The change in the unit value of a country's money relative to goods and other money is permanent too, unless the initiating disturbance is reversed.

The significance of the price changes described, however, also depends on the nature of the disturbance. For where the disturbance is initially confined to one country and is monetary in character and neutral in its impact on demand and supply of goods and securities, an exchange rate change, revaluing the money in question in terms of other money, essentially offsets the initial neutral disturbance. An expansion of one country's money supply by adding a zero to the number on every currency unit and nominal money claim would exemplify such a case. The prices of all domestic goods and claims to goods would rise ten times, along with the price of foreign money, and relative prices and the real value of aggregate money claims would both remain unchanged. Neutrality in the disturbance, however, is an essential ingredient for this outcome. I shall argue in Chapter 5 that an appropriate mix of monetary and fiscal policies can approach this neutrality insofar as the demand and supply for financial assets is concerned, and then with flexible exchange rates it can limit the international implications of discretionary demand management.

When the exchange rate is fixed, the distribution of adjustment costs is different both between and within countries; in particular the timing of bearing the burden is different because the use of international reserves permits part of the adjustment to be postponed.

In respect to the distribution between countries, there is likelihood, under fixed rates, that a special burden falls on the deficit country in the form of unemployment and lost output because of price rigidity. If there is no resource reallocation, the loss of output and earnings may be several times the reduction in imports that would have equilibrated external payments and receipts. In the surplus country there will be, of course, inflationary pressures and perhaps a gain in employment. In that country, however, if spending reaches undesired proportions, the expansion can be neutralized by internal monetary and fiscal policies without concern for a balance of payments constraint. Adjustment is then concentrated in the deficit country where a loss of output is almost certain to occur.

With rigid prices and fixed exchange rates, there is little or no change in the international terms of trade to redistribute income between the two countries. Likewise, there is little or no change in the real value of money and money claims between the two. The international income redistribution centers on changes in employment.

Within countries, too, the burden of adjustment may be borne differently under fixed exchange rates as a result of price rigidity. Without such rigidity, the internal distribution of the burden would in due course be similar under fixed and flexible exchange rates for producers and consumers of tradable goods, and it would differ for holders of net money claims and debts in the currencies involved primarily because of the reversal of gains and losses they would experience. In the deficit country the price level would fall, rather than rise, with fixed exchange rates and would create gains for net money claimants; and in the surplus country it would rise, instead of fall, creating gains for net money debtors. When prices are unresponsive to changing market conditions, however, a payments imbalance produces an adjustment burden for the deficit country that is borne by the unemployed; and in a surplus country, where there is unused slack in the economy's capacity, the payments imbalance may supplement ordinary adjustment gains with employment gains. In circumstances of price rigidity, therefore, the unemployed in a deficit country bear special adjustment costs, and in surplus areas the reemployed enjoy special benefits.

The timing of adjustments differs under fixed and flexible exchange rates. Use of international reserve money to finance a deficit permits the postponement of price and output changes that would otherwise be immediate. It can permit the continuance of a misalignment of prices which misallocates resources. The adjustment and whatever cost is associated with it finally materialize, of course, when a country that has used its reserves rebuilds them; and then, as in any adjustment, the costs for that country fall on its users of internationally traded goods, on debtors whose debt burdens are magnified, and on any factors that become unemployed. But the time when social benefits are obtained and costs are borne is always important to their worth.

When governments modify policies as a result of the state of the balance of payments under either flexible or fixed exchange rates, some of the costs of the adjustment are thrown on those who would have been the beneficiaries of unmodified policies. Government retrenchment on high employment goals can be one example of this. But governments may also initiate trade and payments restrictions, introduce tax and subsidy schemes to mitigate economic distress, or take other measures affecting relative prices and incomes. In the degree that they do so, the internal and external sharing of the adjustment burden is shifted.

A helpful view of the equity aspect of balance of payments adjustment is to see market prices as a means of spreading adjustment burdens over many participants in broad market areas. The cost of a failure of a country's export crop, for example, is borne by the country's other exporters, by users of imports, and by all holders of the nation's money when the exchange rate depreciates as a result of the misfortune. The burden may also be shared in a degree by producers of like and unlike products abroad and by consumers in many nations as the markets seek general equilibrium. Under a fixed exchange rate and *a fortiori* when prices are rigid, the burden tends to be concentrated on the unfortunate producers, except insofar as their distress prompts direct reductions in their demands and supplies vis-à-vis others. Of course, when the time comes that the country's international reserve assets must be rebuilt, the burden will be further shared. If, nonetheless, one believes in collective burden sharing, analogous to collective risk bearing in the case of individual insurance, one is led to opt for maximum price flexibility throughout an economy. In Chapter 8 I analyze why developing countries are pulled into adjustments originating in the markets of industrialized countries more in a regime of flexible exchange rates than when the rates among industrialized countries were pegged. Developing countries have made this a part of their objection to the flexible exchange rate regime.

Efficiency. It is the inefficiency of adjustment under fixed exchange rates that has most often driven academic economists to advocate a flexible rate system. The unemployment a deficit country suffers under a fixed rate arrangement may be offset by a gain in employment in the surplus country if the latter enters the adjustment process with resources less than fully employed. When the surplus country begins the adjustment with a high employment level and resists inflation, however, unemployment in the deficit country is not only unrequited but exacerbated by gains abroad. The frequency with which this situation occurs has led many economists to suggest that a fixed rate system has a deflationary bias. Certainly unemployment that is more than transitional and that accompanies balance of payments adjustment is inefficient both nationally and globally.

Experience since World War I suggests that governments are more prone to adopt uneconomic policies to defend a fixed exchange rate than they are to resist movements of a flexible rate, perhaps because the movement of a flexible rate can be more easily blamed by government officials on impersonal market forces than can protracted unemployment or inflation. For whatever reason, if governments are more willing to tolerate unemployment, impose trade and payments restrictions, or introduce income transfers which serve as disincentives to production when the governments are pledged to a fixed exchange rate than they are when the exchange rate is flexible, this is in itself a condemnation of rates.

Perhaps the chief rationale for flexibility in exchange rates rests on the fact that the demand for labor may develop differently in different countries while wage rates resist change and labor does not move from country to country. Unemployment then appears in some countries while excess labor demand develops and persists in others. Global efficiency then calls for different demand management policies in the two areas. Different demand management policies are difficult to sustain between countries, however, when the exchange rates are fixed, because any effort to enlarge demand in one country spills over to another in the form of an international payments imbalance. Divergent policies are more sustainable when the exchange rates are flexible.

The view that flexible exchange rates make each government the master of its own house by shielding its economy from external disturbances and inhibiting the diffusion of its own policy measures abroad has come under attack in recent years. Criticism has emphasized that monetary and fiscal policy disturbances may be propagated by international capital movements even when the exchange rates are flexible.[5] This criticism is fundamentally correct and important. Yet,

[5] Seminal contributions were J. Marcus Fleming, "Domestic Financial Policies under Fixed and Flexible Exchange Rates," *IMF Staff Papers*, vol. 9 (November 1962), pp. 369-80; and Robert A. Mundell, "Capital Mobility and Stabilization Policy under Fixed and Flexible Exchange Rates," *Canadian Journal of Economics and Political Science*, vol. 29 (November 1963), pp. 475-85. The literature since 1963 has become very extensive. Marina v. N. Whitman's excellent critical survey covers much of the material before 1970: see *Policies for Internal and External Balance*, Special Papers in International Economics, no. 9 (International Finance Section, Princeton University, December 1970).

there can be little doubt that divergent policies are more feasible under flexible than under fixed rates, partly because a number of factors inhibit capital mobility and partly because it is possible so to coordinate the mixes of monetary and fiscal policy that capital accounts are little disturbed by divergent demand policies. I shall return to this matter in Chapter 5.

The other side of the coin, of course, in the matter of independence for monetary policies is that internal monetary changes for a country are exaggerated when they cannot be partially leaked to the rest of the world. This has led some commentators to suggest that the case for fixed versus flexible exchange rates for any country depends on whether demand disturbances for that country typically originate more at home than abroad since movements of the rate shelter the home economy from external disturbances but do not shelter it from domestic disturbances. Since, however, aggregate monetary demand for any large developed country's output *can* be determined at home and since at present governments can be held responsible by their constituencies for only national policies, there seems to be a case for arrangements which require each country to taste the fruit of its own government's monetary policies. In the country of their origin, bad policies then have a chance of being rejected, and good policies a chance of being sustained.

An argument can be made that if monetary disturbances—as opposed to disturbances in the markets for goods and factors of production—are of divergent sorts in different countries, fixed exchange rates will mitigate the problem by permitting the export of one country's excess supply of money to satisfy another's excess demand.[6] Flexible exchange rates deny such opportunities. Nevertheless, since monetary disturbances typically arise from the supply side of the market rather than from the demand side—the demand for money is typically considered, at least in the long run, one of the more stable economic relationships—the argument amounts to saying that one country's money supply excess can offset and be offset by another country's money supply deficiency. While the argument is correct, a proponent of this view must admit that where countries' money supply policies err in similar directions a country with a large error exacerbates the problems of a country with a small error. The possibility

[6] Arthur Laffer, "Optimal Exchange Rate Systems," a paper presented at the December 1976 meetings of the Allied Social Science Associations, Atlantic City, New Jersey, processed.

that monetary problems will be shared is part of the case against fixed exchange rates.[7]

When two countries more or less succeed in achieving their targeted economic objectives but there is a trend in that exchange rate which keeps their overall balance of payments balanced, a freely flexible rate can reflect the trend and insure gradual and continuous balance of payments adjustment. A fixed exchange rate, or exchange market interventions by governments that resist the trend, however, will necessitate rapid catch-up adjustments from time to time. Because adjustment costs are usually lower when there is time for accommodation, gradual adjustments are almost certainly less costly than rapid system-disrupting changes. Another view of this same point recognizes that while flexible exchange rates may stimulate uneconomic and unsustainable production and consumption when the rates fluctuate far from the trend, fixed rates likewise stimulate uneconomic and unsustainable commitments when the fixed rates are prevented from following the trend. The costs of catch-up adjustments are a manifestation of the losses that result from these misguided commitments. In this sense, a part of the efficiency evaluation of fixed versus flexible exchange rates can be seen as one of whether balance of payments disturbances are more likely to be sustained or transient, and as one of how closely a flexible rate can be expected to track a developing trend.

In fact, the relations between some of the currencies of industrialized countries have exhibited pronounced long-term trends going back as far as World War II. The value of sterling and the U.S. dollar, for example, have faced secular downward pressure relative to central European currencies and the Japanese yen since about 1950. Similarly, South American currencies have depreciated relative to the dollar. Other currency relationships have faced less protracted but nonetheless extended periods of monotonic pressure. The trend changes are often due to differences in national priorities and institutions which result through the political process in secularly divergent monetary and fiscal policies, although they may also result from changing trends in population, capital formation, technology, or taste. Whatever their cause, experience with sustained one-sided pressures on the exchange rates suggests that if variations of flexible rates about the

[7] It is not clear that in the period since 1971 governments have fully appreciated the fact that the leverage of their policies on their own economies has been multiplied by the reduction of the areas over which exchange rates are fixed. This point is further elaborated in Chapter 5.

trend equilibrium can be kept small, there is a case for flexible rates over infrequently adjusted fixed rates.

One institutional matter helps to explain why countries intervene in their foreign exchange markets. It can easily be interpreted as a reason why they should, although the interventions represent a matter of considerable risk to the international community. Where they have a degree of independence from their governments, central banks sometimes have legal authority to intervene in the exchange market when government use of other instruments of public policy, such as tax and expenditure changes, is blocked by stalemate in the political process. Under these circumstances, central banks can exploit the capabilities of exchange market intervention to stabilize prices or to achieve other domestic goals pending the authorization of normal policy measures. Similarly, even when a complete range of instruments is available, because of different time lags in the effectiveness of various measures, exchange market intervention can be attractive as a component of a policy directed toward domestic objectives. Use of exchange market intervention for ends other than overall balance of payments equilibrium, however, is dangerous to the world system because each country's exchange rate is also the price of another country's currency. Use by one country of the exchange rate to achieve domestic ends has often been a beggar-my-neighbor policy for other countries. Because of this, governments have conceded to the IMF important surveillance powers over exchange market practices.

The arguments for a more fixed or a more flexible exchange rate need not yield the same conclusion for every government. Countries whose political structures make their internal monetary and fiscal policies less stable through time than those of their trading partners may be attracted to fixing their exchange rates in order to import their partners' stability. Or, as the theory of optimum currency areas suggests,[8] flexible exchange rates may be more burdensome for countries with high ratios of trade to production and consumption than for countries where this ratio is low because the higher this measure of a country's openness, the more any alteration in the exchange rate damages the goal of price stability. It is presumably for this reason that small countries whose markets are highly integrated with specific trading partners have chosen to align their currencies on those of their partners. I consider these problems further in Chapter 8.

[8] See especially Ronald I. McKinnon, "Optimum Currency Areas," *American Economic Review*, vol. 53 (September 1963), pp. 717-24.

Uncertainty. Up to this point arguments of equity and efficiency for fixed and flexible exchange rates have been considered solely on the basis of the adjustment process. Much of the debate on the proper role of governments in the exchange markets, however, boils down to the question of how best to deal with uncertainty about the future course of the exchange rate. Advocates of government intervention to stabilize the exchange rates ask governments to use publicly owned resources in order to limit the short-run risk of exchange rate movements to which individual market participants are otherwise exposed. The argument is often posed as if government intervention to stabilize the rates reduces the risks of international commerce and the international division of labor. Unfortunately, it rarely does. It only shifts the task of bearing uncertainty from one group in society to another, and through time. Hence, questions of the government's role as a bearer of exchange market uncertainty are partly questions of equity.

Equity. In general, when the government has a policy of intervening to limit movement of the exchange rate, it reduces at least short-run risk for all who would have borne adjustment costs under a more flexible rate—primarily users and producers of internationally tradable goods at home and abroad and those holding domestic or foreign money and debts and claims in money—and it raises risks for those who bear them under fixed rates. One can, however, be more specific.

When the government does not intervene, some risk in the exchange markets is borne willingly and for profit by individuals, by banks, and by other firms that take speculative positions. To the extent that these speculators succeed in buying (in either the spot or forward market) when the exchange rate is below its continuing trend and selling when the rate is above trend, they reduce the variation about trend of the exchange rate and consequently the variation about trend of national price levels and variations in the production and consumption decisions resulting from temporary relative price and price level changes. The economic role of the speculator is to make today's prices partially reflect tomorrow's needs and hence to induce preparations for tomorrow.

To the extent that government intervention succeeds in buffering the price effects of transient market forces, the government is substituting its risk bearing (and that of those who will share in the government's gains and losses) for the risk bearing of private speculators. In this shifting of the risk-bearing function from those who do it intentionally to those who do it unintentionally there is a social cost. For even if the private risk-taking funds displaced from this use are reallocated to other productive purposes, the government's act of imposing risk on those who do not take it intentionally distorts behavior based on individual preferences. Economists have not much to say about equity questions in the form of who *should* bear burdens, but unless it can be shown that there are gains in the efficiency with which risks are borne as a result of government participation in risk bearing in the foreign exchange markets, the case for government intervention is weak.[9]

Government intervention affects the nature of risk by unsettling the time pattern and form of adjustment. For while the financing of an overall balance of payments deficit may postpone an adjustment, it does not eliminate the need for it if the forces generating disequilibrium are more than temporary. Ultimately, the adjustment takes place, engineered by a discrete change in the exchange rate, by imposition of trade or capital controls at home or abroad, or by domestic deflation or foreign inflation. The questions of when, how, and to what extent these changes will occur replace the short-run risk avoided, and the bearers of the new risks become the surrogates for those whose short-run risks were relieved.

Efficiency. The efficiency aspect of dealing with uncertainty concerns how errors of prediction can be minimized and the cost of such errors kept small. The possible role that the government might play here can be considered under two headings: (1) the case in which the government pledges to intervene to fix the exchange rate within prescribed (and narrow) boundaries, and (2) that in which the government pledges no rate but does intervene occasionally.

In the first case, when the government undertakes to support a fixed rate, the risks of transitory and moderate disturbances can be shifted for short to intermediate periods away from those who bear adjustments under flexible exchange rates and onto those who bear adjustments under fixed rates. But risks that disturbances will be large or sustained, going beyond credible limits of the government's willingness to finance them or to deal with them by the

[9] One of the benefits the reserve currency country derives from its role is that government actions to stabilize exchange rate movements are executed by foreign governments with resources the foreign countries must accumulate. When the reserve currency country, however, offers other countries the privilege of converting their foreign exchange reserves into an alternative international asset, as the United States did by offering gold convertibility prior to 1971, the gain the reserve country might have had from being spared investment in external assets is reduced.

sacrifice of objectives other than the exchange rate, are not shifted. For the government can shift risk only to the degree it can make believable its pledge that it will employ one adjustment process or another.

In the degree that a government does not eliminate risk but rather shifts it from one group to another, any evaluation of the efficiency of its assumption of risk bearing must take account of the potential costs which are risked by the one exchange rate policy or another. If the defense of a given exchange rate for a time, for example, increases the risk of unemployment or risk that the government will support its efforts by restrictive trade practices or other measures that hamper economic efficiency, then the government's promise of a fixed exchange rate becomes a costly means for society to bear its burden of exchange rate risk.

For the second case, assume the government makes no pledge to exchange market participants but nonetheless intervenes in the exchange market occasionally to moderate fluctuations in the rate. The government then competes directly (although imperfectly because of its size) with other speculators, whose intentions are to buy when the rate is below its trend and sell when the rate is above and hence to make profits. Whether governments can add in any way to the efficiency of this process remains to be seen.[10]

Perhaps most relevant to the matter of whether the government, as speculator, can improve the quantity or quality of services that risk bearers provide is the question whether government officials can be expected to be better forecasters of future market conditions than are unofficial market participants. The recurrent market question is whether given pressures on the exchange rate are an aberration soon to be reversed or the beginning or continuance of a trend. Certainly an unequivocal conclusion about the superior vision of one group or another is impossible. Advocates of increased government intervention seem to reflect faith in the consensus obtainable in official agencies. But unfortunately the published statements of officials offer little evidence that the officials have often known better than others where the exchange rate was going. Nor were the exchange rate estimates provided in such a sophisticated device as the IMF's

[10] While private speculation typically takes place in the market for forward exchange, where leverage for an investment is great, and government intervention is typically in the spot market, since the forward and spot rates are linked by the activities of interest arbitragers, pressures on the one rate are converted into pressures on the other as long as the markets are free of controls. Hence the contribution of speculation to the value of the spot rate is the same whether it originates in the one market or the other.

econometric Multilateral Exchange Rate Model in November–December 1971 (the rates that served as the basis for the Smithsonian settlement) on hindsight very good. In general, every reversed fluctuation in the course of an exchange rate large enough and rapid enough to have yielded its successful predictor a suitable return on a risky investment represents a failure of private risk takers to have anticipated efficiently the transitory disturbance. When a government has no commitment to maintain or achieve a targeted rate, its actions in the exchange market to stabilize the rate should meet a similar test. There is probably abundant truth in the generalization that people usually gamble most wisely when they gamble with their own, not somebody else's money.

The Case for Exchange Rate Management

Several circumstances, nonetheless, may justify limited government intervention: when the government is capable of large-scale operations, when external benefits derive from government action, and when the government, in the very short run, has knowledge that is temporarily not available to the private market.

Consider first the fact that a government's potential for intervention on the exchange is usually so large as to enable it to influence and even determine the course of the exchange rate for a short time. When the international market for goods or securities is subject to large and complex disturbances, uncertainty about the future course of the exchange rate grows among government officials and private individuals alike. In circumstances of little confidence about where the near or intermediate term equilibrium rate lies, market participants may become unduly influenced by *movements* of the rate, and, taking any movement as evidence of at least a direction in which the future equilibrium rate lies (or in which others might think it lies), execute transactions that anticipate continuation of the movement and by that action make the anticipation self-fulfilling. Once a dynamic process of this sort has begun, it can cause the exchange rate to move for a time away from the trend equilibrium level that the speculators in fact seek. Fortunately, such bandwagon processes ultimately self-destruct, either when the rate becomes patently out of line with other evidence about the equilibrium rate, or because the purchasing power of money changes as import and export prices change in sympathy with the exchange rate until market participants look increasingly to the needs of their deficient or excessive cash balances in the various currencies. But in the meanwhile the destabilizing speculation may have imposed uneconomic disruption on decisions about consumption and production.[11] The government, as intervenor in the exchange markets, can by the scale of its operations break such a self-fulfilling chain when smaller and necessarily profit-motivated market participants would still hesitate to move against it. Government interventions for short periods can force market participants to pause to seek new information about the equilibrium rate. But to play this role successfully, such interventions need not be protracted and must be properly timed.

A second case that justifies intervention is one in which the social benefits of exchange market participation exceed the private. This is likely to happen in periods of especially heightened uncertainty, when the degree of risk involved in exchange market speculation may seem so great to private participants as to more than offset the possible rewards to them, so that little private speculative capital is provided to the market. McKinnon has argued that too little, rather than too much, private speculation was responsible for the wide swings in exchange rates of the currencies of the industrialized countries in 1973–1974, and Keynes earlier mentioned the same possibility in connection with the early 1920s.[12] Wide exchange rate swings, however, that might be enforced by day-to-day variations in aggregate exchange market demand and supply have socioeconomic consequences of importance beyond the self-interest that motivates private speculators. Stability in the exchange rates may, for example, contribute to government policy goals such as price stability and stable aggregate output and employment. In such circumstances, limited government speculation aimed at giving depth to the market in the absence of private speculation may be justified.

A third case justifying government intervention may exist on occasions when government officials have knowledge of future policies and events not shared by the public. There is some danger here, however, that officials feel their uniqueness to be greater than it is. While government personnel often have advance information about measures their own government is about to take, and sometimes

---

[11] The phenomenon is an example of what Kenneth Boulding called a "malevolent dynamic process" in society; another example is an international arms race. See *Conflict and Defense: A General Theory* (New York: Harper and Brothers, 1962).

[12] Ronald I. McKinnon, "Floating Exchange Rates, 1973-74: The Emperor's New Clothes," in Karl Brunner and Allen H. Meltzer, eds., *Institutional Arrangements and the Inflation Problem*, Carnegie-Rochester Conference Series on Public Policy, vol. 3, a supplementary series to *Journal of Monetary Economics* (New York: North Holland, 1976), pp. 79-114; and John Maynard Keynes, *A Tract on Monetary Reform* (London: Macmillan, 1923).

confidential information about measures that other governments are about to take, such lead times are typically very short.[13] In appraisals of the longer-term pressures on governments to take given actions, the estimates of outsiders may be more unbiased than those of officials, especially since the latter are prone to be defensive of their own policies. Hence, again, government intervention in the exchange market is justified only for very temporary activity.

The foregoing considerations suggest some conclusions about the design of exchange rate arrangements. For most countries an exchange rate flexible enough to reflect short-run trends is probably desirable. This conclusion, while amply ambiguous, rules out a regime of semipermanently fixed rates, and it condemns too a regime that would depend on frequently adjusted official pegs, since, as noted above, governments cannot be depended on to risk the political consequences of changing their exchange rates until substantial and palpable gains can be identified and attributed to the change. The conclusion also condemns resistance by governments to persistent trends in the exchange rates. No doubt the greatest contribution governments can make to exchange rate stability and to the efficiency of private speculation in the exchange markets lies in what they can do to coordinate and to stabilize monetary and fiscal policies within and between nations. Nevertheless, the discussion here has also suggested that limited government intervention can be useful to rein in variations based on self-fulfilling speculation, to steady the rate when private speculators withdraw from the market, and to direct the rate when information is available to the government and not the market. There is a case, therefore, for official intervention on some occasions to manage the course of the exchange rate in the short term.[14] Management of the rate, nonetheless, must be directed

[13] Charles Coombs' testimony in *The Arena of International Finance* (New York: John Wiley and Sons, 1976) concerning the failure of communications between the U.S. Treasury and the Federal Reserve Bank of New York in 1971-1972 is extreme evidence on this point. More typically, inside information in the government is limited by the fact that decisions are not taken until the last minute.

[14] Herbert Grubel has also offered general arguments in favor of intervention to stabilize the rates in a conference paper on "The Importance of Reserve Control," in Robert A. Mundell and Jacques J. Polak, eds., *The New International Monetary System* (New York: Columbia University Press, 1978), pp. 133-61. His position, however, stems from the view that intervention to reduce departures from any existing rate serves social ends when private speculation has capitalized into the rates the value of all foreseeable events. His contention that movements of the rate can then best be modeled as a random walk implies that changes that are serially correlated can be and are foreseen, an assumption which is dubious. He also fails to recognize that reduction of adjustment costs for some in society (by the reduction of exchange rate variability) typically increases it for others,

solely to the achievement of equilibrium in nonspeculative international payments flows, rather than to the achievement of internal policy goals which may conflict with those of other nations. To ensure that management is not diverted by pressing needs of the latter sort, some international arrangement to monitor national practices can be helpful.

International Supervision of Exchange Market Intervention

The importance of avoiding national measures with respect to the exchange rates that serve one country well but another ill has given rise to widespread demand for international guidelines or rules for permissible and nonpermissible interventions. The remainder of this chapter deals with some general considerations about these guidelines, some problems of making criteria operational, and some specific proposals that have received widespread attention.

The argument that international guidelines for the conduct of exchange rate policy are important is rooted in various purposes. Some advocates of rules want to gain greater stability for the rates through time. Such a desire is misplaced, however, as noted above. A rate that moves too little through time is as much to be avoided as one that moves too much.

Others advocate rules on the ground that they reduce the uncertainty about government interventions. This may be of substantial importance to other governments considering interventions as well as to private market participants. Agreement among governments to consult prior to engaging in exchange market intervention can be at least a partial remedy for this uncertainty, and the informal agreement among Group of Ten countries to consult, reached in December 1975, is a step in the right direction. The present informal international agreement is, however, incomplete since many countries and the IMF are excluded, and the arrangement is only a gentlemen's agreement among officials of good will; its effectiveness under stress is uncertain.

The major rationale for rules is to protect one country from undesired adjustments imposed by another country. The original IMF rules

as has been noted in the discussion of equity issues above. Grubel feels his analysis confirms the existence of an optimal level of reserves for any country. But optimality of policies in general has been shown in economic theory to be dependent upon a social welfare function for income distribution in society, and optimality in foreign exchange reserves is no exception to this rule. The question of the significance of country and world reserve holdings arises again in Chapter 6.

that exchange rates would remain fixed until there was evidence of fundamental disequilibrium was a reaction against the competitive depreciations carried out by nations in the 1930s. In the worldwide inflationary conditions of the early 1970s, the possibility of competitive appreciations by which some countries would export their inflation to others has on a few occasions caused similar concern. It has come to be understood that fixing the rates until they are patently out of line in a period calling for exchange rate change can be as much a beggar-my-neighbor policy as unilateral action to cause a rate to depreciate or appreciate.

While agreed rules may be helpful in avoiding these conflicts, rules appropriate to the variety of potential circumstances are extremely difficult to draft and, while helpful, may not be essential. It is not unfeasible to negotiate conflicts ad hoc, and it could be optimal to do so if the alternatives were rules which themselves gave rise to inefficient policies, as the par value set of exchange rates did. Most governments are not dependent on a set of rules to avoid being beggared by other governments. Insofar as the exchange rate is concerned, the possibility of counteractive intervention and the possibility of pressures in other dimensions of policy always exist.[15]

Some proponents of international guidelines probably want internationalism for its own sake. They want to remove decision making on matters of international concern from national levels, emphasizing that the exchange rate is a crucial price which serves as the transmission mechanism between countries for many market changes and that manipulation of any rate has international consequences.

Accepting the importance of this point, and recognizing that intervention on occasion may be desirable, one may consider the possibility that intervention initiative might be assigned to the International Monetary Fund itself. Resources for the purpose might be subscribed by member countries, as the Fund's original resources were, or created by the Fund as a fiat claim, as SDRs were. Great latitude is possible in the design of such a system.

An institutional innovation of this sort is subject to criticism of several kinds, however. One objection, not totally irrelevant, is the political assessment that nations are unwilling to hand over to

[15] The British plea for foreign cooperation in supporting the pound in November 1976 was accompanied by a suggestion that without such support Britain might well be required to consider withdrawing its troops from Germany. The Germans, at the end of the month, were among the first to pledge financial support for the pound, even before the IMF had completed its negotiation of conditions for an IMF-backed multilateral loan.

an international organization the privilege of manipulating, in some degree at its discretion, a price as vital to each country as its exchange rate. This line of criticism is blunted by the fact that no country has unilateral control over its exchange rate relative to any other country in any case, since at the very least that rate may be influenced by the government of the other country. Assigning a limited intervention role to the IMF is, in particular for the United States, in large degree a matter of entrusting the function to an international organization as opposed to entrusting it to the country's trading partners. Nonetheless, delegation of authority and responsibility to an international organization requires the drafting of very tight rules to define the extent of the authority and responsibility delegated. Otherwise, a reserve currency country, finding itself in conflict, might prefer to be arrayed against one or a few of its trading partners than against them plus a surrogate for global morality. In any case it is not clear that governments could be prevented from intervening, and where this is the case the addition of the IMF to the group of interveners would not constitute an obvious advantage.

Another basis for objecting to internationalization of the intervention role is that while intervention in the form of purchases and sales in the markets for exchange is perhaps the most direct means of influencing the exchange rate, it is by no means the only way. Governments may influence the rate by borrowing their foreign exchange needs instead of purchasing them, or by borrowing abroad for domestic needs, or they may induce private firms to do so by regulation, by tax subsidies, or by action to influence domestic interest rates. They may also use commercial policies to influence trade, even though international agreements have circumscribed such activity, or of course they may take other actions, such as expansion or contraction of aggregate demand or internal structural changes, which may or may not be desirable in themselves but which have implications for the rate of exchange. In view of the dependence of the exchange rate on all economic policies, the IMF might find the assumption of exchange market management a task for which any authority it might be given was not commensurate with the responsibility it was expected to assume.

The compromise that has emerged from the monetary reform deliberations endows the Fund with responsibility for surveillance over the international monetary system and the exchange rate policies of member states. The compromise gains in breadth what it lacks in specificity and opportunities for sanctions. Power to enforce a judgment against any nation's practices remains in the hands of other states which may feel themselves aggrieved by the practices. Resolution is a matter of negotiation in which the Fund may participate but in which the trump cards are held by the several national governments, since the various means discussed at length in the Committee of Twenty for providing preorganized pressures against governments found no place in the comprehensive amendment.

Fundamental to the task of both writing and implementing guidelines is the problem of identifying operationally the equilibrium exchange rate. It was argued above that intervention is justified in order to halt or slow movement of the rate away from its trend equilibrium value or in order to move, or in some cases accelerate movement, toward the trend value. But government and central bank officials are usually as much in the dark as are private market participants in assessing the myriad of forces at work in the market, or about to be at work, and hence in knowing whether any present rate is on trend or off. Guidelines might assign priority to the present exchange rate on the ground that it is, or was, at least a resolution of actual market forces at some moment of time; such guidelines would then authorize intervention only to inhibit movement of the rate. The procedure, however, would only be meaningful if there were reason to believe that forces influencing the equilibrium rate were unchanging, or else were offsetting, through time. Guidelines might use other objective indicators, among which are past exchange rates and their trend, balance of payments data, reserve stock changes marking recent interventions, and price level or money supply changes to indicate forces currently at work on the future equilibrium rate. This evidence is of course subject to its own limitations.

Another part of the task of defining an equilibrium rate is defining the time interval over which one wants or expects nonspeculative demand and supply for foreign exchange to be equated. Since the exchange rate, like any price, performs multiple functions, certain costs are incurred when the rate does not resolve its market demand and supply forces at each moment of time. On the other hand, since adjustments involve costs, a case can be made for minimizing those movements of the rate that are correctly seen as temporary by some but not all market participants. On the basis of the reasoning offered earlier in this chapter and the experience of the past several years, one might hazard a guess that governments should not undertake intervention designed to generate a rate on the ground that it will be an equilibrium value of a period longer than, say, a few weeks. This horizon is of course markedly shorter than any employed in the defense of the adjustable peg arrangements of pre-1971. It is also shorter than the period envisaged in the IMF guidelines proposed in 1974 and discussed below. The period is short because the possibilities for an erroneous forecast grow with longer periods and because a longer period offers a rationale for more prolonged commitment to an official estimate made at one point in time in lieu of sensitivity to accumulating market evidence.

An ideal equilibrium set of rates from a global standpoint balances out payments flows when all nations are following policies that simultaneously determine targeted ranges for their important economic variables. Loosely, this may be interpreted to mean that the rates are equilibrium rates when they achieve overall balance of payments equilibrium and are at the same time consistent with universally high levels of employment, stable prices, reasonable rates of growth, and tolerable terms of trade. But in fact all these targets are virtually never simultaneously achieved; some countries are always redirecting policy measures toward the improvement of performance. An ideal equilibrium set of exchange rates, then, is not one that will balance payments flows with markets as they are, but as governments would like them to be. The OECD and the U.S. Treasury, among other groups, have attempted estimates of high-employment balances of payments which might be used for the estimation of high-employment equilibrium exchange rates. The LINK model pioneered by econometricians at the University of Pennsylvania also provides material for such estimates. Econometric work toward the estimation of high-employment equilibrium exchange rates is, however, not far advanced.

Surveillance of intervention policies may need to deal with the selection of the currency or currencies in which intervention is executed. Any one country need intervene in only one currency, of course, in order to influence its exchange rates against all currencies to the extent that private arbitrage maintains consistency among the various rates. If the currency appreciates against one other money it will appreciate equally against all, except insofar as other rates are simultaneously changing relative to each other. When one currency is used as the intervention medium by many countries, however, that currency's rate against any other currency is less violatile than the other rates may be among themselves. When the dollar serves as intervention medium for other members of the dollar bloc, for example, and those members support their rates within ± 2.25 percent about central rates on the dollar, the rates among outer members of the bloc may vary by ± 4.5 percent. This is so because any two countries that move oppositely against the dollar by 2.25 percent each, will have moved by 4.5 percent relative to each other.[16]

During the long reform exercise that culminated in the report of the Committee of Twenty, representatives of the United States expressed the view that it was desirable to have a system in which the dollar could experience as much flexibility against other currencies as other countries enjoyed. This goal led to consideration of two schemes for achieving greater symmetry in exchange flexibility. One of these called for multiple currency intervention (MCI) in which a number of currencies would be used as intervention media; the other called for the SDR to be used. Both proposals were explored by the reform negotiators in terms of a fixed exchange rate regime in which countries would maintain rates within given margins around a common denominator. In fact, multiple currency intervention and possibly SDR intervention could be employed in a world of managed floating, although with some complications.

A country engaging in multiple currency intervention would, under a regime of maximum exchange rate margins, buy or sell any one of its intervention media when the price of that currency reached its maximum permitted divergence from official parity. In a regime of floating exchange rates, with no established intervention points, much greater freedom would be available to a country in its selection of the intervention medium. The selections made, however, would have some significance since the value of the currency bought or sold would tend to be supported or depressed relative to third countries along with that of the currency of the country undertaking the intervention. The country whose currency is used will suffer some part of the deflation or inflation of the intervening country that it would not have experienced had its currency not been used. The matter of selection need not be one of great importance if interventions do not cause the effective exchange rates of the intervening countries seriously to depart from relatively short-run equilibrium values. But countries whose currencies are being used for intervention will want to exercise vigilance that other countries do not employ intervention to maintain effectively over- or undervalued currencies.[17]

---

16 At the Smithsonian negotiations in December 1971, the United States wanted a band for the dollar at least 4.5 percent wide (± 2.25 percent), but members of the Common Market found that the 9 percent band that this implied for them was uncomfortably broad. This led to the special arrangements for the maintenance of narrow exchange margins in Europe that came to be called the snake.

17 Massive interventions against the dollar by Germany, Switzerland, and Japan to keep their currencies from appreciating provide a case in point.

The possibility of using SDRs as a common intervention medium is discussed in Chapter 7. In general, steps in this direction raise problems that probably should not be precipitated at this time. If the SDR's character were changed so as to make it holdable and transferable by private parties, for example, as a step toward making a market in which intervention could take place, one would have to reckon with the supply of the medium becoming more elastic than it is as a result of credit created by banks; banks could be expected to accept deposits and make loans in SDR terms.[18] Furthermore, if the SDR continued to be defined in terms of a bundle of currencies, interventions to insure parity between the SDR and the bundle would require providing the SDR on demand and would eliminate any possibility of managing the money supply by managing the stock of SDRs. The technical group on intervention and settlement of the Committee of Twenty discussed a limited form of private participation in SDR transfers according to which banks would buy and sell SDRs for transfer on the IMF accounts of official holders.[19] The technique, however, merely shifted the initiative for intervention from official to private hands without changing the monetary consequences of the tranfers, and its relevance was limited to the parity exchange rate system the group was charged to explore.

As noted, there is some case for official intervention in the exchange market when private speculators are underinvolved in the market or when they are overinvolved in the sense that they are engaged in a dynamic process driving the rate away from an equilibrium value. But how does one identify speculative from nonspeculative activity in the actual market or know whether there is too little or too much exchange rate movement? Many adaptations, such as changes in the leads or lags in the timing of international payments or changes in the degree to which foreign exchange exposures are covered in the forward market, contain elements of speculation. But the facts concerning changes in these patterns, completed or in progress, are largely unknown at any point. Some evidence is discernible from balance of payments estimates after a lag that is so long as to make the data useless for this purpose. But on any given day, the chief evidence is typically the talk of the street, what a few customers have gratuitously confided in their bankers, or what bankers have confided to their foreign exchange brokers.

[18] A few banks, including Chase Manhattan, have in fact already indicated their willingness to maintain SDR denominated accounts, and the SDR has of course been used as the numeraire of a number of long-term loans.

[19] See International Monetary Fund, *International Monetary Reform: Documents of the Committee of Twenty*, p. 123.

In the United States the Federal Reserve Bank of New York intervenes in the exchange market on behalf of the system to prevent erratic movements of the rates and a disorderly market. Chief among the objective criteria for its decision whether to intervene in the market for a given currency seem to be the rapidity of the movement of a rate and the widening of the margins between dealers' buying and selling prices. Rapid movement of a rate during a day attracts attention because it might represent either the absence of stabilizing speculation or the presence of self-fulfilling speculation based on expectations of continued movement in the rate. The circumstance may also, however, reflect rapid change or rapid spread of the perception of change in fundamental nonspeculative market forces. Awareness of the news that has reached the market through the wire services, together with conversations with traders and brokers in the street, then have to provide the additional evidence on the basis of which Federal Reserve officials take a decision. Widening of the margins at which foreign exchange traders are willing to buy and sell may reflect increased uncertainty among the traders about where the market is headed. It is often accompanied by increased reluctance by the banks to "make a market." The Fed's involvement in this situation is expected to improve the "tone" of the market, presumably meaning a reminder to the market of the Fed's presence and its willingness to trade at existing rates. For such purposes, the Federal Reserve would usually disclose its interventions. On other occasions, such as when it might wish to end a flurry of speculation by private traders without having appeared to do so, it might take care not to disclose its actions. These subtleties deriving from the need to make decisions on the basis of fragmentary evidence illustrate the problems of articulating guidelines to prescribe or proscribe activity in terms that are both operational and sufficiently general to cover the variety of cases that arise.

Of the many rules for the management of exchange rates that have been widely discussed, three are chosen to illustrate the problems: (1) a gliding or self-adjusting peg, (2) the U.S. proposal for using reserve changes as indicators of adjustment needs, and (3) the IMF guidelines proposed by the Committee of Twenty and adopted by the executive directors, June 1974.

The Gliding Peg. The proposal that official exchange rates around which intervention is mandatory be reset periodically (daily, weekly, or monthly) on the basis of a moving average of recent market exchange rates came forward in the mid-1960s from independent sources.[20] In the minds of many the gliding or self-adjusting peg was associated with still other proposals that have come to be called crawling pegs,[21] although in fact the two sorts of proposals are distinguished because crawling pegs make changing the exchange rate a discretionary decision on the part of government authorities while gliding pegs are characterized by automaticity. A gliding peg's appeal lies in the degree of exchange stability it offers, both within the periods for which parities are fixed and over longer periods to the degree that parities move slowly, and in its automatic tendency to adjust secularly to market forces. Speculation that would drive a rate away from its intermediate-term equilibrium level would largely be eliminated under the arrangement, insofar as the intermediate-term equilibrium was discernible. There is no assurance, however, that the rate would ever correspond to such an equilibrium level. Movements of the parity rate, and hence the allowed market rate, could lag seriously behind rapid changes in market conditions.[22]

Kenen has simulated a number of exchange rate rules, including one in which the difference between a present parity rate and a six-month moving average of market rates is used to trigger a limited change in the parity.[23] He finds that when speculative capital movements in his model are stabilizing around the true comparative static equilibrium rate and the trade adjustment to rather low price elasticities is fast, such a glide generates greater stability in export volume after a specified disturbance than does even a freely fluctuating exchange rate. It is also superior, by this test of stability in export volume, to arrangements in which changes in the parity are triggered by changes in reserves or by changes in the "basic balance" of payments. When expectations are made stabilizing to the momentary parity rate, however, the glide based on market exchange rates performs less well than alternative schemes.

[20] J. Carter Murphy, "Moderated Exchange Rate Variability," *National Banking Review*, vol. 3 (December 1965), pp. 151-61; and J. Black, "A Proposal for the Reform of Exchange Rates," *Economic Journal*, vol. 76 (June 1966), pp. 288-95.

[21] James E. Meade and John Williamson were the inspiration for these proposals. See Meade, "The International Monetary Mechanism," *Three Banks Review*, no. 63 (September 1964), and "Exchange Rate Flexibility," in *International Payments Problems* (Washington, D.C.: American Enterprise Institute, 1966); and Williamson, *The Crawling Peg*, Essays in International Finance, no. 50 (International Finance Section, Princeton University, December 1965).

[22] See Henry N. Goldstein, "Moderated Exchange Rate Variability: A Comment," and J. Carter Murphy, "Reply," *National Banking Review*, vol. 4 (September 1966), pp. 97-106, for a further discussion of these matters.

[23] Peter B. Kenen, "Floats, Glides, and Indicators: A Comparison of Methods for Changing Exchange Rates," *Journal of International Economics*, vol. 5 (May 1975), pp. 107-52.

Another kind of simulation of the gliding peg can be constructed by asking what the actual rates experienced over a several-year period would have been had market pressures remained what they actually were while the exchange rates were constrained within boundaries based on a moving average of past rates. The limitations of this test arise from the fact that the pressures on the rates would have been different had the actual rate been the constrained one; among other things, it must be remembered that the actual rates have been mitigated by policy measures, including substantial official exchange market intervention, which were induced by the actual pressures. With these limitations in mind it is still interesting to look at the data shown in Figure 2 (a) and (b), which plot the actual exchange rates of the dollar on the deutsche mark and the pound sterling, July 6, 1973–August 4, 1978, and the rates that would have materialized had the rate changes been constrained by a rule that each week's parity be the unweighted average of the previous fifty-two weeks' market rates with the market rate in any week permitted to vary in a ± 1.5 percent band about its parity. It can be seen that some of the swings of the dollar to deutsche mark rate would have been reduced in amplitude by the scheme, but that in the face of strong secular pressures on both the pound and the mark the formula would have generated a very serious lag in adjustment. It is possible that the more appreciated values for the pound indicated by the moving average formula could have been sustained with a smaller outlay of reserves than the Bank of England actually experienced if speculators had maintained a conviction that the formula rate would have been defended, but about this there can be no guarantee.

It is often contended that a discretionary form of gradual adjustment in the parity exchange rate (the crawling peg) can escape anticipatory speculation if the monetary authority of a country announcing a discretionary crawl will promptly adjust that country's interest rates to offset the announced rate of exchange rate change; an announced 3 percent rate of currency depreciation, say, could be countered by a 3 percentage point increase in the interest rate on assets denominated in that currency. But such a safeguard against speculation is in fact spurious since speculators would in any case flee from assets expected to fall in relative value (securities on which the market yield is about to rise). An arrangement based on discretionary decisions cannot escape speculation concerning what that decision is going to be. Similarly, an automatic rule such as a gliding peg cannot escape some speculation based on anticipation of the exchange rate movements the rule will allow when the rate lags so

FIGURE 2(a)

ACTUAL EXCHANGE RATE AND EXCHANGE RATE CONSTRAINED BY GLIDING PEG, JULY 5, 1974–AUGUST 4, 1978

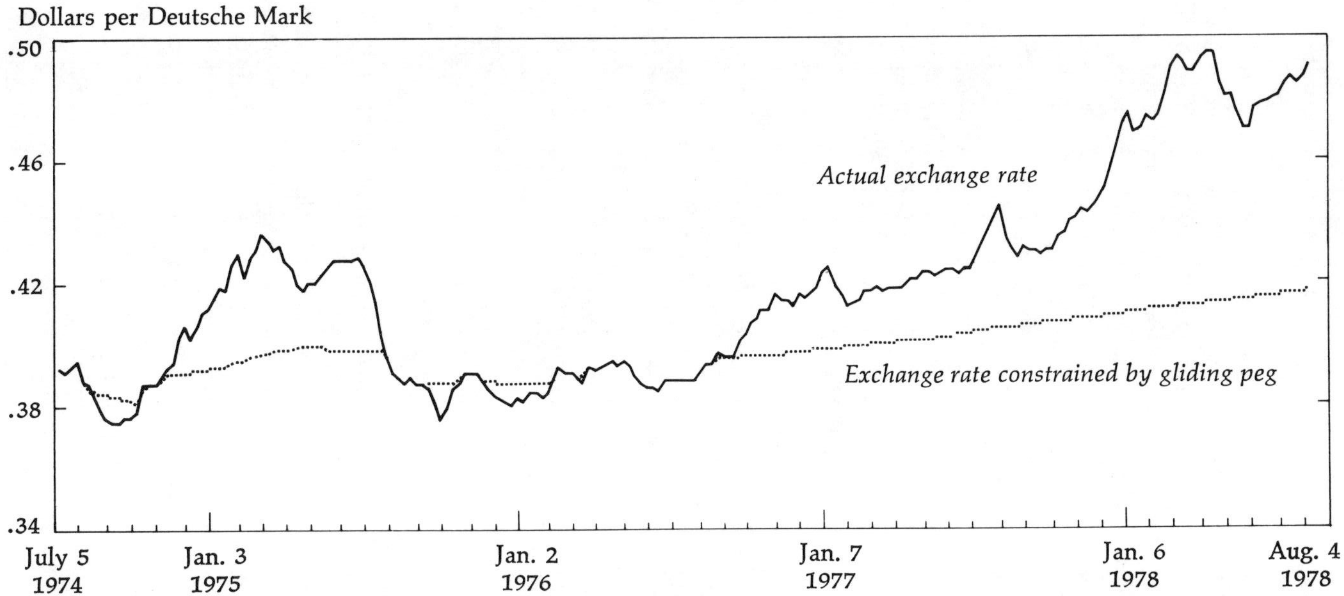

NOTE: Gliding peg is calculated as fifty-two-week moving average of constrained rate; constrained rate is actual rate except when outside gliding peg plus or minus 1.5 percent. If actual rate is outside the support band, constrained rate is at the boundary of gliding peg plus or minus 1.5 percent.

SOURCE: Calculated from daily noon buying rates reported by Federal Reserve Bank of New York.

FIGURE 2(b)

ACTUAL EXCHANGE RATE AND EXCHANGE RATE CONSTAINED BY GLIDING PEG, JULY 5, 1974–AUGUST 4, 1978

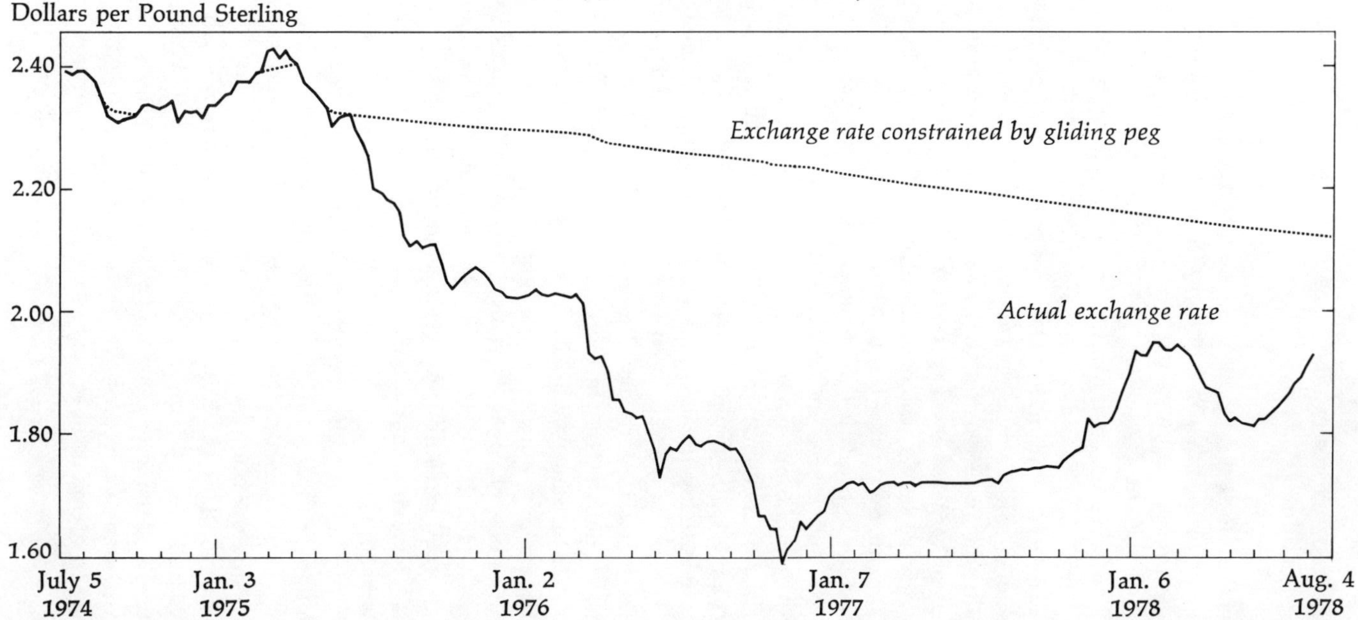

NOTE: Gliding peg is calculated as fifty-two-week moving average of constrained rate; constrained rate is actual rate except when outside gliding peg plus or minus 1.5 percent. If actual rate is outside the support band, constrained rate is at the boundary of gliding peg plus or minus 1.5 percent.

SOURCE: Calculated from daily noon buying rates reported by Federal Reserve Bank of New York.

seriously behind market events as to make the rate's future course broadly predictable.

Maintenance of Reserve Levels. As noted in Chapter 2, one rather detailed set of proposals for monetary reform was submitted to the C-20 negotiations by a national government—the plan offered by the United States in December 1972.[24] The proposal centered on the use of reserves as an indicator of the need for balance of payments adjustment. The indicator was to be presumptive, rather than mandatory, up to certain limits, and adjustment could be implemented by an exchange rate change or any other policy measure compatible with liberal trade and investment. The rule was aimed at maintenance of a normal or targeted level of reserves by each country, with outer points for reserve levels which could ultimately trigger a requirement that adjustment measures be undertaken. International sanctions were proposed for countries persistently resisting policy adjustments called for by the reserve indicator.

Kenen's simulation of an automatic version of such an arrangement, in which annual changes in parity were limited to 5 percent and in which changes were triggered when reserves differed by ± 15 percent from the base level, was, in his word, disastrous. Prolonged oscillations in the exchange rate were set up by the marriage of a flow control to a stock target, and the simulated exchange rate did not settle at the model's static equilibrium rate even after a ten-year run, a 5 percent disturbance in prices in the first year having served as the stimulus for adjustment. Kenen got better results with a reserve indicator in which *changes* in reserves triggered changes in the exchange parity. Further difficulties were encountered here, however, in repeated small periodic reserve level changes, since each reserve change was less than sufficient to trigger a secularly appropriate exchange rate adjustment.

Either of the foregoing rules suffers from problems of enforcement although both are based on objective criteria. Much criticism of a gliding peg focused on the possibility that governments would intervene inside the boundaries around parity to influence the market exchange rate and hence the future of the parity. Much criticism of a reserve indicator has emphasized the problem of defining reserves in an entirely satisfactory manner: governments may commit resources in a great variety of ways while they retain some measure of authority to marshal those resources once again in time of balance

---

[24] See the *Economic Report of the President*, supplement to Chapter 5, January 1973.

of payments need. The use of international credit by many governments since 1974 illustrates the difference between a country's potential official claims on the rest of the world at any moment and its official reserves. If reserves could be defined satisfactorily, a rule combining gliding parity with reserve neutrality might be enforceable. But in a world characterized by very rapid changes that bring pressure for monotonic movements in the exchange rates, any scheme that causes exchange rate adjustment to lag significantly would very likely be less than ideal.

IMF Guidelines and Surveillance. In June 1974, when the exchange rates of many member countries were floating in violation of the members' IMF charter obligations, the executive directors of the IMF adopted a decision recommending that members use their best endeavors to observe a set of six guidelines for the management of floating exchange rates. The decision was taken in connection with members' general obligations under the old charter "to collaborate with the Fund to promote exchange stability, to maintain orderly exchange arrangements with other members, and to avoid competitive exchange alterations."[25] The first three guidelines said that a country *should* intervene to prevent or moderate sharp and disruptive exchange rate fluctuations from day to day and from week to week, and that it *might* act to moderate movements from month to month and quarter to quarter. The member was not to act aggressively to depress a falling exchange rate or to enhance a rising one. But it could act aggressively to move its rate toward a target zone that was determined in consultation with the Fund and projected as a three- to four-year equilibrium value for the currency. The guidelines expressed a policy of leaning against the wind in conjunction with the view that it was appropriate to defend a rate officially estimated to be a three- to four-year equilibrium rate.[26]

A great deal has been said earlier in this chapter about the hazards of commitments to official estimates of what the multiyear equilibrium exchange rates are. Similarly, the costs of a bias toward exchange rate stability when the markets are in fact providing pres-

---

25 Article 4, section 4 (a) of the charter before its comprehensive amendment.

26 The guidelines had a kinship to the "reference rate proposal" of Wilfred Ethier and A. I. Bloomfield according to which governments could (but need not) intervene to move the market rates for their respective currencies toward preannounced reference rates but would never intervene to move market rates away. See Ethier and Bloomfield, *Managing the Managed Float*, Essays in International Finance, no. 112 (International Finance Section, Princeton University, October 1975).

sure for monotonic change have been emphasized. It is fortunate, therefore, that the guidelines passed into history with the comprehensive second amendment to the IMF charter. In their place have come IMF responsibilities and authority for surveillance of the international monetary system and the exchange rate policies of members. The principles and procedures that are emerging under this legal framework are promising.

Article 4, section 1, of the amended charter places a general obligation on members to collaborate with the Fund and other members to assure orderly exchange arrangements and to promote a stable system of exchange rates. In particular, each member is to:

- endeavor to direct its economic and financial policies toward the objective of fostering orderly economic growth with reasonable price stability, with due regard to its circumstances
- seek to promote stability by fostering orderly underlying economic and financial conditions and a monetary system that does not tend to produce erratic disruptions
- avoid manipulating exchange rates or the international monetary system in order to prevent effective balance of payments adjustment or to gain an unfair competitive advantage over other members.

While the general obligations mention a stable system of exchange rates as a goal, the particular undertakings clearly emphasize the avoidance of exchange rate manipulation to prevent adjustment, along with the fostering of orderly economic growth, financial conditions, and price stability.

Under the authority of section 3 of the same article, which assigns the Fund responsibility for overseeing the international monetary system and for exercising firm surveillance over the exchange rate policies of members, the Fund has announced the broad criteria it intends to follow.[27] Members are to avoid manipulating exchange rates with the intent of preventing effective balance of payments adjustments or of gaining an unfair competitive advantage over other members. They are, nonetheless, to intervene to counter disorderly conditions, and they must take into account the interests of other members. Particular actions by members may precipitate Fund consultations. Those actions include protracted large-scale intervention in one direction in the exchange market, extensive official or quasi-

[27] The statement on surveillance is published in *IMF Survey*, May 22, 1977, p. 131.

official borrowing or lending for balance of payments purposes, maintenance of restrictions on trade or capital movements, the pursuit of domestic policies providing abnormal encouragement or discouragement to capital flows, and other actions resulting in behavior of the exchange rate that appears to be unrelated to underlying economic and financial conditions. The principles and procedures have been acknowledged by the Fund's managing director to amount to dealing with matters case by case.

The difference between the surveillance criteria of 1977 and the guidelines of 1974 is the difference between the new charter and the old. The new criteria replace the bias in favor of exchange rate stability with a bias in favor of balance of payments adjustment. They acknowledge a role for limited intervention while they call for concern for the interests of other members. They condemn protracted, large-scale intervention in one direction and identify other actions that justify special scrutiny. They are a great step forward. Enforcement of the Fund's views will rest on moral suasion and, more fundamentally, on the pressure that may be brought against uncooperative members by other members. This recognizes the present state of economic nationalism but places no barriers to the evolution of supranational authority.

Since the Fund's surveillance work will be carried out mostly in private, some time must elapse before any attempt to judge its effectiveness will be appropriate. What can be said at this time is that the criteria are well drafted, as measured against the principles that have been argued in this chapter, and the procedures prescribed seem appropriate for the present circumstances of international economic relations. Together, the principles and procedures seem more promising than any explicit rule for exchange rate management yet offered. The problems necessarily associated with having legitimatized ad hoc national government interventions in the markets for foreign exchange after having condemned beggar-my-neighbor results are nevertheless not completely solved. They will become apparent in the years ahead, and observers of the scene must be prepared continually to learn from experience.[28]

---

[28] Two especially cogent essays on the problems of establishing guidelines for the surveillance of the exchange market policies of countries are Richard N. Cooper, "Exchange Rate Surveillance," in Mundell and Polak, *The New International Monetary System*, pp. 69-83; and Jacques R. Artus and Andrew D. Crockett, *Floating Exchange Rates and the Need for Surveillance*, Essays in International Finance, no. 127 (International Finance Section, Princeton University, May 1978).

4
Experience with Floating Exchange Rates

A general assessment of the performance of the markets for foreign exchange under managed floating must conclude that they have behaved reasonably well, and in the circumstances the markets probably performed better than they could have under any feasible alternative arrangement. They have not, however, performed entirely according to prediction. On the positive side, some of the worst fears expressed over the years about floating exchange rates—in particular that the volume of international trade and real capital movements would be depressed—have not observably materialized. Surprisingly, use of the forward markets for hedging seems to have been less in the period of floating exchange rates than in the preceding period of fixed rates. The rates have moved broadly to equalize competitive conditions among some countries, but they have not always served this function well. Furthermore, economists have been shown to be wrong in predicting that the use of official reserves for intervention would be less under floating than under fixed exchange rates. The combination of needs seen by governments to supplement or replace private stabilizing speculation in periods of strong uncertainty and to brake exchange rate movements that were very rapid when expectations of change gathered strength have drawn authorities into exchange rate management on a large, probably a too large, scale. A summary of some of the evidence on these matters follows.

Volume of Trade and Investment

During the 1960–1970 decade world trade grew something like 70 percent faster than world output; IMF estimates indicate that in that period the volume of trade expanded at a compound annual rate of

8.5 percent while real output grew at 5 percent. During the period of generalized floating (1973–1977), although trade's growth rate slowed, it did not slow as much as production. World trade in this period managed to grow, despite recession, approximately twice as fast as output, with trade growing an average of 5.1 percent per annum in volume while output grew only 2.6 percent. While many variables at work are not accounted for here, the prima facie evidence does not show that trade was inhibited much by the advent of greater flexibility in the exchange rates, except insofar as exchange rate flexibility may have had some adverse effect on production itself.

The borrowing inspired by countries' efforts to gain time for adjustment to the increase in petroleum prices after 1973 makes an assessment of the possible effect of floating exchange rates on international borrowing difficult. It can be said, nonetheless, that nominal debt continued to grow at a very rapid rate under flexible rates, and debt grew faster in 1973–1975 than in the earlier 1970s even when deflated for price increases. World Bank data show external public debt of eighty-four developing countries growing at an average rate of $11.2 billion per annum (1969–1972), a 13.4 percent growth rate on 1971 debt, and then more than doubling to an annual average of $25.2 billion in 1973–1975, still a 17.1 percent growth on the 1974 base. While export prices of nonoil developing countries increased by approximately 85 percent between these two periods, real borrowing was clearly up by more than 20 percent. Table 10 in Chapter 7 shows that borrowing by developed as well as by developing countries continued to grow rapidly in 1976 and 1977.

Exchange Rates and Changing International Cost Comparisons

Figures 3 and 4, reproduced from the OECD's *Economic Outlook*, show exchange rate movements against the dollar and effective (trade-weighted average) exchange rate changes of the currencies of a group of European countries, the United States, Canada, and Japan, from January 1973 into 1978. At the beginning of that period, the exchange rates negotiated at the Smithsonian Institution in December 1971 were still in effect, except for the British pound which had been set afloat some six months earlier. The Canadian dollar had been floating since 1970. The Swiss franc was set free in January 1973, and in February in connection with the second devaluation of the dollar most European countries appreciated sharply in dollar terms, and the Italian lira and Japanese yen were floated. By March 1973, when the peg against the dollar for the snake countries was removed, the currencies of most of the industrialized countries were without formal support margins. The striking changes illustrated in Figure 3 are, of course, the doubling of the value of the Swiss franc against the dollar during the five-year period and the 30 percent depreciations of the pound sterling and the Italian lira. The Canadian dollar is marked by its stability against the U S. currency until 1977, after which it depreciated some 10 to 15 percent. Continental European currencies, on the other hand, were marked by volatility against the dollar, the deutsche mark having three times before 1976 breached a premium of 35 percent above its January 1973 value only to recede each time. In mid-1976 the continental currencies began a sustained two-year climb.

The effective exchange rates—that is, exchange rates of countries against a trade-weighted average of their partners' currencies—in Figure 4 display, of course, somewhat less volatility than do the rates against the dollar alone.[1] The effective rate of the dollar, it can be seen, stayed for more than five years within 5 percent of its level of March 1973 when generalized floating began. Similarly, the effective rates of most European countries participating in 1978 in the snake arrangement moved horizontally from the middle of 1974 to the middle of 1976 and then drifted upward. The Swiss franc and Japanese yen appreciations and the pound sterling and lira depreciations, however, are as marked in trade-weighted terms as they are against the dollar alone.

Of perhaps greater interest than the exchange rate movements themselves is the question of the degree to which the exchange rates have mirrored, and hence compensated for, changes in prices and costs in the countries concerned. The doctrine of purchasing power parity hypothesizes that trade in goods and services dominates the foreign exchange markets, that trade is directed by relative prices and costs, and that exchange rates will consequently mirror changing international relative price and cost conditions. A narrow form of the hypothesis suggests that exchange rates should make the prices of similar tradable goods the same when quoted in different currencies, provided transportation costs are small. This form amounts only to

---

[1] There are various meaningful ways of weighting the exchange rates of a country's trade partners to obtain an "effective" exchange rate for the country, and each way has advantages and disadvantages for alternative uses to which the measure might be put. The OECD measure uses 1972 trade weights with allowance for third market effects along the lines of the IMF Multilateral Exchange Rate Model. The effective exchange rates shown in Figures 6-16 are not identical to the OECD rate because they were compiled by the Morgan Guaranty Trust using bilateral trade data for 1976 as weights.

FIGURE 3
EXCHANGE RATES AGAINST THE DOLLAR

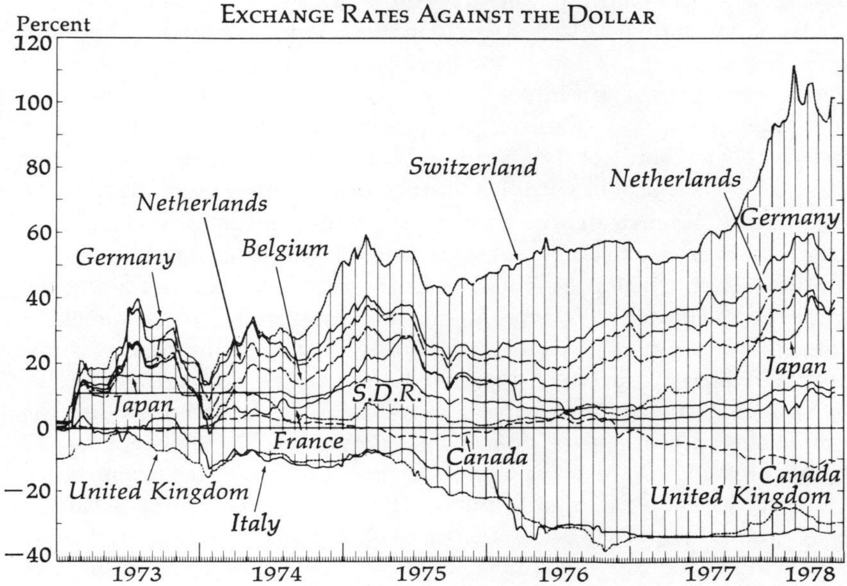

NOTE: Percentage deviations are from dollar Smithsonian parities as of December 1971. Weekly averages of daily figures are in U.S. dollars per unit.

FIGURE 4
EFFECTIVE EXCHANGE RATES

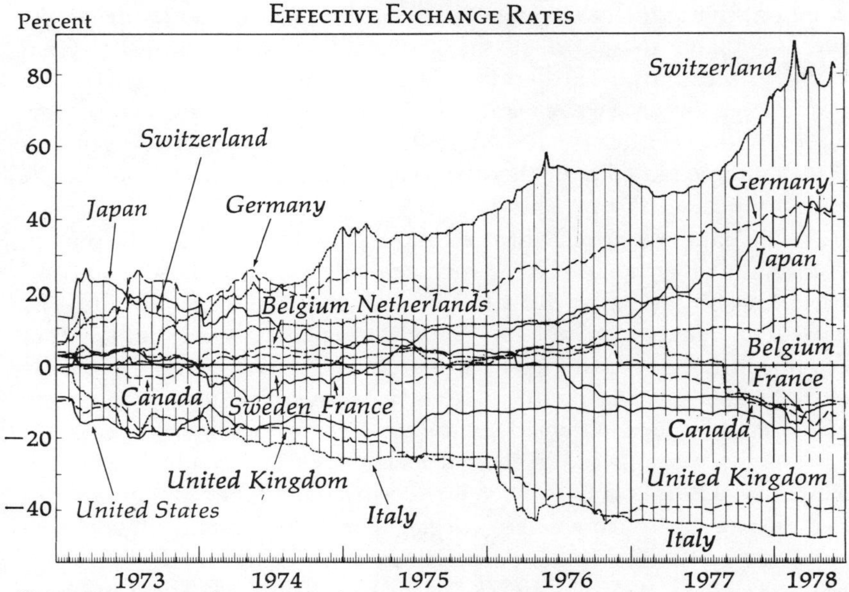

NOTE: Percentage changes are from first quarter 1970; weekly averages of daily figures.

SOURCES: Adapted from *Economic Outlook*, July 1978, OECD, Paris.

saying that competition operates on a global scale and that for tradable goods the world is a single marketplace. A broader and more meaningful interpretation of the hypothesis states that exchange rates and costs of production interact with each other so as to equalize costs of production across countries, as the costs are quoted in any one of the currencies, and to stabilize the competitive abilities of countries around levels that will generate balance of payments equilibriums.

Figure 5 illustrates in a rough way the movements of relative labor costs and exchange rates of several countries relative to the United States. In that figure a rise in the solid line signifies a relative increase in a country's unit labor costs (generally, total wages in manufacturing divided by manufacturing output in the named country relative to the United States), and a rise in the dotted line denotes a depreciation of the country's currency. The broad form of the purchasing power parity doctrine is supported, then, where movements of the lines are in the same direction and in similar proportions. (The vertical scale is logarithmic.) The picture that emerges can be only approximate for several reasons. One is that the data are highly aggregated, and the weights in the unit labor cost indexes are not necessarily those appropriate for indicating either the significance of particular cost changes on trade and investment flows and hence significance for the exchange rates, on the one hand, or a relationship that would flow from the exchange rate to costs, on the other. In addition, the industry coverage of the cost indexes, the nature of the raw data, and the form of the statistical construct all vary from country to country. Furthermore, between some of the countries, for example, between Sweden and the United States, there are so few direct trade relations that competition is largely effective only in third markets. In spite of these shortcomings, nonetheless, one might expect the data to be revealing.

The data of Figure 5 for the United Kingdom, Canada, Germany, France, and Italy suggest that the exchange rates of those countries' currencies on the dollar did move broadly to offset a good deal of the measured relative change in labor cost per unit of output that developed over several years. In particular, if one takes the middle of 1974 as a starting point, relative costs and exchange rates moved about equiproportionately over the next three and a half years for each of those countries. In the particular cases of Canada, the United Kingdom, France, and Italy, all experiencing higher inflation rates (as measured by consumer prices) than the United States, cost increases generally led the depreciation of the currency in both timing and extent. In the case of Germany, on the other hand, where

FIGURE 5

Unit Labor Costs and Exchange Rates, Selected Countries in Comparison to the United States, by Quarters, 1973–1977

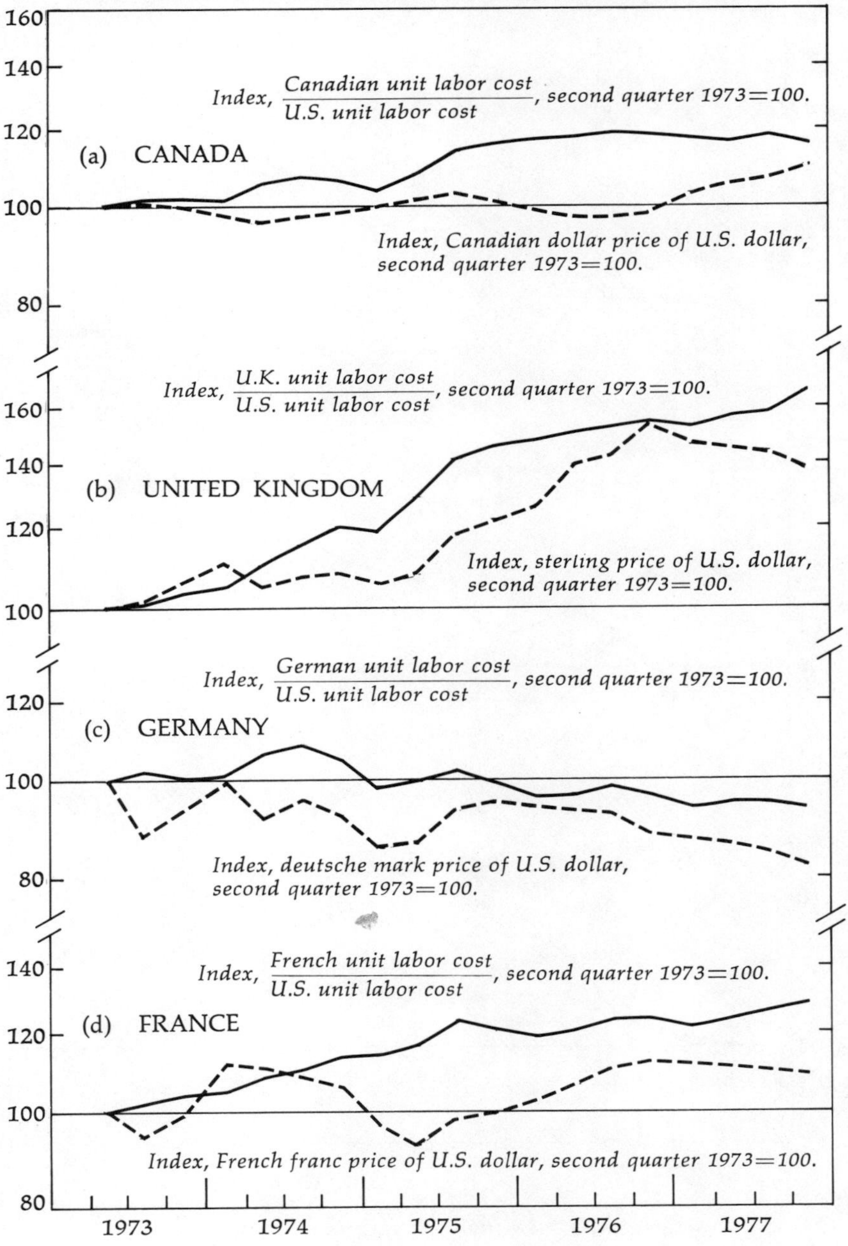

FIGURE 5

Unit Labor Costs and Exchange Rates, Selected Countries in Comparison to the United States, by Quarters, 1973–1977

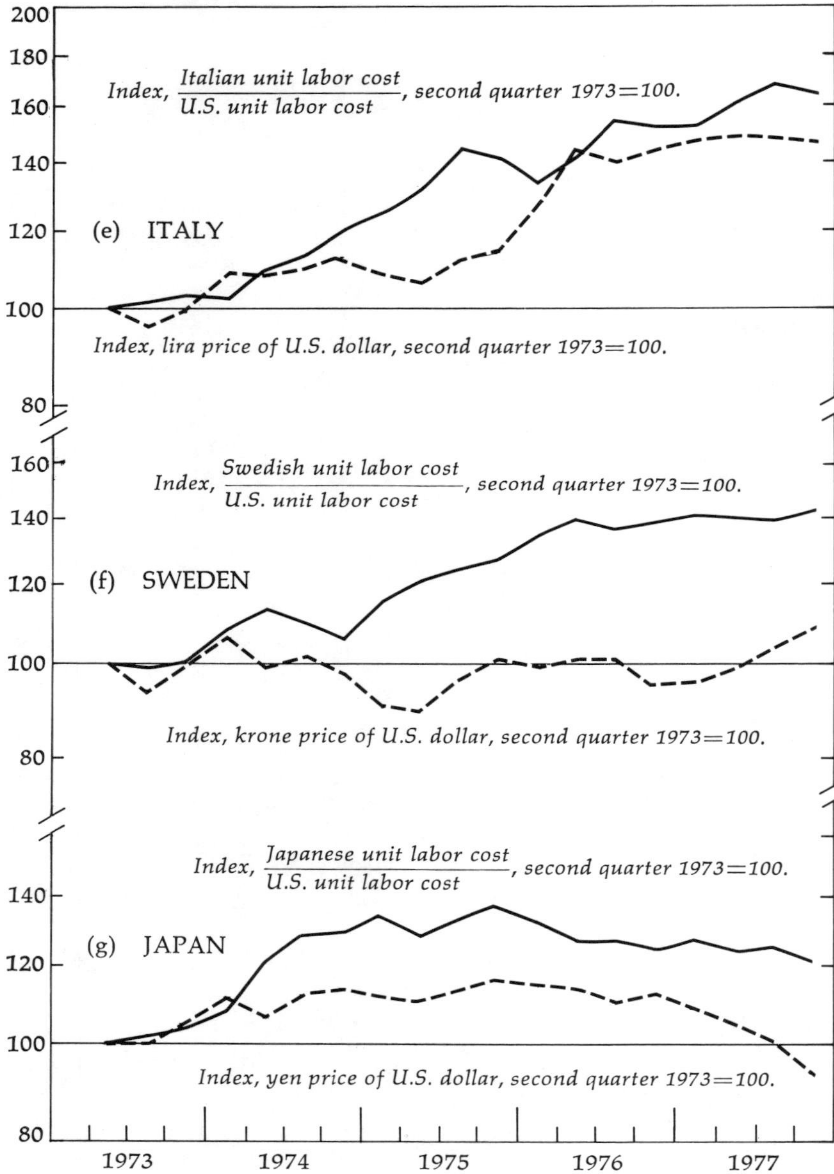

Source: Unit labor costs, OECD, *Main Economic Indicators* and *Economic Outlook*; Exchange rates, IMF, *International Financial Statistics*.

the inflation rate in 1974 and subsequent years was only about half that in the United States, changes in the exchange rate seemed to lead relative costs, both upward and downward. If one accepts mid-1974 as a time at which the deutsche mark was not overvalued (the German payments surplus for goods and services was at an all time high that year), the currency was almost surely undervalued, exaggerating Germany's international competitiveness, in much of 1975, 1976, and 1977. These were in fact years of continued strong surplus in Germany's current international balance of payments.

The divergence of the exchange rates from cost changes in either time or amount (divergence that is not due to failures in the available statistical base) can be seen in part as an information lag phenomenon—asset holders recognized the nature and extent of changes in the values of currencies only somewhat after the fact. But everywhere the exchange rate adjustments also reflected explicit actions by governments to resist changes. Governments of countries with appreciating currencies tended to intervene directly in the exchange markets to accumulate foreign exchange, while governments of countries with depreciating currencies tended to be borrowers of foreign currencies. Evidence concerning these interventions is reviewed below.

The experiences of Sweden and Japan are more anomalous than the others. Until 1977 Sweden was associated with the snake, the narrow exchange rate margins arrangement in Europe. The rise in Swedish costs, unrequited by currency depreciation, was accompanied by a growing current balance of payments deficit in 1974–1977. In spite of the current account deficit, official reserves grew in 1975 and 1977 and for the four-year period as a whole, indicating that external borrowing was more than enough to finance the current deficit. In 1977, to reverse the deteriorating trade situation, Sweden at last left the snake, devalued the krone, and tied the currency to a trade-weighted index of other currencies.

Japan's ability to improve its current account balance in 1974, in spite of labor cost increases relative to the United States of as much as 36 percent that were offset by only a 14 percent depreciation, must be understood in terms of Japan's unique response to cyclical changes. Labor contracts in Japan that essentially guarantee workers continuous employment give rise to sharply rising unit costs of output when demand for final product declines. Slack domestic demand also limits imports and causes a redirection of output to external markets. The result is an improvement in the current trade balance when per unit costs are at a cyclical high. Employers regularly absorb losses in this phase of activity and use foreign markets to minimize the loss. It is less easy to explain the continued improvement of Japan's current account balance into 1976, 1977, and 1978. Currency appreciation in that period offset the Japanese relative unit cost reductions associated with the recovery so that Japan sustained an international cost disadvantage in those years as compared with 1973. The international surplus on current account nevertheless reached an historic high of nearly $11 billion in 1977 and went on at an annual rate of $16 billion in the first quarter of 1978. The appreciation of the yen, which had begun at the opening of 1976, accelerated in 1977 and in the middle of 1978, despite measures taken by the government of Japan to liberalize imports. One is led to surmise that the exchange value of the yen in 1973–1974 was the anomaly: the yen was undervalued. Certainly that exchange rate turned the Japanese trade balance around from deficit in the first half of 1974 to strong surplus thereafter. In fact the increase in Japanese relative costs that is unrequited in the exchange rate is a trend phenomenon, as are Japanese current account surpluses. Both the unrequited cost increases and the surpluses predated 1973. Profound changes in cost-price relationships in Japan as compared with the United States seem to underlie the experience.

The conclusion that for a number of countries, although not all, the exchange rates have moved so as broadly to equalize international cost conditions is supported by other studies. The IMF, for example, has charted the ratio of the GNP price deflator for each of seven industrialized countries to a trade-weighted index of the deflators of other countries, along with the effective exchange rates of the seven.[2] When the relative GNP deflators for four of the countries were adjusted for effective exchange rate changes, they came in early 1976 within 5 percent of their levels of early 1973 in spite of broad price changes in three of the four. The remainder were at or within 10 percent of their early 1973 values. French and Canadian exchange rate oscillations were greater than those countries' relative price level movements, but the two countries were exceptional in this regard.

In connection with a set of calculations in which the wholesale price index for each of eight countries is expressed relative to that index for fourteen industrial countries and then deflated by the index of the country's effective exchange rate, the IMF also has noted that the competitive positions of six of the eight countries in early 1977 were not much different from their positions in the first half of 1973.

---

[2] IMF, *Annual Report*, 1976, p. 33.

(The six were the United States, the Federal Republic of Germany, France, the United Kingdom, Japan, and Canada.) Only the competitiveness of Italian and Swiss goods had changed much by this measure, since Italy's external prices fell relative to those of competitors by some 10 percent as a result of excessive lira depreciation and Swiss prices rose by 10 percent as a result of excessive Swiss franc appreciation.[3]

Calculations at the Bank for International Settlements (BIS) using relative wholesale and consumer price indexes adjusted for exchange rate changes tell a similar story, as do OECD estimates of relative export prices of manufactures.[4] For a majority of industrialized countries, then, the exchanges rates have tracked price and cost indexes rather well, though not all countries conform to the pattern.

There remain questions about the direction of causality in these observed relationships. An appreciating exchange rate lowers the domestic currency price of a country's imports and exports and therefore tends to keep domestic currency prices and costs down This effect makes the causality run from exchange rate to prices, rather than vice versa, and there can be no doubt that price and exchange rate movements interact on each other in a mutually supporting way. Still there is reason to believe that changes in a country's supply of money predominantly affects prices and the exchange rate rather than the exchange rate determining price movements. Donald Kemp, of the Federal Reserve Bank of St. Louis, has put it this way: pointing out that not only prices but also national money supplies are negatively and significantly correlated with exchange values, he notes that these results are consistent with a theory that makes causality stem predominantly from money supply changes. A theory suggesting that causality runs from exchange rates to prices, on the other hand, leaves the negative correlation between money supply and exchange value of the currency unexplained.[5]

Failures of the purchasing power parity doctrine also require explanation, but reasons for the failures may be legion. Low short-run price elasticities may cause the payments flows to pressure exchange rates adversely for a number of quarters following price level disturbances at home or abroad. Expectations of a continuing trend in an exchange rate may induce money flows that prolong the trend beyond a price level justification for it. Bunched short- and

[3] IMF, *Annual Report*, 1977, pp. 30-31.

[4] BIS, *Annual Report*, 1976; and OECD, *Economic Outlook*, July 1978, p. 37.

[5] Donald S. Kemp, "The U.S. Dollar in International Markets: Mid-1970 to Mid-1976," Federal Reserve Bank of St. Louis *Review*, August 1976, pp. 7-14.

long-term capital movements move the exchange rates about without affecting prices, as do shifts in governmental measures to affect trade and capital flows and to bring about variations in output. In view of these and other such possibilities, it is perhaps a testament to the power of the relationship between prices and exchange rates that the relationship is visible at all in relatively short-run periods.[6]

The 1973–1977 period was a profoundly unsettled one as most countries experienced heavy disturbances in exchange market conditions from both internal and external sources. The movement of the exchange rates probably exacerbated the internally generated inflationary differences between countries but at the same time mitigated the external consequences. Apart from the petroleum crisis, the most acute disturbances have arisen from the tendency of countries to finance inflation with too much money creation for too long. This matter is considered further in Chapters 5 and 7.

Interest Rates, the Exchanges, and Interest Parity

In well-functioning international money and capital markets interest rates on assets which are identical except for being denominated in different currencies will be equal except for expectable gains or losses to investors because of the exchange rates. Borrowers and lenders will engage in international interest arbitrage until loss expected from movement of the exchange rates offsets gains due to differences in nominal interest earnings. Those who shift assets and liabilities on a covered basis, hedging possible exchange rate gains or losses through use of the forward exchange markets, will shift their positions among currencies as long as the discount (in relation to the spot rate) at which a currency has to be sold forward is less than the interest differential to be earned by holding the currency for the interim. The relationships between interest rates and exchange rates are, however, complex and mutually interacting, and some of the interactions may be suppressed or deflected when governments impose or threaten to impose exchange controls which impede the movement of capital through particular channels into or out of an area.

Interest rates are prices that resolve, within closed economies, forces of many kinds, among them saving decisions, investment decisions, and asset demand and supply decisions including the monetary and fiscal actions of governments. Nominal interest rates

[6] A useful critical survey of the literature on purchasing power parity is L.H. Officer, "The Purchasing Power Parity Theory of Exchange Rates: A Review Article," *IMF Staff Papers*, March 1976. Also of note is the entire issue of *Journal of International Economics*, vol. 8 (May 1978), which was given over to a symposium on purchasing power parity.

may be, and in recent years no doubt have been, affected by expectations about inflation—expected changes in the purchasing power value of the numeraire of loans. High nominal interest rates have in some circumstances probably reflected high real costs of credit, as in Germany in 1974 when long-term government bond yields averaged 10.4 percent while the German consumer price inflation rate reached only 7.0 percent and was at that time the lowest inflation rate of any industrialized country. On the other hand, nominal interest rates have more frequently been dominated by inflationary fears as, for example, in Japan in 1974 when long-term government interest rates approached 10 percent as inflation soared to more than 20 percent but then receded with the lessening of inflation, or in Italy and the United Kingdom where both interest rates and inflation rates were, in 1974–1976, the highest of any of the industrialized countries. Nominal interest rates have generally been much higher in the 1970s than in the 1960s as a result of the inflation, and both the long- and the short-term rates have been more volatile as a result of shifting expectations. Real interest rates have been low and often negative when real rates are viewed ex post as nominal rates less the rates of price change actually experienced during the loan periods.

It should be emphasized that when interest rate differentials between countries have appeared to reflect differing conditions of supply and demand for financial assets in real terms, the exchange rates have been affected by movements of private funds toward higher interest returns. Where interest rate differentials have been dominated, however, by expectations about loss in the purchasing power of the money numeraire, the same expectations that created high nominal interest rates have often led to expectations of exchange rate depreciation and have not induced movements of funds. The former relationship is illustrated by a close association between the deutsche mark to dollar three-month interest differential and the mark to dollar exchange rate between 1975 and 1976.[7] The latter is illustrated by corresponding sterling to dollar relationships in which premium interest rates in London were associated with sterling depreciation rather than appreciation. The market's long-term expectations throughout 1975–1978 about the future dollar values of deutsche marks and sterling, respectively, were indicated by the chronic tendency for German long-term interest rates to be less than those in the United States and for those in sterling markets to be higher.[8]

[7] The data are plotted in IMF, *Annual Report*, 1976, chart 9, p. 29.

[8] The U.S. long-term government bond yield in July 1978 was 8.65 percent while in Germany it was 5.68 and in the United Kingdom it was 11.43.

When exchange markets are free of government controls, *forward exchange rates* between currencies for each of which there is a well-organized money market tend to stand at interest parity in relation to spot exchange rates. The forward rate is at interest parity when the loss that a trader makes by swapping his currency spot for a claim on his own currency forward exactly offsets the interest differential he might earn as a result of a further transfer of funds from his own to the foreign money market. Where opportunities exist for interest arbitrage with the exchange rate risk hedged in this way, the opportunities may be expected to be exploited. And where the markets have been free of controls, they have indeed functioned largely as predicted. The *covered* interest differential on three-month commercial paper, for example, between the U.S. dollar and the Canadian dollar was regularly less than 1 percent after the second quarter of 1975, and throughout 1976–1978 it remained almost continuously within 0.5 percent per annum, typically in favor of investments in Canada. Similarly, the covered differential between three-month Eurodollar deposits and deutsche mark interbank deposits was very small, typically less than 0.5 percent per annum, following the easing of exchange controls in both countries in 1974.[9] The covered differential between Eurodollar and Swiss franc deposits, on the other hand, was steadily of the order of 2 to 3 percent in favor of the franc in the same period as a result of the Swiss regulations restraining the inflow of foreign funds. And the Eurodollar-sterling differential favored dollar assets as a result of British restraints on capital outflows.[10] When such covered differentials exceed transactions costs and are not due to differences in risk and other properties of investment securities available, they mark unexploited differences in the marginal productivity of liquid capital between the markets and hence a less than optimal international usage of this resource.

[9] Jacob Frenkel and Richard Levitz, "Covered Interest Arbitrage: Unexploited Profits?" *Journal of Political Economy*, vol. 83 (April 1975), pp. 325-38, and "Transactions Costs and Tranquil vs. Turbulent Periods," *Journal of Political Economy*, vol. 85 (December 1977), pp. 1209-27, have suggested that the 0.5 percent, largely risk free, covered interest differential that money managers did not allow to be exceeded corresponds to a measure of transactions costs for financial portfolio balancing operations. Their estimate of transactions costs is obtained from observations of trilateral currency arbitrage that are independent of the interest arbitrage explained. Herbert Grubel, on the other hand, has explained the unexploited differential as due to differences in international security characteristics, noting that some differential in rates of return is likely even when portfolio equilibrium exists. See, for example, his *International Economics* (Homewood, Ill.: R. D. Irwin, 1977), pp. 251-59.

[10] A number of interest arbitrage calculations are conveniently charted each week in Board of Governors of the Federal Reserve System, Division of International Finance, *Selected Interest and Exchange Rates: Weekly Series of Charts.*

Short-Period Exchange Rate Movements and Buy and Sell Spreads

Traders and professional observers of the foreign exchange markets complained from time to time, especially in 1973–1974 and 1977–1978, of wide daily and weekly movements in the exchange rates and of the development of unusual spreads between the buy and sell prices offered by foreign exchange dealers. Temporary movements in the exchange rates are normally expected to be kept small by speculative position taking by exchange dealers and others, and spreads are normally kept small by competition and by the same willingness of dealers to take short-term positions in order to accommodate customers from hour to hour and day to day. Widening of the spreads and of the short-term movements of the rates presumably reflect an unwillingness by banks and nonbank speculators to take uncovered positions that involve risk and that would deepen the market around the daily or weekly average rates and smooth the rates' paths. The experience must reflect either heightened uncertainty on the part of the potential position takers at the times referred to or increased risk aversion, or both of these. Any failure of professional risk bearers to fulfill that function means, of course, that the risk is shifted to others.

Ronald McKinnon noted that bid-ask spreads for a number of currencies on three separate dates in September 1972, June 1973, and October 1974 successively became wider in the U.S. market, with the widening more pronounced for the longer forward-dated contracts than for the spot rates.[11] He reported a selling rate 0.03 percent above the buying rate for spot sterling and a selling rate 0.05 percent above the buying rate for six-month forward sterling on October 1, 1974, and 0.11 and 0.21 percent, respectively, on comparably dated deutsche marks against the dollar. These compared with only 0.02 and 0.05 percent for sterling and 0.02 and 0.06 percent for the deutsche mark on September 29, 1972. Spreads tended to narrow in 1976, except in limited periods of enhanced exchange rate uncertainty between selected currencies,[12] but they widened again in the disorder accompanying the depreciation of the dollar in 1977 and 1978.

Daily and weekly movements of the rates have been examined in detail by several researchers. Hirsch and Higham[13] calculated weekly averages of the daily movements of sterling against six other

[11] "Floating Foreign Exchange Rates 1973-74," pp. 79-113.

[12] IMF, *Annual Report*, 1976, p. 28.

[13] Fred Hirsch and David Higham, "Floating Rates—Expectations and Experience," *Three Banks Review*, no. 102 (June 1974), pp. 3-34.

currencies for ten months beginning April 1, 1973, and found the weekly averages ranged from 0.8 percent against the dollar to 1.5 percent against the deutsche mark in that disturbed period. On two occasions, the weekly change of sterling against the deutsche mark was over 9 percent—in June and again in July 1973. Even the effective rates for several currencies changed by 0.75 to 1.0 percent per week *on the average* during that ten months. The maximum weekly change of an effective rate was 6.4 percent, experienced by the yen. Hirsch and Higham assessed these rates of change as large against the 2.0 percent total movement of a rate permitted under IMF rules prior to 1971 and even against the widened 4.5 percent band introduced in connection with IMF central rates in December 1971. The period that Hirsch and Higham examined, however, was an especially troubled one; its early end included the months immediately following the introduction of generalized floating, when central banks held back from stabilizing interventions, and its final four months were the time of the global petroleum embargo. The high weekly rates of change reported were not reversed fluctuations but rather parts of broader movements of the rates in those periods of transition and heightened uncertainty.

An alternative assessment has been made by Donald Kemp, who calculated mean daily, monthly, and quarterly percentage exchange rate movements between the dollar and each of nine other currencies from June 1970, when the par value system began to rupture, to June 1976, with the standard deviation for each country's change about its mean. Kemp further broke the period into two parts, one prior to March 1973, the date when generalized floating materialized, the other after. He concluded that "in no instance did the mean of the percentage change . . . exceed 4.5 percent over either daily, monthly, or quarterly intervals. In addition, in no instance did the standard deviation of the percentage exchange rate changes exceed 4.5 percent for either the daily or monthly data."[14] Only against the European snake currencies and Italy did the quarterly standard deviations of the dollar exchange rates exceed 4.5 percent during the period of the generalized float. Focusing on the dollar and disregarding maximum weekly changes, then, Kemp arrived at a more sanguine view of exchange rate performance.

Exchange rates between the dollar and snake currencies tended to settle down to smaller weekly (and also daily) movements from mid-1975 to mid-1976. The average weekly change in the effective

[14] "The U.S. Dollar in International Markets: Mid-1970 to Mid-1976," Federal Reserve Bank of St. Louis *Review*, August 1976.

value of the deutsche mark in that period was only 0.48 percent, whereas it had been 0.70 in the prior portion of the period of generalized floating. Similarly, the weekly changes in effective value of the yen averaged only 0.31 percent in the final two quarters of 1975 and the first two of 1976, whereas it had been 0.57 percent from July 1973 to June 1975. In the latter half of 1976, however, in anticipation of currency realignments within the EEC snake, and again in 1977–1978 in connection with rapid readjustment of the value of the dollar, disorder returned. In January 1978 the U.S. Federal Reserve authorities announced a policy of more aggressive intervention to defend orderly conditions.

Use of the Forward Markets

Most economists predicted that a substantial increase in volume in the markets for forward exchange would accompany the advent of floating rates. The prediction did not materialize in the U.S. market between 1973 and 1976, although it apparently did in Sweden. Information concerning other countries is scanty.

In the United States, while firm data on foreign exchange volume for exchange contracts of all maturities are limited, bankers report that the volume of forward exchange trading was less in 1975–1976 than in 1971. The widened spreads on forward buying and selling rates, mentioned above, seem also to testify to increased thinness in the forward market. For Sweden, on the other hand, data collected by the Swedish Central Bank and reported by Sven Grassman, show a trebling of forward contracts outstanding in 1973 and 1974 as compared with earlier years, although those contracts still represented only a small percent of the value of Sweden's imports and exports.[15]

Why greater use of the forward markets has not developed in the United States is not clear. It may be partly because the share of U.S. trade executed by smaller firms is largely denominated in dollars so that the American transactor incurs no foreign exchange risk, while the share executed by multinational corporations and denominated in other currencies has been increasingly hedged by offsetting positions internal to the firm and by borrowing and lending foreign currency. Ronald McKinnon has suggested that uncertainty has caused the banks not only to widen their bid-offer spreads on forward contracts but to raise the margins (that is, the cash deposits) they require of those with whom they make forward contracts. Both

[15] "Currency Distribution and Forward Cover in Foreign Trade," pp. 215-21.

these measures raise the cost to customers of using the forward market to obtain a hedge. Importers, then, could have been induced to acquire foreign currency needs in advance via the spot market rather than through a purchase of forward exchange, and exporters could have learned to borrow foreign currency for immediate conversion in lieu of selling expected foreign currency proceeds forward. McKinnon feels this phenomenon not only occurred but also contributed to the general pressure on bank liquidity, which he feels in turn contributed to bank unwillingness to take stabilizing speculative positions in the foreign exchange markets.

In view of the proclivity of some countries to invoke exchange controls to protect exchange rates, traders may have felt, too, some uncertainty about the ability of banks to fulfill forward exchange contracts. Public concern about the liquidity and solvency of the banks themselves at times no doubt heightened such feelings.

Exchange controls also inhibited interest arbitrage, as noted above, and this limited the volume of forward trading.

A number of countries took steps in 1974–1976 to protect exporters against the risk of losses arising from exchange fluctuations by offering them exchange rate insurance. The IMF reports that Denmark, France, Norway, and Switzerland offered such insurance in 1976.[16]

Forward markets, then, are only one means of providing hedges to individuals who are exposed to foreign exchange risk because of their involvement in international commerce. But they are an efficient way insofar as they clear traders' risks which are offsetting or transfer traders' risks to professional risk bearers. Heightened uncertainty in 1973–1978 because of large differentials in inflation rates, sudden and massive international payments imbalances caused by the petroleum crisis, intensified international borrowing and concern for the safety of banks, political scandals, and other significant irregularities in the international payments fabric very likely caused some withdrawal of professional risk taking from the foreign exchange markets with consequent higher costs for hedging to nonbank traders and arbitragers. It seems reasonable to expect that if there is a continued slowing of global inflation and especially an easing of inflation differentials among countries, exchange rate variations will become smaller and risk bearing less costly to bankers and traders alike. The Swedish experience supports this view since the growth in forward exchange trading in Sweden may be related to the fact that, as com-

[16] IMF, *Annual Report on Exchange Restrictions*, 1976.

pared with the dollar, the krona had a stable value against the currencies of Sweden's main trading partners during the period for which the data were reported (see Figure 4).[17]

McKinnon has complained that the forward markets have been poor predictors of the future course of the spot exchange rates in that premiums of the forward over the spot rates have not accurately presaged rises of the spot rate, and discounts have not presaged spot rate declines.[18] Mussa, however, has properly commented that in fact one cannot expect the position of a forward rate relative to spot to reflect the future course of the spot rate.[19] All the information about the future available at any time will be embodied in all prices, including the spot exchange rate, the forward rate, and the interest rates in the respective countries. The forward premium or discount will, when official regulations do not interfere, reflect interest parity considerations—the value of holding assets denominated in one currency or the other with the exchange risk covered, and this will depend on interest rates alone. A change in expectations about future exchange rates might affect first the forward rates if speculators prefer that market, but the spot rate will move in close tandem with the forward rate because of the link between the two enforced by interest arbitraging activities.[20]

Patterns of Exchange Rate Variability and Official Intervention

Official purchases and sales in the foreign exchange markets to limit or slow movements of the exchange rates have been larger, taken as totals over periods as long as, say, a year, in 1973–1977 than they were under fixed exchange rates prior to 1971.[21] The interventions, however, have rarely been as massive or sudden as they were during short periods of exchange market crisis in the fixed exchange rate

---

[17] The mid-1977 devaluation of the krona, however, was a break in this pattern.

[18] "Floating Exchange Rates, 1973-74."

[19] Michael Mussa, "Our Recent Experience with Fixed and Flexible Exchange Rates: A Comment," in Karl Brunner and Allan H. Meltzer, eds., *Institutional Arrangements and the Inflation Problem,* Carnegie-Rochester Conference Series on Public Policy, a supplementary series to *Journal of Monetary Economics,* (New York: North Holland, 1976) p. 135.

[20] The IMF has published data on failure of the three-month forward rate to reflect the spot rate subsequently achieved, but has offered it as a measure of uncertainty in the market. By that measure uncertainty was lower in 1976 than in 1973-1974. See IMF, *Annual Report,* 1977, pp. 27-29.

[21] Weir Brown, *World Afloat: National Policies Ruling the Waves,* Essays in International Finance, no. 116 (International Finance Section, Princeton University, May 1976).

period, except among the countries continuing to maintain narrow exchange rate margins, especially in Europe.

The interventions have been undertaken partly to temper the exchange rate movements inspired by heightened market uncertainty about where a medium-term equilibrium rate might lie and to provide day-to-day tone to the markets. Especially following eruption of the petroleum crisis in late 1973 they were also rationalized as measures to slow the trend movements of exchange rates in the conviction that exchange rate changes among the oil-consuming countries could only reallocate, not eliminate, the massive collective deficit of those countries vis-à-vis the oil-producing countries. Furthermore, the interaction between exchange rate movements and domestic inflation trends were often a cause of concern. In countries where inflation was high, currency depreciation was resisted because it intensified inflationary pressures. In countries where inflation was low, exchange rate appreciation often sparked fears that the appreciation, induced by anticipation of price level developments, would be premature and would price exports out of their foreign markets and expose domestic producers to unacceptable external competition.

The interventions have taken a variety of forms and are poorly reported. In their most direct form, they have consisted of official purchases and sales of foreign currencies making use of existing or borrowed reserves. In a broader sense, they have consisted also of redirection of the borrowing (lending) of publicly controlled agencies and private firms toward the foreign or domestic market, changes in bank regulations, and other measures.

Changes in countries' reported official reserves reflect to a substantial degree their exchange market intervention activities. Unfortunately, however, they provide only a rough approximation. The reserves measured, say, in dollars also change as a result of a number of other influences, for several of which no data exist. The reserve aggregates change, for example, as a result of revaluations of the gold, SDR, and foreign exchange components of the series as the market prices of these assets change. While the first two of these influences can be accounted for, the influence on foreign exchange holdings of changes in exchange rates cannot be removed because of the absence of data on the currency composition of countries' foreign exchange assets. Furthermore, the data on short- to intermediate-term official borrowings from Eurobanks and from other governments, including drawings under bilateral swap arrangements, are not complete, and there is no public information concerning the rate at which these borrowings or the borrowings of publicly owned enterprises or other pseudo-official agencies have been entered in the official reserve reports.

In spite of these difficulties, and because there is no alternative time series, a partially adjusted series showing monthly reserve changes for the Group of Ten countries plus Switzerland is shown in Figures 6 through 16 along with an effective exchange rate index for each country. The reserve changes shown there are based on reserves reported in the IMF's *International Financial Statistics,* measured in dollars, with several adjustments. The gold component of the reserve aggregate for each country has been eliminated because there were no significant purchases or sales of gold by the countries involved.[22] The SDR component and the reserve position in the Fund component are deflated to compensate for changes in the SDR's dollar valuation. And each country's use of IMF credit and its loans to the Fund (under the general agreement to borrow and under the oil facility) are removed from its reserves. Monthly changes in the adjusted reserve aggregates are then shown as bars on the charts. Drawings and repayments under bilateral swap agreements between the Federal Reserve System and other central banks, available only on a quarterly basis, appear as bars without shading. Since drawings under the bilateral credit lines augment reserves of both drawer and drawee countries, they are shown as negative for each pair of countries so that they can be used visually to offset or augment the changes in "adjusted reserves" if the viewer wishes to give attention to the quarterly data. Repayments on the swap lines are shown as positive reserve changes. Dashed line bars on some of the charts show a corrected series resulting from the removal of long-term public and public agency borrowing on the international capital markets from the "adjusted reserves" series. None of the data reflect the very considerable amount of intervention activity which was completed and reversed within the periods for which the data are reported. Nonetheless, the series do suggest some generalizations.

Intervention activity in the sixty-four months, March 1973 to June 1978, appears to have been greatest in the market for deutsche marks, with the market for Swiss francs in second place. Table 3 shows monthly average absolute changes in the adjusted reserve series for each of the eleven countries, with no correction made to exclude the effects of central bank swap drawings or other borrowing or

[22] Exceptions to this rule are a small purchase of IMF gold by France for dollars and small open market gold sales for dollars by the United States (in 1974 and again in 1978). None of these purchases or sales directly involved the foreign exchange market.

FIGURE 6

UNITED STATES: ADJUSTED RESERVE CHANGES AND EFFECTIVE EXCHANGE RATE, MARCH 1973–JUNE 1978

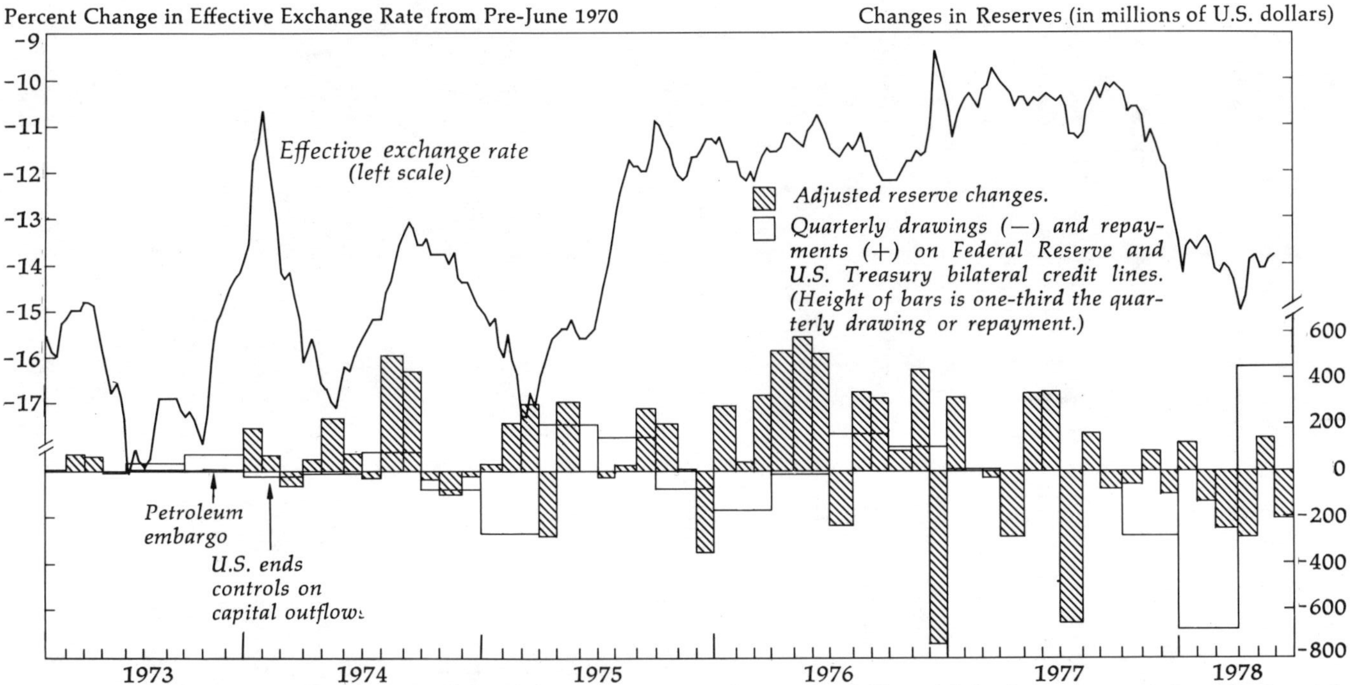

SOURCES: Adjusted reserve changes are calculated from data in IMF, *International Financial Statistics* (see text for adjustments). The effective exchange rate series is that of Morgan Guaranty Trust. Quarterly net drawings and repayments on Federal Reserve bilateral credit lines, where shown in Figures 6–16, are from *Federal Reserve Bulletin*. Long-term agency borrowing, where shown, is from Table 4.

FIGURE 7

CANADA: ADJUSTED RESERVE CHANGES AND EFFECTIVE EXCHANGE RATE, MARCH 1973–JUNE 1978

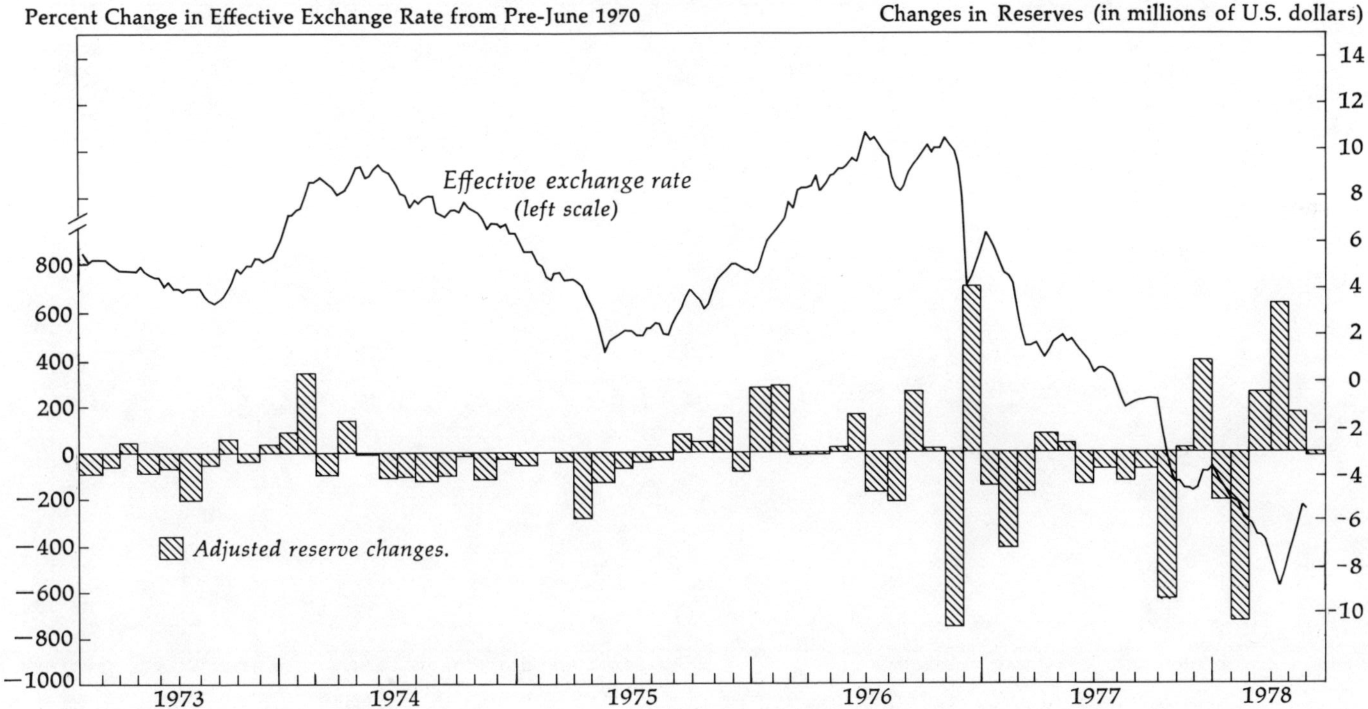

SOURCES: See Figure 6.

FIGURE 8

JAPAN: ADJUSTED RESERVE CHANGES AND EFFECTIVE EXCHANGE RATE, MARCH 1973–JUNE 1978

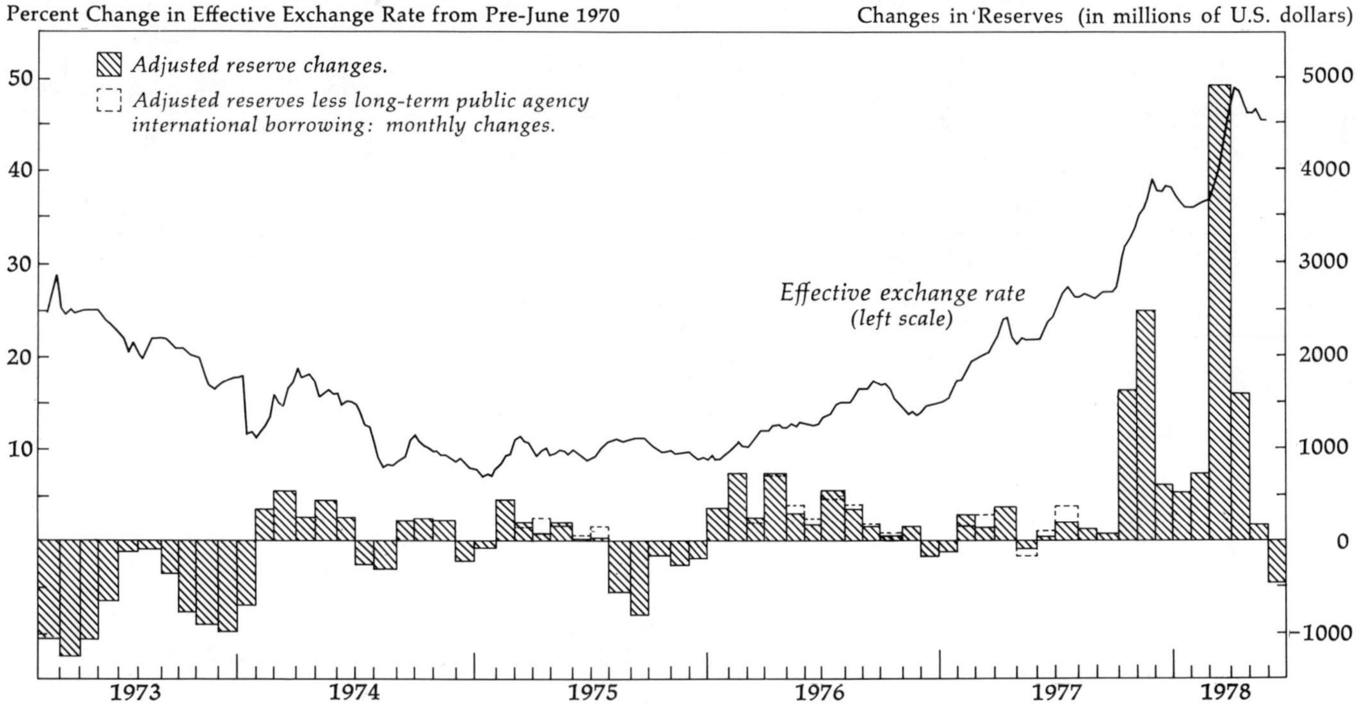

SOURCES: See Figure 6.

FIGURE 9

UNITED KINGDOM: ADJUSTED RESERVE CHANGES AND EFFECTIVE EXCHANGE RATE, MARCH 1973–JUNE 1978

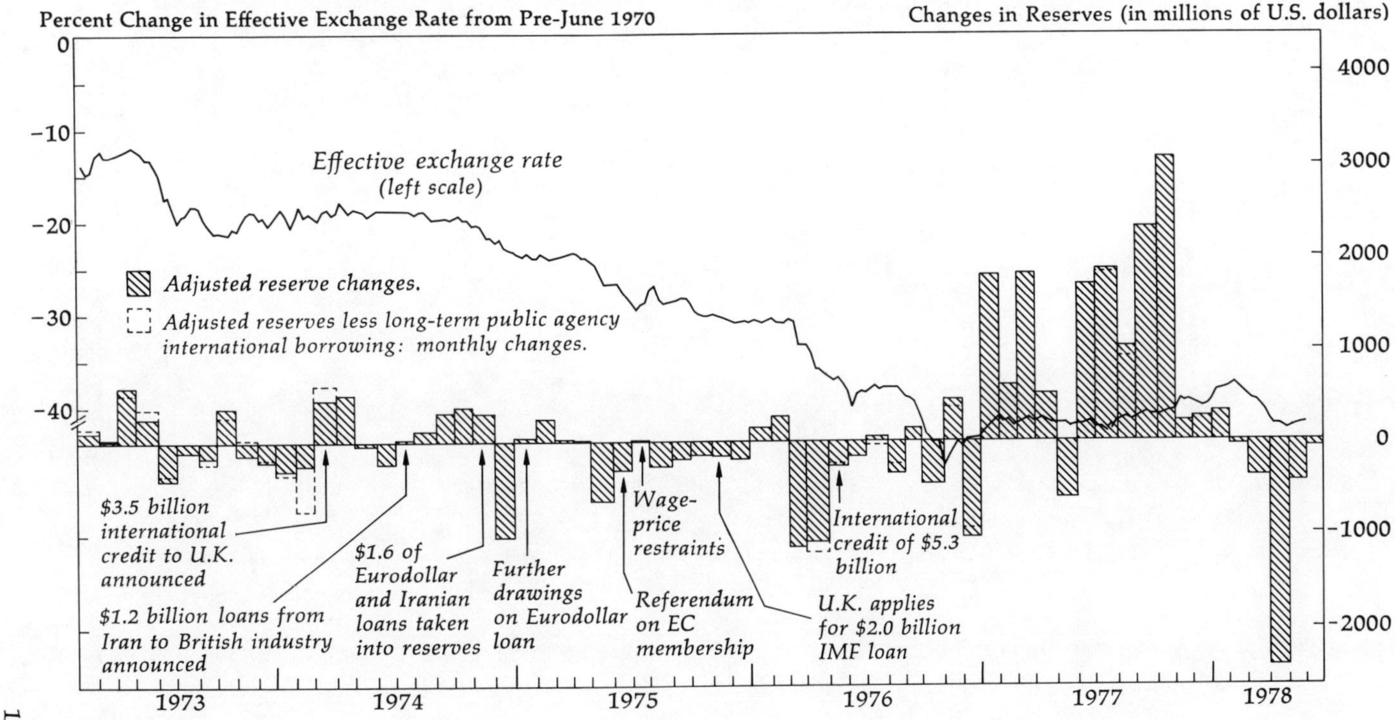

SOURCES: See Figure 6.

FIGURE 10

GERMANY: ADJUSTED RESERVE CHANGES AND EFFECTIVE EXCHANGE RATE, MARCH 1973–JUNE 1978

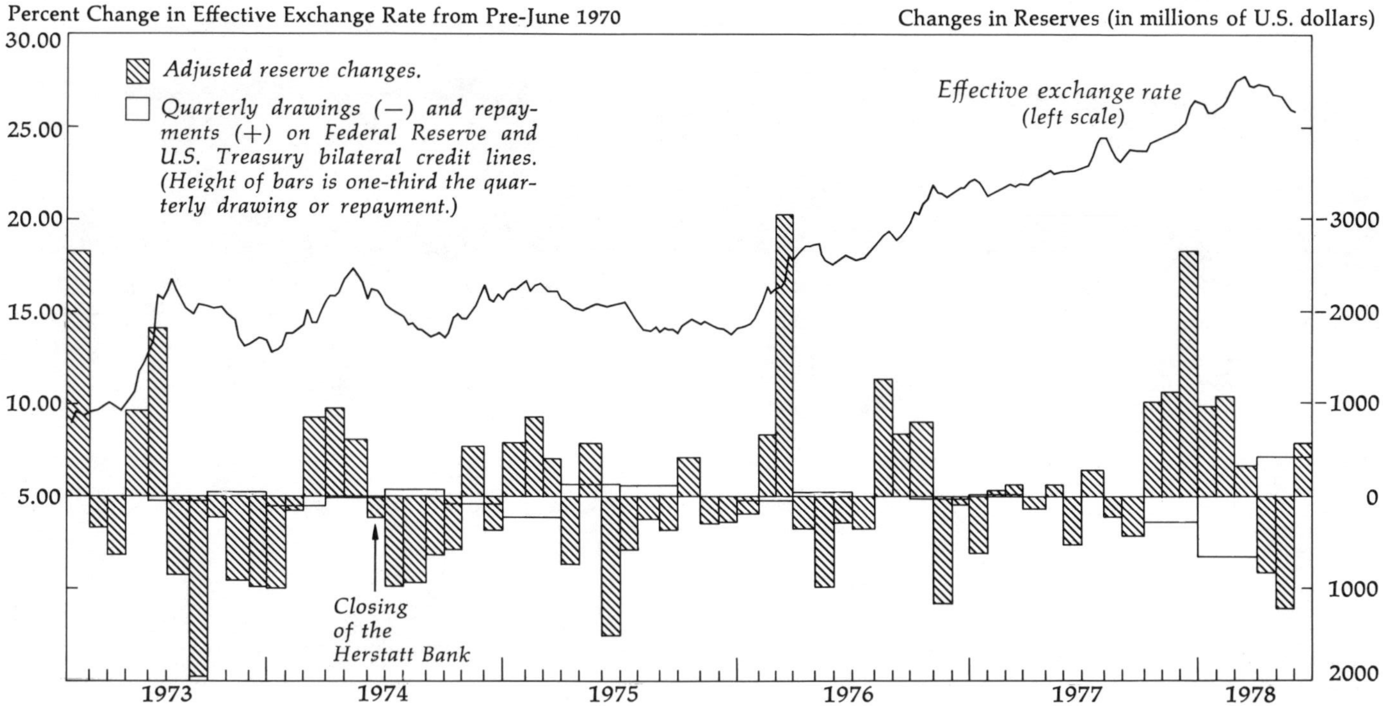

SOURCES: See Figure 6.

FIGURE 11

FRANCE: ADJUSTED RESERVE CHANGES AND EFFECTIVE EXCHANGE RATE, MARCH 1973–JUNE 1978

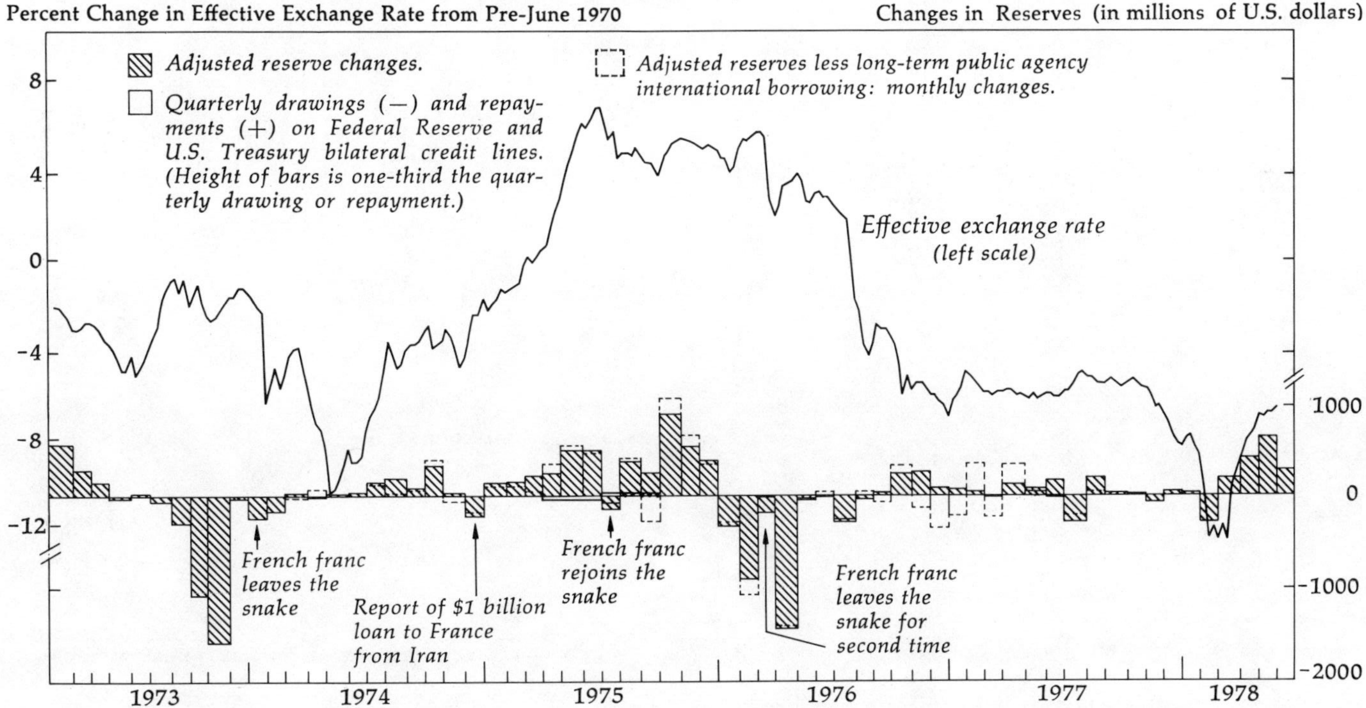

SOURCES: See Figure 6.

FIGURE 12

ITALY: ADJUSTED RESERVE CHANGES AND EFFECTIVE EXCHANGE RATE, MARCH 1973–JUNE 1978

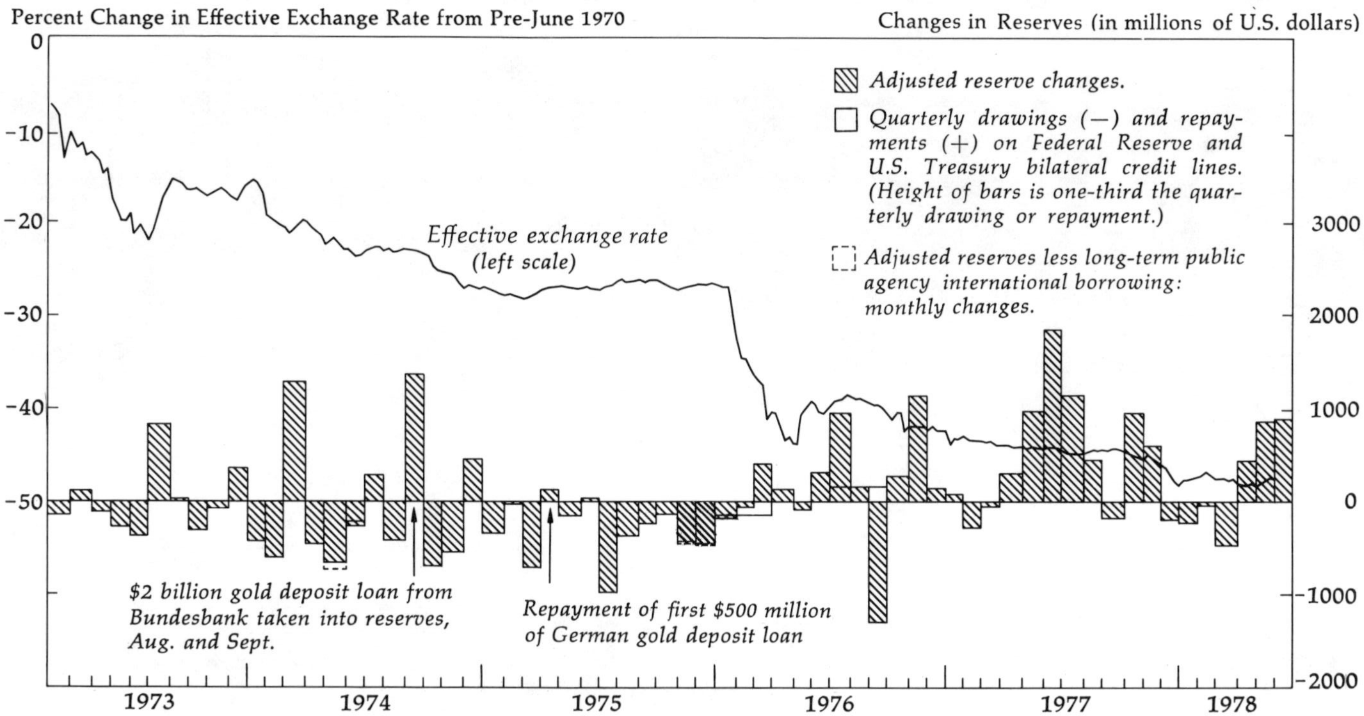

SOURCES: See Figure 6.

FIGURE 13

BELGIUM-LUXEMBOURG: ADJUSTED RESERVE CHANGES AND EFFECTIVE EXCHANGE RATE, MARCH 1973–JUNE 1978

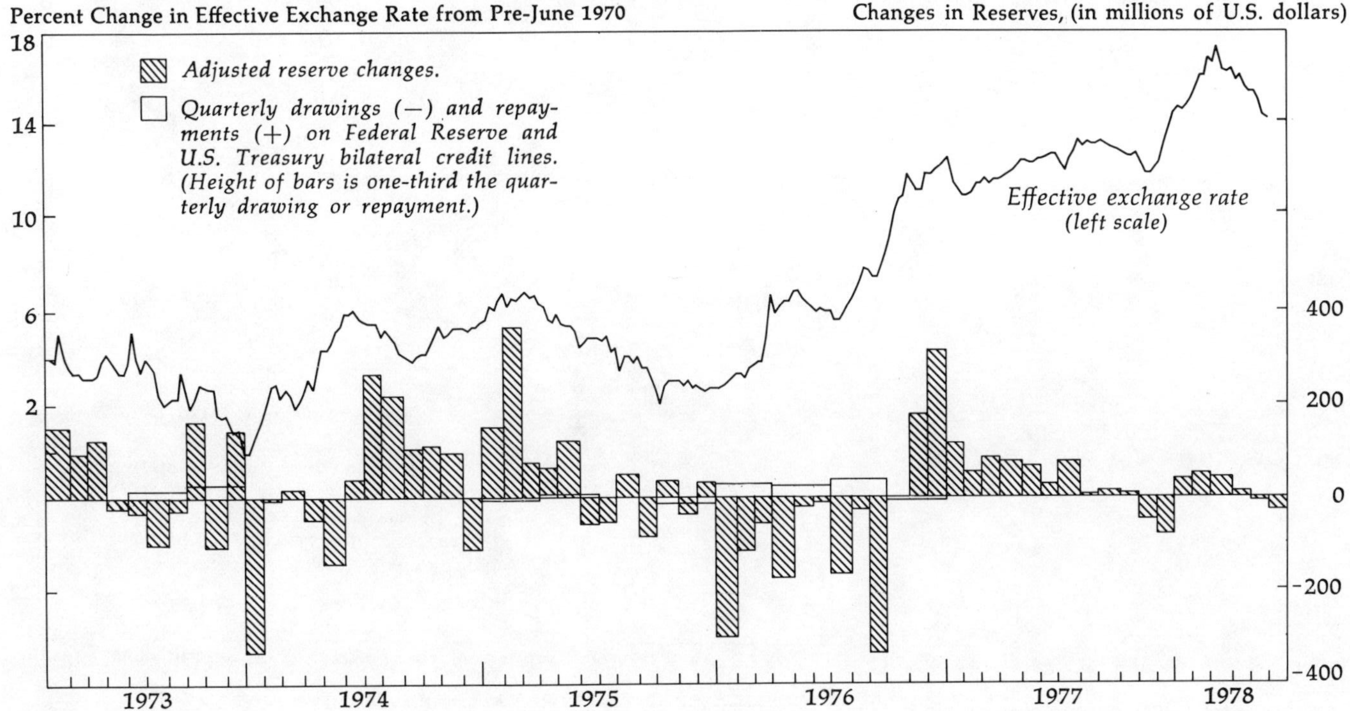

SOURCES: See Figure 6.

FIGURE 14

NETHERLANDS: ADJUSTED RESERVE CHANGES AND EFFECTIVE EXCHANGE RATE, MARCH 1973–JUNE 1978

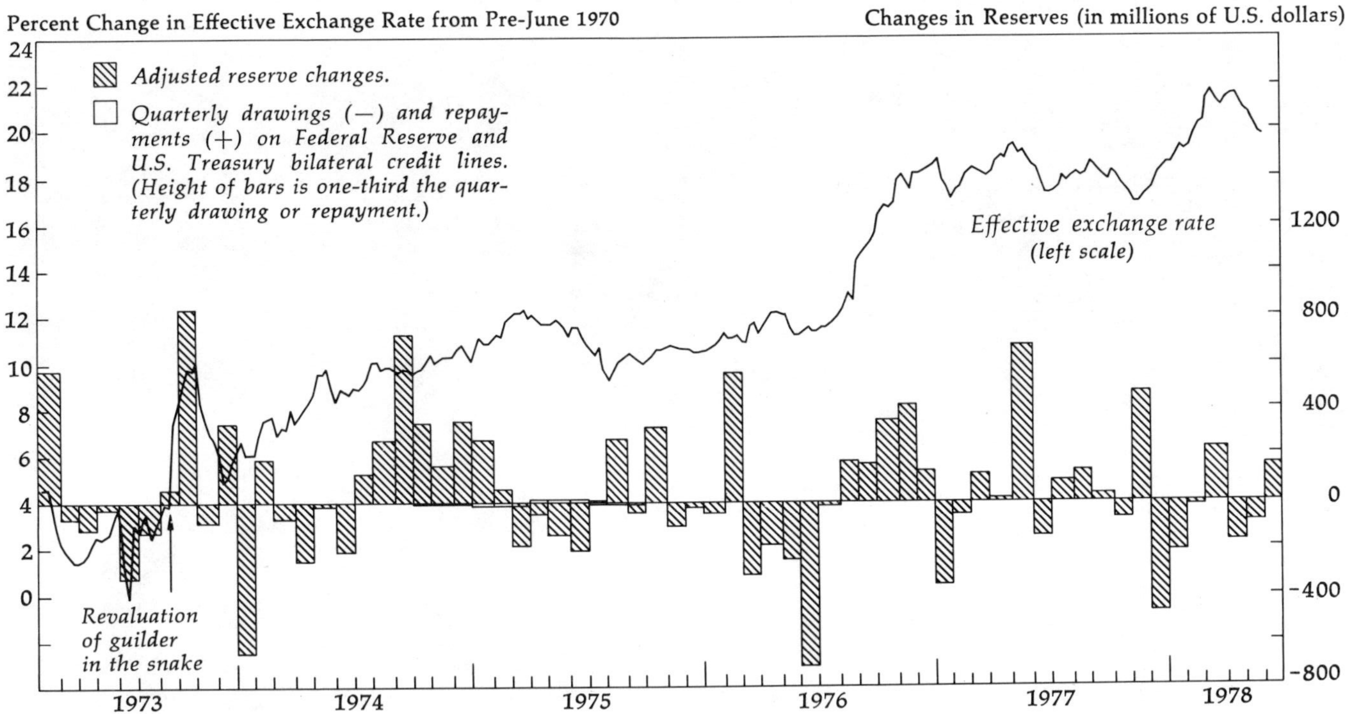

SOURCES: See Figure 6.

FIGURE 15

SWITZERLAND: ADJUSTED RESERVE CHANGES AND EFFECTIVE EXCHANGE RATE, MARCH 1973–JUNE 1978

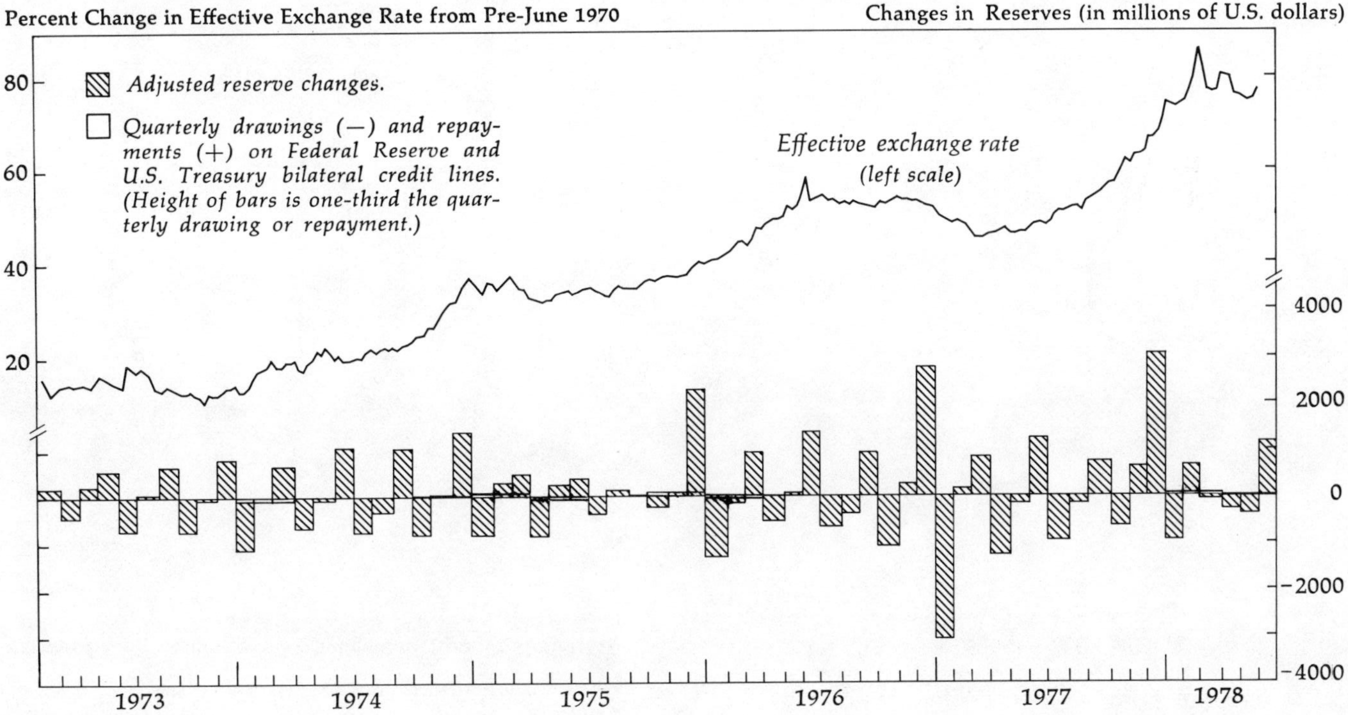

SOURCES: See Figure 6.

FIGURE 16

SWEDEN: ADJUSTED RESERVE CHANGES AND EFFECTIVE EXCHANGE RATE, MARCH 1973–JUNE 1978

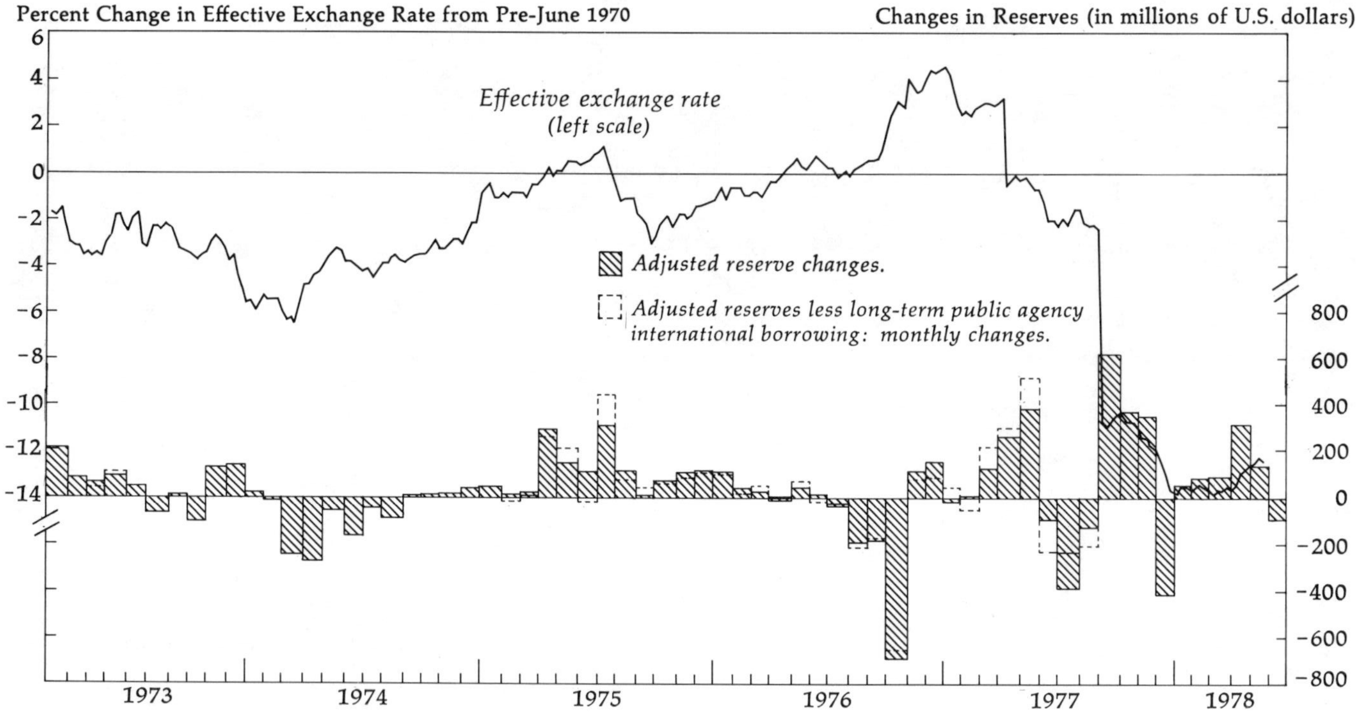

SOURCES: See Figure 6.

TABLE 3

MONTHLY AVERAGE ABSOLUTE CHANGE AND TOTAL NET CHANGE IN ADJUSTED RESERVES, ELEVEN COUNTRIES, MARCH 1973–JUNE 1978
(millions of dollars)

Country	*Monthly Mean of Absolute Reserve Changes, 64 Months*	*Total Net Change in Adjusted Reserves Over 64 Months*
Germany	754	8,130
Switzerland	704	5,637
United Kingdom	521	7,989
Japan	517	9,026
Italy	457	4,943
France	256	227
Netherlands	224	1,826
United States	187	4,247
Canada	157	−1,687
Sweden	139	2,302
Belgium	92	962

SOURCE: Calculated from data in IMF, *International Financial Statistics;* for adjustments, see text.

lending outside the IMF. Germany's adjusted reserve changes, at $754 million per month, averaged $9.0 billion per year during the period. The Swiss changes, at $704 million per month, averaged $8.4 billion per year. Intervention activity was also heavy in the markets for sterling, for Japanese yen, and for Italian lire. It was lighter in absolute amount for the currencies of France, the Netherlands, Canada, Sweden, and Belgium, currencies for which the markets are in any case smaller. The data of Table 3 cannot be used to imply intervention activity on the part of the governments named since the reported reserves of any country are influenced by the activities of other governments as well as those of the country itself. SDR holdings, for example, are influenced by the IMF's direction of SDR transactions; countries' reserve positions in the Fund are influenced by the drawings and repayments of other countries; and foreign exchange reserves respond to drawings and repayments under intergovernmental reciprocal swap lines. Switzerland is a case in point. The National Bank of Switzerland began a policy of active exchange market intervention only in early 1975. Changes in adjusted Swiss reserves, however, were greater in 1973–1974 than in the early months of the more aggressive Swiss policy. Imperfect as they are, the data shown probably reflect orders of relative magnitude of intervention activity in the countries' respective currencies.

When the heavy external borrowing undertaken in 1974–1977 by Italy, France, the United Kingdom, and, in lesser degree, Sweden, and Japan (see below) are taken into account, the data of the second column of Table 3 suggest that intervention was heaviest in those currencies that were under trend pressure to appreciate. Germany, Switzerland, the United Kingdom, and Japan were the large net accumulators of reserves, and their currencies apparently experienced the heaviest intervention activity, as measured by aggregated absolute reserve changes.

The data on the figures indicate that intervention was often against the wind in the period covered, in accordance with the IMF 1974 guidelines for exchange market policies, but it was by no means entirely so. Table 4 gives the percent, for each country, of the monthly adjusted reserve changes that were of the same sign as the change in the effective exchange rate, where the latter was measured as the change between the final weekly observations of successive months. The percentages in Table 4, therefore, represent the shares of the monthly reserve changes that were in appropriate directions to resist the observed end-of-month to end-of-month exchange rate changes. Germany's score by this count was 73 percent, while Switzerland's was only 44 percent. Only eight of the eleven scores were over 50 percent.[23]

The tabulation is an inexact measure not only because the quality of the data is poor for the purpose, but especially because many substantial intervention actions were completed and more or less reversed within the monthly periods. Furthermore, neither the effective exchange rates nor the aggregate reserve changes reveal offsetting tendencies and perhaps offsetting interventions in various currencies. Since the exchange rate changes recorded are also those after and not before the interventions, in each case they reflect the effect of the intervention as well as the need for it. Indeed, in some cases the appearance of a destabilizing intervention may be spurious because the intervention itself reversed the rate's tendency. And

[23] The Federal Reserve Bank of New York has reported that its intervention operations between August 1971 and the end of 1977 have been profitable in each year, netting $29.3 million overall. ("Treasury and Federal Reserve Foreign Exchange Operations: Interim Report," *Federal Reserve Bulletin*, June 1978, p. 451, table 6.) This is evidence that the U.S. operations had the effect of limiting movement of the dollar exchange rate yearly and over the entire period although it does not prove that the interventions were against the wind in most cases.

TABLE 4

PERCENTAGE OF MONTHLY ADJUSTED RESERVE CHANGES STABILIZING TO OBSERVED MONTHLY CHANGE IN EFFECTIVE EXCHANGE RATE, ELEVEN COUNTRIES, MARCH 1973–MAY 1978

Country[a]	*Percentage*
Germany	73
Switzerland	44
Japan	68
Italy	56
France	57
United Kingdom	68
Netherlands	57
United States	52
Belgium	47
Sweden	48
Canada	76

[a] In order of average size of monthly adjusted reserve changes in Table 3.
SOURCE: Data from Figures 6-16.

among countries participating in the snake arrangement, interventions were often large in order to prevent exchange rate changes.

Table 5 shows reported external long-time borrowing by official agencies of Group of Ten countries which borrowed significantly during the March 1973–August 1977 period. Several countries used such borrowing from time to time to strengthen their international reserves and converted the currencies at the central bank to add to official international reserves without directly affecting the exchange market. Unfortunately, data on public agency short-and intermediate-term borrowing from banks are not available in detail although such borrowing was undoubtedly large. It is also not clear to what extent and when the long-term official and pseudo-official borrowings were marked up in international reserves.

Long-term borrowing from the capital market by public agencies in the United Kingdom was largely bunched in 1973 and 1974 when it amounted to $643 million. Most of this borrowing was presumably converted into sterling at the Bank of England under the exchange cover arrangement initiated by the government in March 1973. French borrowing began only as British borrowing tapered off and totaled $4,131 million in the forty-four months from 1974 through August 1977. Swedish and Japanese public agencies became active international borrowers beginning in 1975. Canadian borrowing was

TABLE 5

Government and Public Agency International Bond Issues, March 1973–August 1977
(in millions of dollars)

Year	*Month*	*United Kingdom*	*France*	*Italy*	*Canada*	*Japan*	*Sweden*
1973	3	25	—	—	67	—	—
	4	40	—	—	36	—	—
	5	125	—	—	—	—	13
	6	25	—	—	49	—	—
	7	—	—	—	—	—	—
	8	—	—	—	—	—	—
	9	70	—	—	—	—	—
	10	164	—	—	—	—	—
	11	10	—	—	—	—	—
	12	—	—	—	11	—	—
1974	1	50	—	—	30	—	—
	2	134	25	—	80	—	—
	3	—	60	—	182	—	—
	4	—	—	—	3	—	—
	5	—	—	50	18	—	—
	6	—	—	—	118	—	—
	7	—	25	—	225	—	—
	8	—	—	—	—	—	—
	9	—	25	—	70	—	—
	10	—	—	—	200	—	—
	11	—	77	—	250	—	—
	12	—	59	—	10	—	—
1975	1	—	91	—	310	—	—
	2	—	131	—	250	—	21
	3	—	296	—	25	92	37
	4	—	192	—	51	—	67
	5	—	131	—	375	21	—
	6	—	146	—	350	43	134
	7	—	67	—	350	—	—
	8	—	50	—	38	—	30
	9	—	—	—	340	—	—
	10	—	160	—	182	—	7
	11	—	34	15	665	—	19
	12	—	72	—	330	—	20
1976	1	—	119	—	478	—	31
	2	—	281	—	1,171	—	50
	3	—	108	—	894	74	28
	4	37	99	—	94	100	21

TABLE 5 (continued)

Year	Month	United Kingdom	France	Italy	Canada	Japan	Sweden
	5	—	123	—	240	39	—
	6	—	93	—	289	—	27
	7	109	115	—	3,306	100	20
	8	—	50	—	282	61	42
	9	—	172	—	493	40	35
	10	—	93	—	2,204	—	—
	11	75	265	—	500	—	30
	12	—	—	—	6,965	—	103
1977	1	—	306	—	460	—	40
	2	—	—	—	234	150	92
	3	—	219	—	100	—	—
	4	—	—	—	197	—	132
	5	—	50	—	320	100	20
	6	—	221	—	34	193	160
	7	14	156	—	96	—	—
	8	100	20	—	454	—	80
Total		978	4,131	65	23,526	1,013	1,259

NOTE: Dashes = zero or negligible.

SOURCE: Compiled from Morgan Guaranty Trust, *World Financial Markets.* Issues in currencies other than the dollar were converted at monthly average market exchange rates as reported in IMF, *International Financial Statistics.*

heavy and continuous throughout the period but was probably not motivated much by the state of the balance of payments; it came to $23,526 million in the three years. Germany, Belgium-Luxembourg, and the Netherlands were borrowers in 1976–1977 but only of insignificant amounts.

Removing the borrowings shown in Table 5 from the previously adjusted reserve totals and recalculating the month-to-month changes does not much change the apparent intervention picture. The dotted line bars on the figures for the United Kingdom, France, Italy, Japan, and Sweden show the adjusted reserve changes that could have been attributed to exchange market interventions under the assumption that all public agency long-term international borrowings were entered in the reserves in the month reported for bond issues. The differences in the two series are small, and the direction of change in the reserves is different, as a result of removing the long-term borrowing, only twice for the United Kingdom, ten times for France, four times for Sweden, and not at all for Japan and Italy.

It is clear, however, that the borrowings shown in Table 5 are only part of the totals that the listed countries have borrowed. In his semi-annual review of "Treasury and Federal Foreign Exchange Operations" for March 1974, Charles Coombs reported that total Italian public agency borrowing, from mid-1972 through January 1974, exceeded $6 billion, largely from banks.[24] In addition, the Italians borrowed $2 billion from the German Bundesbank, securing the loan with gold, in mid-1974. Coombs reported French public sector international borrowing in February 1974 of over $1 billion,[25] and press reports indicated an Iranian deposit in the Bank of France of $500 million late in the year. The deposit was subsequently raised to $700 million and targeted to be $1 billion but was drawn back to $500 million in May 1976. French banks borrowed abroad at government invitation specifically for the purpose of relending francs at home, and the amounts of such intermediation were put by the Bank of France at F4.2 billion ($0.9 billion) in 1974.[26] The British Treasury borrowed $2.5 billion from a commercial banking consortium in 1974 and turned to the International Monetary Fund and governments of several Group of Ten countries for a combined standby credit of $5.3 billion in June 1976. In January 1977, in connection with a further $3.9 billion IMF credit, the United Kingdom negotiated a standby credit of $3 billion from a group of governments to ensure the convertibility of non-U.K. reserve currency balances in sterling and arranged a further commercial bank syndicate loan of $1.5 billion.

World Bank estimates of total public and private borrowing in international capital markets by major industrialized countries, 1974–1977, are shown in Table 6. The data do not include the government to government credits and IMF advances mentioned above, but they do reflect the magnitude of French official borrowing in private markets in 1976, Italian and British use of the Eurocurrency markets in 1974, and the expansion of Japanese and Swedish borrowing in the capital markets in 1975, 1976, and 1977.

Manipulation of the exchange controls was another means by which governments sought to influence their foreign exchange rates during the early period of generalized floating. In January 1974 the United States abandoned its restraints on outward movements of capital, although this action was probably to take advantage of a moment

---

[24] "Treasury and Federal Reserve Foreign Exchange Operations," *Federal Reserve Bulletin*, March 1974.

[25] "Treasury and Federal Reserve Foreign Exchange Operations," *Federal Reserve Bulletin*, September 1974, p. 644.

[26] Cited in Brown, *World Afloat*, p. 33.

TABLE 6

Borrowing in International Capital Markets, Selected Industrialized Countries, 1974–1977
(millions of U.S. dollars or equivalent)

Borrowing Country[a]	Total Bonds: Public borrower	Total Bonds: Private borrower	*Total*	*Euro-currency Credits*	*Total Bonds and Credits*
Belgium					
1974	24.8	—	24.8	—	24.8
1975	18.5	—	18.5	—	18.5
1976	—	133.9	133.9	—	133.9
1977	—	174.1	174.1	—	174.1
Canada					
1974	1,248.3	1,153.4	2,401.7	75.0	2,476.7
1975	3,385.9	1,167.0	4,552.9	113.0	4,665.9
1976	4,881.6	4,208.4	9,090.0	935.0	10,025.0
1977	3,482.7	1,724.0	5,206.7	537.0	5,743.7
France					
1974	205.8	466.0	671.8	3,330.6	4,002.4
1975	1,459.0	343.1	1,802.1	506.1	2,308.2
1976	2,052.3	764.6	2,816.9	733.8	3,550.7
1977	1,491.0	468.0	1,959.0	1,712.0	3,671.0
Germany, Fed. Rep.					
1974	49.4	83.9	133.3	9.0	142.3
1975	92.2	135.2	227.4	—	227.4
1976	160.7	213.1	373.8	—	373.8
1977	150.0	120.4	270.4	—	270.4
Italy					
1974	50.0	—	50.0	2,390.0	2,440.0
1975	9.9	51.1	61.0	120.0	181.0
1976	85.0	—	85.0	20.0	105.0
1977	237.8	61.8	299.6	826.4	1,126.0
Japan					
1974	162.7	84.7	247.4	326.0	573.4
1975	1,131.5	519.7	1,651.2	331.8	1,983.0
1976	1,317.7	690.2	2,007.9	368.4	2,376.3
1977	1,499.9	376.7	1,876.6	67.5	1,944.1

(Table continued on next page)

TABLE 6 (continued)

Borrowing Country[a]	Total Bonds: Public borrower	Total Bonds: Private borrower	Total	Euro-currency Credits	Total Bonds and Credits
Netherlands					
1974	18.9	457.5	476.4	587.7	1,064.1
1975	225.1	454.4	679.5	75.9	755.4
1976	135.9	360.5	496.4	99.0	595.4
1977	186.8	345.8	532.6	—	532.6
Sweden					
1974	40.3	83.4	123.7	188.5	312.2
1975	630.0	438.2	1,068.2	281.8	1,350.0
1976	655.0	455.1	1,110.1	439.7	1,549.8
1977	1,169.6	410.5	1,580.1	1,345.7	2,925.8
Switzerland					
1974	—	11.6	11.6	10.0	21.6
1975	102.8	67.4	170.2	—	170.2
1976	164.0	28.2	192.2	—	192.2
1977	—	7.5	7.5	—	7.5
United Kingdom					
1974	136.1	169.0	305.1	5,723.0	6,028.1
1975	415.5	282.6	698.1	601.9	1,300.0
1976	807.1	435.2	1,242.3	2,154.0	3,396.3
1977	1,400.1	236.8	1,636.9	2,054.3	3,691.2
United States					
1974	150.6	38.1	188.7	1,354.3	1,543.0
1975	254.6	201.0	455.6	547.2	1,002.8
1976	285.0	147.6	432.6	381.8	814.4
1977	905.8	646.9	1,552.7	418.0	1,970.7

NOTE: Dashes = zero or negligible.

[a] Includes loans that have not been allocated to a single month.

SOURCE: *Borrowing in International Capital Markets, Fourth Quarter 1977*, World Bank Document EC-181-/774, March 1978, table 2.2.

of dollar market strength rather than to engineer a dollar depreciation. The Swiss steadily inhibited the inward flow of funds by allowing only zero or negative interest rates on foreign-owned bank deposits and limiting foreign ownership of other assets. But after the petroleum embargo in late 1973 most countries moved to encourage inward flows of funds—which meant the dismantling of some restraints imposed in earlier years—and to restrain outward movements. The Italian controls on payments abroad provide a notable example of this policy.[27]

Concluding Comments

It is clear that once again a regime of flexible exchange rates began its trial in a setting so economically disrupted that alternative exchange rate regimes were untenable. It should not be surprising that the rates went through such broad swings that the swings appeared to many to be a significant cause of the general economic disruption rather than a symptom. That governments have been under pressure to restrain the swings is understandable.

Some new and old truths can be gleaned from the experience. Private speculation seems to work well in buffering temporary disturbances to an expected norm only when there is a basis for establishing the expectation. In periods of high uncertainty speculators withdraw from the market, leaving the price, in this case the exchange rate, to be pressed up or down by transitory disturbances with little resistance and opening the way for bandwagon speculation for limited periods. The speculators who retire from their role of buying and selling in response to price deviations from an expected norm include the bankers who in less volatile circumstances make markets in currencies and keep exchange transactions costs to other traders small. In periods of high uncertainty there appears to be a role for public authorities to play, therefore, in providing some temporary depth to the market.

Monetary authorities, however, did much more than that after 1973. Data reviewed in this chapter indicate substantial interventions direct and indirect, to slow the trend of the exchange rates. In the long run these interventions could not be successful, and they were probably ill-advised when taken, except insofar as they may have facilitated political decisions that led to more appropriate monetary policies.

In particular, countries engaged to some degree in beggar-my-neighbor policies when their purchases of foreign exchange accentuated the depreciation of their currencies or—more commonly—resisted appreciation. They protected their own markets, internal and external, at the expense of sales by their competitors.

[27] Gottfried Haberler has properly criticized the use of these techniques in "The Case against Capital Controls for Balance of Payments Reasons," A. K. Swoboda, ed., *Capital Movements and Their Control* (Leiden: A.W. Sijthoff, 1976); reprinted as Reprint no. 62, American Enterprise Institute, February 1977.

Better data on intervention activity will be necessary before unofficial observers can make appraisals of the short-run behavior of governments in this regard. It is especially regrettable that intervention data are not yet provided to the IMF on a daily basis, even though the facts are shared among a number of governments. The Fund can hardly fulfill its responsibility for surveillance of the international monetary system without them.

Flexible exchange rates have been associated with growing international trade and investment in spite of strong divergences in international demand policies and massive current account imbalances because of the petroleum crisis. Effective exchange rates of most major industrial countries except Switzerland, the United Kingdom, France, and Italy moved within a range of $\pm$ 5 percent for a two-year period from mid-1974 to mid-1976 although the trough of the recession arrived at different times in various countries. The rates have in many cases faithfully mirrored changing international price and cost levels, which have in turn reflected divergent monetary conditions. In the light of the evidence reviewed, it would be difficult to conclude that exchange rate changes were excessive for more than temporary periods.

5
Floating Exchange Rates and Inflation

Managed floating of the exchange rates from 1973 to 1978 coincided with inflation that, as a global matter, had no precedent for half a century. Is a claim that the floating has contributed to the inflation mere guilt by association or has floating indeed been a substantial cause? The theme of this chapter is that while floating may have contributed to ratcheting prices upward in some degree for a limited time, and that it has certainly accelerated inflation in some countries and decelerated it in others compared with what would have happened in a fixed exchange rate regime, the fundamental cause of the global inflation is not to be found in the flexibility of the exchange rates. Rather, the cause of the inflation lies in the demand management policies of governments. Governments have repeatedly expected more of such policies than they could deliver and have abused them.

Furthermore, governments do not yet seem to have appreciated the importance of international coordination of the mixes of monetary and fiscal policies they pursue. Failure to do so has probably exacerbated inflationary pressures in some countries and frustrated the achievement of policy objectives elsewhere.

Floating Exchange Rates and Monetary Discipline

In the traditional debate on fixed versus flexible exchange rates, opponents of flexible rates asserted a belief that without the discipline of having to redeem the currency in terms of an external asset, governments would be prone to profligacy in their monetary and fiscal policies, thereby causing inflation. The coincidence of protracted inflation and greater flexibility for the exchange rates in recent years seems to offer support for the hypothesis. To concentrate too much on the exchange rate regime, however, would be to mistake the symptom for the disease. For the disease is older than the flexible exchange rate period, and it threatens to be chronic. The disease is the inflationary bias in public policy decisions which has steadily grown in most industrialized countries since World War II. Beguiled by the frequently useful diagnosis that unemployment is a problem of deficient demand, democracies have, by turning too often to demand expansion, numbed other adjustment processes.

The roots of the inflation of the 1970s antedate the floating of the exchange rates by nearly a decade. Between 1950 and 1970 the annual rate of inflation of consumer prices in the industrialized countries of Europe, North America, and Japan, taken collectively, nearly trebled from 1.9 to 5.6 percent per annum, with most of the change occurring after 1964.[1] Efforts to slow demand expansion in the late 1960s generated some unemployment but did not succeed in slowing the by then well-entrenched inflation. In 1971 and 1972 the rate of price increase in these countries did diminish as a result of wage and price controls and other incomes policies in both Europe and North America. But under cover of these same controls money supply growth was accelerated, the M_1 measure (currency plus demand deposits) jumping from a 6.2 percent growth rate on the average for industrialized countries in 1970 to 11.8 percent in 1971; the growth then continued at double-digit levels for the next two years.[2] When in 1973 and 1974 the wage-price ceilings and guidelines became untenable as a result of demand pressures and cost increases, including the rise in petroleum prices, the temporarily suppressed inflationary forces reerupted; consumer prices in industrialized countries advanced 7.5 percent in 1973, 12.6 percent in 1974, and another 10.7 percent in 1975. The facts, then, that inflation was a problem attracting worldwide concern even in the late 1960s and in 1970–1971 and that it failed to be more apparent than it was in 1971–1972 because of temporarily effective controls, tends to shift the search for its cause away from the exchange rate regime and toward forces already at work before 1972.

The New Economic Policy declared by President Nixon in August 1971 will be cited by some as an example of a country pursuing a more expansionary monetary-fiscal policy in connection with greater exchange rate flexibility. But it must be remembered that the U.S. government in 1971 sought release from balance of payments deficits

---

[1] IMF, *International Financial Statistics*, world tables for prices.

[2] Ibid., world tables for money growth rates.

which had been accumulating over a number of years in a regime of fixed exchange rates. The demand expansion policies in the 1960s had been accompanied by only limited domestic inflation because of the availability of the nation's foreign exchange reserves, and particularly its foreign credit, to finance the overall deficits. But by 1971 the exhaustion of these assets was near. Relief from the convertibility obligation was essential for the nation to be able to resume demand expansion, and, in a degree not appreciated at the time, inflation could no longer be so easily avoided. The import surtax and other protective steps taken in 1971 give evidence that measures other than the exchange rate would have been employed to facilitate the dominant strategy had not exchange rate depreciation been won and had it not seemed to provide the necessary leeway.

It must be acknowledged that under a flexible exchange rate regime the absence of pressures on the monetary reserve stocks of countries whose balances of payments tend to overall deficit removes what has sometimes been a significant cause for less inflationary policies. Flexible exchange rates avoid what was once deemed a deflationary bias in the system, a bias that took the form of a compulsion on deficit countries without a counterpart in surplus countries. That deflationary bias, however, turned inflationary when the central reserve currency country itself became a deficit nation and began to multiply the money supplies and monetary reserves of surplus countries. Flexible exchange rates now intensify deflationary pressures in countries whose currencies appreciate in the same degree that they intensify inflationary pressures in depreciating countries, and are consequently more evenhanded on the inflation issue.

That all countries can inflate or deflate in parallel without effects on the pattern of exchange rates raises issues for the system, but none that were not also present under fixed rates.

The Anatomy of Inflation

The roots of the inflation of the 1960s and 1970s go much deeper than the system of exchange rates. The title Jacques Rueff gave to a collection of his lectures in 1963, *The Age of Inflation,* was prophetic.[3] The root of the inflation of the 1960s and 1970s was the work of "an academic scribbler of a few years back," to quote well-known words of the scribbler himself, John Maynard Keynes. Keynesian truths about significant causes of mass unemployment in the 1930s became orthodoxy after World War II and formed the rationale under

[3] Paris: Les Editions Payot.

which it was hoped that monetary and fiscal strategies would obtain full employment growth in most industrial countries. As is often the case, however, interpreting the master led to oversimplification of his views. While Keynes himself had a lifelong respect for the danger of inflation, his views on the economics of the 1930s depression introduced building blocks to economic thinking which in the forge of pressure politics became justifications for dramatically inflationary policies.

Among these building blocks, two deserve mention. One is the idea that whenever unemployment, measured as persons not working but looking for work, exists beyond a "frictional" amount, it is caused by deficient aggregrate demand. Associated with this view is the thought that frictional unemployment—that caused by the transition of workers from one job to another even when jobs exist in the national labor market—is subject only slowly to change. Hence whenever measured unemployment is greater than the 4 percent, 4.5 percent, or 5 percent that an average of past periods indicates to be an irreducible minimum, it must be due to demand deficiency and calls for government deficit spending and increased monetization of the public debt. This focus on relative constancy in the lowest obtainable unemployment rate, however, can be, and has been, misleading. The shifts in resource reallocation required in the United States, for example, in the mid-1960s to mid-1970s as a result of war and demobilization, a sudden quadrupling of energy prices, extensive action to satisfy environmental concerns, income redistribution, the depreciation of the dollar, changing mores concerning schooling of young people and the role of women, and continuing technological change, seem to have been large in the aggregate relative to historical standards.[4] They called for microeconomic adjustments rather than aggregate demand expansion, and the demand expansion that was employed, while calling new recruits into the labor force, left some of these plus a substantial hard core of unemployed without jobs and simultaneously caused inflation.

A second idea fostered by Keynesian orthodoxy was that "money doesn't matter much." Looking at a world characterized by extraordinarily pessimistic price expectations in the 1930s, Keynes was convinced that, at least in the short run, increasing the supply of money—especially increasing it by simply monetizing existing government debt—would not generate the spending necessary to lead economies like that of Britain and the United States out of depression. He argued that increases in the money supply would at best ease

[4] See *Economic Report of the President,* January 1977, pp. 45-57 and 136-69.

interest rates and then induce spending only if investors' expectations were such that they would respond to lower credit costs, and he was not optimistic about this. Keynes's view of the efficacy of money, voiced after a money supply collapse, became part of orthodoxy in the 1940s, 1950s, and 1960s. A corollary to pessimism about monetary efficacy was monetary apathy, a view that even in a period of inflation, as long as nominal interest rates were not low, increases in the stock of money would not change circumstances much, although they might lower interest rates and increase employment opportunities in particular industries. There can be little doubt that such views helped to rationalize the monetary policies of the 1960s and 1970s that led to excessive worldwide monetary growth rates.

A central inference of Keynesian thinking was that fiscal deficits can and should be used to enlarge aggregate demand when unemployment exceeds traditional amounts. Some critics of the dominant view, however, contend that, to the contrary, fiscal policy does not matter much. There can, in fact, be little doubt that such deficits do add to total spending in a closed national economy. The effects are often envisioned as a simple increase in the velocity of money—government gives money a once-for-all thrust that is propagated by respending in the manner described by the familiar multiplier. But the effects of the deficit can also be seen in society's perception of its wealth. A burst of public expenditures covered by borrowing rather than by taxes creates incomes, and perhaps expectations of incomes, that are not offset by perceived tax liabilities, and hence society's perception of its net wealth is increased. If in a subsequent period taxes more than cover public expenditures, with the surplus equal to the preceding deficit, the privately perceived wealth is destroyed. Protracted deficits, however, are especially stimulative because they create expectations of permanence in net private incomes that correspond to the government expenditures not covered by taxes. This is the wealth facet of the spending process that results in the cumulative income multiplier when government deficits are sustained. That a government finances its deficit by issuing bonds, rather than money, makes a difference in the effect of the deficit only because of considerations of liquidity discussed below. A bond or its value in money represents an immediate or deferred claim on society which, if not subsequently extracted from private hands by fiscal surplus, manifests the holder's perceived claim to wealth. Bonds take their value from their claim to interest and a deferred return of principal, while money's value lies in its immediate acceptability in exchange for goods. A government decision to finance deficits with bonds rather than money has an obvious fiscal cost since interest on the debt requires subsequent taxes to be higher or expenditures lower than they otherwise would have had to be. (The parallel effect of financing with money is that money is more inflationary than bonds in a high-employment economy, reducing the purchasing power of tax revenues.) But the central fact of government deficit spending is that the deficits introduce into the private sector of the economy financial claims that are perceived by individuals as real wealth and that therefore lead to private spending which can either enhance aggregate output or be inflationary. This generalization is valid whether the deficits arise from expanded government expenditures or reductions in taxes. Expenditures are more expansive than taxes only as a result of the temporary increase in the velocity of money that results from the initial government outlay.

There are some offsets to the demand-expanding effects of government deficits. In particular, if the deficits are financed by borrowing, and if increased government cash balances (from the flow of funds through government accounts) drains cash from the economy and causes private spenders to rebuild their own cash positions by slowing spending or by selling off securities, the government's increment to aggregate spending will be in some degree compensated by a decrease in private spending.[5] The private spending reduction will persist as long as the deficits continue, since only a sustained reduction in private spending can make the reduced cash balances available to that sector—caused by increased cash holding through government transactions—stand in the preferred ratio to spending. In spite of an offset to government net spending, nevertheless, it would be erroneous to understate the wealth effects of deficits. A government outpouring of bonds may be regarded as leading to a process of private portfolio balancing in which people exchange some of their new bond holdings for money and some for producer and consumer goods; the demand for goods constitutes a demand for both the existing stock and the flow of society's output.

The reference to cash balances emphasizes that the degree of liquidity of the stock of financial assets in private hands, as well as the size of the stock, influences spending. This is because only money, the most liquid claim, is generally acceptable in exchanges, and

[5] In a recent effort to reassess the effect of government expenditures on total spending, Robert Hall has concluded that the expenditure multiplier is indeed neither as high as the factor embodied on Keynesian grounds in many large-scale econometric models—about 1.5—nor as small as a simple monetarist view would make it—zero. Hall puts it in between these two positions, at about 0.7. See "Investment, Interest Rates, and the Effects of Stabilization Policies," *Brookings Papers on Economic Activity*, vol. 1 (1977), pp. 61-103.

because transactions costs of uncertain magnitude may be incurred in shifting from nonmoney assets to money. Given the pattern and uncertainty of such transactions costs, payments practices, interest rates, and the magnitude and distribution of perceived real wealth, there is a private demand for money to hold for each level of total output and prices. A supply in excess of this demand gives rise to private purchases of goods and securities until the excess demand is removed through a rise in the money value of financial wealth and of current production. On the other hand, where the money supply is deficient, spending agents will liquidate real and financial assets, raising interest rates and causing prices or output to fall until the demand for cash is reduced to the available supply. These ideas constitute part of the rationale for the unique emphasis that contemporary monetarists and a long line of classical and neoclassical economists have put on the regulation of the supply of money. It is no doubt widely agreed today that the degree of liquidity in the entire set of financial assets influences people's aggregated propensity to spend.

The degree of liquidity that exists in society's stock of claims at any time depends on past interactions of the public and the society's financial intermediaries and in a critical way on the actions of the central bank. Financial intermediaries, and particularly commercial banks, engage in maturity transformation and increase the liquidity of the nonbank public's existing wealth when the intermediaries exchange their own short-term liabilities for longer-term assets—for example, when banks loan demand deposits to their customers against longer-term promises to pay.[6] While a process of general portfolio adjustment would presumably establish for any economy a balance in its more and less liquid assets if there were no regulation, in most countries the ability of the commercial banks to intermediate to increase liquidity is restrained by bank reserve requirements. The central bank then regulates the liquidity of the market (for which various measures of the money supply are proxies) by its own maturity transformation decisions, which change the society's base money (government issue money plus central bank credit), and by its control of bank minimum reserve ratios. The central bank's willingness to tolerate growth in the liquidity of the economy and hence private adaptations to greater liquidity constitutes its monetary policy.[7]

---

[6] See James Tobin, "Commercial Banks as Creators of 'Money'," in Deane Carson, ed., *Banking and Monetary Studies* (Homewood, Ill.: R. D. Irwin, 1963), pp. 408-19.

[7] The stock of liquidity, whether commodity money or bank deposits, that society has accumulated in response to liquidity demand generated by economic growth constitutes part of society's real wealth. See Boris P. Pesek and Thomas R.

Fundamentally, therefore, the rate at which monetary demand for goods and services grows, in an area that is closed to external transactions, depends on (1) the deficits of governmental units which add to the perceived financial wealth of the private sector; (2) the growth in liquidity of wealth, which can be interpreted over any short to intermediate period as the growth in the society's money supply; and (3) the growth in its real income and wealth, including technology and human and physical capital, and the extent to which these are effectively employed. Growth in the real income and wealth of society adds to the aggregate supply of goods and services as well as to demand and is therefore not of itself inflationary. Inflation, which is the result of demand for goods and services outrunning supply at existing money prices, is caused primarily by excessive government deficits and too rapid monetary expansion.

The discussion of the roots of inflation has proceeded as if it concerned one nation that could be considered apart from the rest of the world, but as indicated below, especially in the discussion of the international transmission of economic disturbances, this is a dangerous simplification. Particularly when exchange rates are flexible, and both financial capital and goods and services are internationally mobile, a single nation's monetary and fiscal policies may well have their chief initial impact abroad. It therefore becomes imperative to coordinate policies, both internally and externally, with a view to global developments. The principles set out for a closed national economy nevertheless remain applicable to a necessarily closed world economy, although the distribution of effects among nations takes on special significance in the world view.

Once begun, inflation in a less than perfect market economy stubbornly resists reduction and cannot be slowed without cost. It is protracted because price setters apprehensively hedge against its continuance, and each seeks to set prices which will at least maintain that market participant's relative position. A few prices change flexibly in the light of changing conditions, but most move only in discrete jumps. A change in the rate of inflation that falsifies a previously expected rate then introduces new distortions into the relative price pattern. A government attempting to wind down inflation must expect to encounter disbelief in the probable success of its policies and rigidity not only in those prices that have previously been bargained

---

Saving, *Money, Wealth, and Economic Theory* (New York: Macmillan, 1967), Chapter 4; and Harry G. Johnson, "Inside Money, Outside Money, Income, Wealth, and Welfare in Monetary Theory," *Journal of Money, Credit and Banking* (February 1969), pp. 30-45.

but also in those that continue to be bargained in anticipation of continued high rates of inflation. Prices that then become excessive give rise to sales declines, loss of output, and unemployment when the anticipated growth of demand fails to materialize.[8]

The idea that some wage and price setters can and do raise prices regardless of the level of demand, causing perennial cost-push inflation, received encouragement in both the United States and Western Europe when prices continued to rise after output slowed its growth in 1969 and then again in 1974–1975. Cost-push, however, is rarely an instigator of inflation; it is a perpetuator which will eventually yield to change in demand growth. Each price setter who exploits some element of monopoly has an optimal relative price, and his adjustment to a given and expected level (or rate of change) of demand and prices therefore seeks to be a once-for-all adaptation to markets as they exist or are expected to exist. The search for a new optimal price (or rate of price change) begins again when expectations about other prices (or rates of change of prices) change. An economy suffering inflation is therefore like a freight train, moved fundamentally by demand-pull but characterized by inertia. When demand-pull slows, price setters, like freight cars, find themselves pushed hard from behind and are tempted mistakenly to see fundamental forces as cost-push. Only removal of the demand-pull, however, can ultimately slow the inflationary process.

The U.S. inflation of 1969–1970, for example, was surely an extension of the inflation of the preceding several years caused by the temporary inflexibility of previously determined inflationary expectations. The inflation in the face of declining output in 1974–1975 had similar roots but was exacerbated by a number of special influences—the removal of wage and price controls in 1973–1974, the worldwide increase in prices of energy and of other raw materials, and the exchange rate changes. Especially because of the universality of these disturbances, individual price setters could raise prices without fear of competitors failing to follow.

If fears of a return to legal ceilings on wages and prices were permitted to abate in the United States as the 1980s begin and demand growth were slowed, a broad upward surge of administered

---

8 William Fellner argues cogently that macroeconomic theory must be reconstructed to take into account expectations and their formation. In particular he argues that macroequilibrium must be conceived in terms of satisfaction of the aggregate budget equation at a rate of price level change that market participants regard as sustainable. Other rates of price level change may be unstable. See Fellner, *Towards a Reconstruction of Macroeconomics: Problems of Theory and Policy* (Washington, D.C.: American Enterprise Institute, 1976).

prices need not be encountered again. Nevertheless, price increases set in longer contracts, prices belatedly catching up, and especially prices of intermediate goods, which feel slackening demand only after final goods demand is affected, would continue for a time to reflect past inflationary experience. For this reason, some unemployment and production dislocation that would appear to be attributable to deficient demand would be a concomitant of lower levels of demand growth.

A major political constraint on winding down inflation is that the costs of doing so are unequally distributed, since they fall especially on those who lose employment altogether. Transfer payments to soften the blow on this group are justified when the transfers are financed by taxes so that inflationary effects of the transfer program are minimized. Meanwhile, it must be remembered that a continuation of inflation also imposes very unequal burdens that, like unemployment, tend to fall on those with least market power, and, unlike unemployment, are not well requited by government policies.

How Inflation Became a Global Matter

While any nation's inflation is due basically to excessive government deficit spending and expansion of the monetary base, the fact that inflation was a global phenomenon in the late 1960s and early 1970s requires further explanation. We must ask why so many governments opened the floodgates at once. A small part of the phenomenon may have derived from a ratcheting effect on prices as a result of changing the exchange rates. But the ratcheting might have been insignificant had other broad inflationary forces not been at work. Most important was the fact that many countries simultaneously experienced circumstances which induced them to persist in unwise and excessive demand expansion. U.S. monetary policies of the 1960s were an important prime mover of events. A subtle factor may have been that many governments perceived their inflation as imported and thus discounted their own contribution to the worldwide process.

The discussion begins with the possibility that ratcheting of prices which are flexible only one way has resulted from up and down movements of the exchange rates.[9] If prices were flexible upward but

[9] This diagnosis is attributed to Arthur Laffer and Robert Mundell. See J. Wanniski, "The Case for Fixed Exchange Rates," *Wall Street Journal*, June 14, 1974. It is an extension of the contention that prices ratchet upward in a largely closed economy as a result of shifts in the pattern of demand. See Charles Schultze, *Recent Inflation in the United States*, Study Paper no. 1, Joint Economic Committee, Study of Employment, Growth, and Price Levels, 86th Congress, 1st session, September 1959.

not downward, a country's price rises associated with periods of exchange rate depreciation would not be compensated by price falls when the exchange rate appreciated. The evidence for one-way price flexibility, however, is inconclusive.[10] What is clear is that many prices are reasonably inflexible both upward and downward in the short run when the price level is expected to be stable because the act of carrying out a price change has costs. Both buyers and sellers in imperfectly competitive markets find comfort in multimonth or multiyear contracts to govern valued buyer-supplier relationships; risks to such relationships arise in price negotiations, and uncertainty and other costs are incurred in any search for a new optimal price.[11]

Whatever the usual case—and one may suspect that prices, adjusted through time for expected changes in the value of money, have substantial short-run rigidity both upward and downward—the mid-1970s were not usual. In particular, business firms and trade unions were just escaping the yoke of incomes policies and wage and price controls in Europe and the United States when the exchange rates were made flexible, and there was excess demand in most national markets. In this circumstance, price setters were unusually willing to take competitive risks on the upside of price changes and reluctant to take them on the downside. The experience with price controls had taught them that it was a great advantage to have a high price in effect in the event that ceilings should be retroactively reimposed.[12] Given the coincidence in time of the ending of price ceilings (amid much talk in both the United States and in some countries of Western Europe that they should be continued or reimposed) and the advent of flexible exchange rates, it would be surprising if upward ratcheting did not occur. The experience, nonetheless, cannot be used to infer that flexible exchange rates are generally incompatible with a stable price level.[13]

---

[10] See Charles Pigott, Richard James Sweeney, and Thomas D. Willett, "Some Aspects of the Behavior and Effects of Flexible Exchange Rates," a paper presented at the Conference on Monetary Theory and Policy, Konstanz, Germany, 1975; and Morris Goldstein, "Downward Price Inflexibility, Ratchet Effects, and the Inflationary Effect of Import Price Changes," *IMF Staff Papers*, vol. 24 (November 1977), pp. 569-612.

[11] W. D. Nordhaus, "Recent Developments in Price Dynamics," in Otto Eckstein, ed., *The Econometrics of Price Determination* (Washington, D.C., Board of Governors of the Federal Reserve System, 1972), pp. 16-49.

[12] The British did return to an incomes policy in 1975, Canada imposed controls in 1976, and Sweden followed in 1977. Unfortunately, wage and price standards again came under discussion in the United States in the summer of 1977 and the fall of 1978.

[13] A careful analysis of the ratchet hypothesis is included in Andrew Crockett and

More important than the move to flexible exchange rates for understanding the universality of inflation in the mid-1960s to mid-1970s is the occurrence of a series of changes worldwide. In a milieu of excessive faith in the capability of demand expansion, these changes induced countries to embark simultaneously on policies of enlarged deficit spending and monetary creation. A prime mover of this sequence of events was the inflationary policy on which the United States embarked in 1964. It was a policy that might have been brought to a halt under an international monetary arrangement that either required asset settlement of all participants or imposed currency depreciation on leading inflators. But the United States, as provider of a reserve currency, had unusual license to borrow abroad, to prolong inflationary measures, and to export the inflationary consequences to the rest of the world.

Both monetary policy and fiscal policy were inflationary in the United States between 1963 and 1972, although the critical extravagance was in monetary policy. The net federal debt of the United States (debt held outside the government itself) increased by 31 percent (from $250 to $327 billion) as a result of the Vietnam hostilities, undertakings to build a Great Society at home, and then a recession induced to combat the incipient inflation and balance of payments deficit. The central problem, however, was in monetary policy, for the authorities of the Federal Reserve System monetized approximately half the additions to the federal debt of that period and in the process increased the monetary base of the economy no less than 130 percent. Commercial banks and the public responded to the central bank's outpouring of reserve money by increasing the rate of growth of bank deposits. The narrowly defined money supply (M_1) grew more than twice as fast in the five years after 1964 as it had in the preceding five years (4.8 percent in the later period compared with 2.2 percent in the earlier), and the growth rate reached 7.0 percent per annum by 1971. The broader money measure (M_2), which includes time deposits at banks and which had grown at a rate of only 5.0 percent, on average, in the five years 1959–1963, reached annual growth rates of 11.6 and 10.5 percent, respectively, in 1970

Morris Goldstein, "Inflation under Fixed and Flexible Exchange Rates," *IMF Staff Papers*, vol. 23 (November 1976), pp. 509-44. Stanley Black, *Floating Exchange Rates and National Economic Policy* (New Haven: Yale University Press, 1977), p. 189, after a review of U.S. and German policies and experiences, also expresses the view that ratcheting has not significantly affected inflation in the two countries.

and 1971. As a stock, M_2 approximately doubled between the end of 1963 and the end of 1972.[14]

In the process of this monetary expansion, inflation spurted in America and, more important in the light of subsequent events, spilled out overseas and contributed to making inflation a worldwide problem. As a result of U.S. current trade deficits, overseas investments, and shifts of short-term funds abroad, the United States spent gold reserves in the amount of $5.7 billion between 1964 and the end of 1972, and it almost trebled its liquid liabilities to foreigners (from $29.4 to $82.9 billion). Most of the increase in short-term dollar obligations to foreigners was acquired by foreign monetary authorities endeavoring to keep the exchange rates from changing; the acquisitions then increased the monetary base of each of the countries concerned. Altogether, U.S. official reserve deficits in the balance of payments, 1963–1972, added to the consolidated monetary base of other countries an amount more than twice the combined 1964 money supplies of Germany and Switzerland—an addition of $52 billion, of which $12 billion was added in 1964–1970 and $40 billion in 1971–1972. While foreign governments and central banks could and did offset to some degree the liquidity effects of their purchase of dollars through other open market operations, their offset efforts were incomplete. They could also, of course, have reduced the rates of accumulation of net financial assets in their economies by running government budget surpluses, but they did not. Rather, they themselves increased their deficit spending in 1963–1968 and again in 1971–1972, and thereby made their own contribution to the world's inflationary process.[15]

By the end of the 1960s, inflation had come to be recognized as an international problem. The IMF's average of consumer price indexes in industrial countries rose by 5.6 percent in 1970, as opposed to 2.7 percent in 1964, in spite of counterinflationary measures begun by some countries as early as 1967. The anti-inflation measures, which came to include incomes policies and wage and price controls, only mildly slowed inflation but sharply increased unemployment. In

[14] Jürg A. Niehans, "How to Fill an Empty Shell," *American Economic Review*, vol. 66 (May 1976), pp. 177-83, has pointed out that the dramatic change in Federal Reserve policy in fact occurred as early as 1961-1962 and then was sustained. Before 1961 the twelve-year compound annual growth rate in Federal Reserve credit was about 1.5 percent; following 1961 it was about 8.5 percent.

[15] Data on the aggregated budget balances of Group of Ten countries outside North America are tabulated in Richard James Sweeney and Thomas D. Willett, "The International Transmission of Inflation: Mechanisms, Issues and Evidence," *Kredit und Kapital*, Special Supplement, 1977.

1972–1974, therefore, following the realignment of exchange rates and then the floating, many governments moved anew toward expansive demand policies. The result of this combined effort was a virtual explosion of money supplies and prices throughout the world in 1972–1976. Widespread efforts in 1976–1977 to stem the tide were then once again blunted by the appearance of uncomfortably high levels of unemployment.

In general, the worldwide economic difficulties of the decade from the mid-1960s to the mid-1970s were associated with a tendency toward increased synchronization of the business fluctuations in many countries. U.S. abuse of its reserve currency position in the 1960s set in motion the initial tidal current. Simultaneous efforts by a number of countries to suppress inflation in 1968–1971 then resulted in widespread unemployment; following this, synchronous use of expansive demand policies in 1972–1974 led to the worldwide inflation of special virulence in 1973–1974.[16]

Of course restraints on supply—the energy crisis, crop failures, and capital shortages—played a part in inflation. But except for the crop failures of 1972 and 1974, the factors of supply in inflation were not entirely independent of the inflation itself and of misguided government efforts to suppress it. These factors are considered at greater length in connection with the problem of unemployment.

In a subsequent analysis of the transmission of inflation among countries it will be shown that some governments, especially in the 1970s, may have failed to be sufficiently critical of the inflationary consequences of their own policies simply because they were able to export their own dominant inflationary impulses while the inflation they themselves experienced appeared to come from abroad. There is much yet to be learned about this process.

The Anatomy of Unemployment

Mass unemployment and inflation are not bedfellows in the simple Keynesian image according to which output and employment, rather than prices, respond to changes in demand so long as resources are

[16] Duncan Ripley, working at the IMF, did not find any significant tendency toward international synchronization of output fluctuations in the 1950s and 1960s, but her data for the early 1970s, including that for 1975, do show a marked concurrence. Her pooled correlation of the cyclical positions of twelve industrial countries, for example, increased from 0.56 for 1958-1963 to 0.75 for 1967-1970 and to 0.87 for 1971-1975. See "Cyclical Fluctuations in Industrial Countries, 1952-1974" (IMF, 1976; processed) and added computations for 1975, which she kindly provided the author.

idle. Yet unemployment increased with prices in the United States in 1970–1971 and again in 1974–1975, and measured unemployment exceeded the 4.8 percent average of the 1960s in every year of the 1970s through 1978. Unemployment did decline with high demand levels in the later 1960s, falling from 5.7 percent in 1963 to 3.5 percent in 1969. And the unemployment rates of 1970–1971 (4.9 and 5.9 percent, respectively) and of 1974–1975 (5.6 and 8.5) must be seen in part as the social costs of adjusting to slower rates of demand growth in those years, a phenomenon considered above. Other factors, however, added to the measured unemployment rate observed in the United States in the 1970s. They helped keep unemployment as high as 4.6 percent even at the crest of the 1973 boom and deceived policy makers into continued excessive use of demand expansion. To some extent, U.S. experience in this connection paralleled that of other countries.

A factor contributing to measured unemployment was the sharp change in the structure of the labor force in the late 1960s and early 1970s, in part because of inflation and social unrest. Teenagers and women sought paid employment in the United States in unprecedented numbers during this period, and the proportion of the total population that was working for pay or seeking work grew from 59.6 percent in 1964 to 62.1 percent in 1976. These entrants to the labor force came with little previous employment experience and with family ties to given localities, as compared with the average for the labor force as a whole. As a result, they were not easily absorbed. Teenage unemployment was exacerbated by demographic trends which increased the relative numbers of young people in the population. Wage rigidity enforced by union contracts and by the minimum wage law especially slowed the rate at which the economy could accommodate their needs.

Another factor was the disincentive to search for work which was heightened by the public welfare programs initiated or expanded in the United States in the 1960s. Federal outlays on programs for cash income maintenance and for helping people buy essentials increased by six times between 1960 and 1975,[17] while the price level increased at less than a third that rate. Without denigrating the motive of social justice that inspired the revolution in public expenditures, one must acknowledge that it reduced the cost of leisure for many people. The magnitude of its effect on measured unemployment in the 1970s is uncertain, but its direction is undoubtedly positive. In

[17] B. M. Blechman, E. M. Gramlich, and R. W. Hartman, *Setting National Priorities: The 1975 Budget* (Washington, D.C.: Brookings Institution, 1974), p. 168.

many income maintenance programs, in particular unemployment compensation, only those who make some gestures toward seeking work are eligible to receive income support, and hence unusual numbers have been counted "in the labor force and unemployed" regardless of the intensity of their job search.

A variety of regulatory rigidities inhibited adjustment. Some regulations held prices too high, limiting the quantity of product demanded in the industries involved—interstate rail, truck, and airline transportation come to mind for the period before 1973—and others kept prices too low, limiting supply and the incentive to invest. Other regulations imposed new costs on production. Price rigidities enforced by regulation would have created no more difficulties than any static monopoly or monopsony position had the economy not been called on to make especially substantial adjustments in the late 1970s. But under the impact of broad disturbances—a 10 to 20 percent depreciation of the dollar, demobilization of the armed forces, the energy crisis, income redistribution and changing labor force composition associated with inflation, and efforts to reverse environmental deterioration—the rigidities, along with the cost-increasing regulations, became significant. Of special importance were (1) wage and price controls of 1971–1974, which threatened the rewards to risk taking in numerous fields for a substantial time; (2) price controls on oil and gas, which vitiated an all-out effort to increase domestic supplies of those products and their energy substitutes while domestic spending for petroleum and associated products was being deflected abroad; and (3) environmental and health and safety regulations, which reduced the prospective returns to investors in many undertakings.

More serious than the regulations themselves was society's indecision about them. Clamor for wage and price ceilings, both before and after the U.S. experience with these controls, prolonged the incentive they gave to businesses to raise prices and to limit output. Indecision about the form, extent, and financing of environmental and health and safety controls hampered private capital investment decisions in electrical power production, transportation, and innumerable other undertakings. And the inability of Americans to resolve their differences over energy pricing was, by 1977–1978, little short of a national calamity.

Supply constraints outside the control of national economic policy makers contributed to both unemployment and inflation, although their effect could easily be overestimated. The extraordinary toll that drought and freezing took on agricultural production over several years beginning in 1971 was one such constraint. And the price rise for oil imposed by OPEC was another, although it may be cogently argued that the surprising success that OPEC found in its move was a direct result of the inflationary decisions made in the industrialized countries. Nevertheless, nothing happened by way of an exogenous supply constraint in the 1970s that could not have been overcome by well-guided human endeavor. The real supply problem was that human and physical capital formation was limited by regulatory inefficiency, policy indecision, and inflation, while wage and price rigidities, reinforced by regulation, inhibited the substitution of labor for capital.

In general, concerns for income distribution and the environment outweighed concerns for incentives and efficiency in producing marketable goods in the public policy of the period, and the efforts to move toward satisfying these major concerns were then frustrated by inflation, the persistance of unemployment, and capital shortage. With investment hampered by taxes, wage and regulatory costs, and uncertainties about future policies, demand for output could be sustained only through public programs to sustain consumption.

Fortunately, time and fluid markets will heal the structural maladjustments of the mid-1970s if governments can be induced to relax their own distorting interventions and to take steps to decelerate demand inflation. Forecasters trained in Keynesian traditions certainly erred in viewing the 1975–1978 recovery as if it should follow a pattern typical of cyclical change during the 1947–1967 period. Similarly, observers erred who saw the world in an irrevocable stagnation phase of a long (Kondratieff) cycle.[18] The poor performance of a number of industrialized countries in the 1970s has been to a great extent a result of poor policies. Amendment of the policies could liberate many output constraints and set the stage for the resumption of sustained growth.

The International Transmission of Disturbances

Before 1961 it was common to disregard capital movements in much balance of payments analysis; attention focused instead on current accounts and on international movements of reserve money. Since then, however, developments in international banking and surges of funds across the foreign exchange markets have made it unrealistic to disregard the origins and implications of these flows. As a result of theorizing about macroeconomic changes in terms which make

[18] The *Wall Street Journal*, June 12, 1978, characterized the 1978 Annual Report of the Bank for International Settlements as taking this view.

international capital movements an endogenous variable, some hoary pieces of conventional wisdom about the way economic disturbances are transmitted from country to country have been discarded, and a more general view of the process has been obtained.[19]

One result of the new theory is the recognition that under a flexible exchange rate the intended result of an expansive fiscal policy, where a government deficit is financed by public borrowing, may be largely lost through a deficit in the country's current international balance of payments. In a more traditional view, deficit spending by a government would have been expected to crowd out some private domestic spending as a result of its upward pressure on interest rates; but deterioration of the balance of payments on current account would have been prevented by depreciation of the exchange rate, so that whatever demand expansion materialized at home was at least bottled up there. When international capital mobility is acknowledged, however, one must conclude that any upward pressure on interest rates—at least pressure that carries interest rates above some threshold—will be mitigated by a capital inflow from abroad. Upward pressure on the exchange rate from the capital flow then induces deterioration of the balance of payments on current account, and the crowding out materializes through the window of the balance of payments. Wealth effects of the government spending are shifted overseas by international borrowing and the current account deficit. The conclusion negates a view that flexible exchange rates, by keeping a country's balance of payments on current account in balance, provide a country independence to manage its internal demand as it chooses without transmitting spending changes to or receiving them from the rest of the world. Under flexible exchange rates with capital mobility, debt-financed fiscal policies become slippery means of demand management because there is no assurance that their effects can be kept at home. These forces are illustrated by the U.S. budgetary deficits associated with unprecedented international current account payments deficits in 1977 and 1978, for the current account deficits could not have been sustained had not a capital inflow kept the dollar's exchange value relatively high. The U.S. budget deficit of the period was not, therefore, much of an automatic stabilizer to the U.S. economy, although it did provide an increment to demand for the output of our trading partners and through them some feedback.

Monetary policy becomes an effective tool of demand management for a country with a flexible exchange rate when capital is mobile, but in an unconventional way. A central bank's open market

[19] Bibliographical references are cited in note 6 to Chapter 3.

operation that increases liquidity in a closed economy, in a way that has not been wholly discounted in expectations, presumably affects spending by temporarily lowering interest rates and increasing money-measured wealth. Interest rates fall because the monetary action has created an excess demand for securities and an excess supply of money at unchanged interest rates. (There may also be an excess demand for goods.) When the economy is open to international transactions, however, and capital is mobile, any unexpected tendency for internal interest rates to decline causes capital to depart the country, depreciates the exchange rate, and for this reason directs worldwide spending onto the goods of the economy concerned. Hence monetary expansion at least temporarily succeeds in enhancing demand for the country's goods, but in large part the gain arises from a deflection of demand from other countries; the one country's demand expansion is at the expense of demand expansion elsewhere. This conclusion that one country's increase in effective demand may be at another country's expense is at odds with the traditional Keynesian multiplier theory.

Where exchange rates are fixed, the presence of capital mobility does not overturn conventional wisdom so often. But an analysis of the transmission mechanism nonetheless must be somewhat revised. Starting from macroequilibrium and zero inflation, debt-financed fiscal expansion under a fixed exchange rate succeeds in expanding demand for domestic output because any tendency for interest rates to rise attracts reserve money from abroad which, when purchased by the domestic monetary authority, creates the liquidity which supports additional domestic demand. Some of the government's addition to the illiquid financial wealth of the community is in effect exchanged on international markets for liquid assets. This action then permits growth in the aggregate of domestic spending without significant change in the level of interest rates. The current account of the balance of payments deteriorates in the way expected by traditional analysis, and some, but only part, of the successful domestic expansion of demand spills out overseas as demand for foreign goods.

Monetary policy under fixed exchange rates becomes, on the other hand, a not very effective means of influencing domestic demand. Monetary expansion, undertaken alone, tends temporarily to ease nominal interest rates, and this in turn induces a capital outflow and loss of monetary reserves, thus offsetting the central bank's open market operations in bonds. An effort to increase the liquidity of one economy in this circumstance results in an increase in the liquidity of the world, and only to the extent that world liquidity and interest rates are affected will the economy that initially adds to its money stock feel any more than the most transitory demand stimulus. It was in this way that the United States to a great extend avoided the effects of its own inflationary measures in the 1960s.

What may be called the new theory of the balance of payments has been explored in a great variety of models, and particular results depend, of course, on the design of the model. Some approaches feature fixed wages and prices and emphasize adjustments in output, while others feature full-employment output and demonstrate the international transmission of price level changes. In some, the asset variables are in terms of flows, revealing short-term responses, while in others demand and supply for assets are in terms of stocks revealing conditions of portfolio balance. Some models include nontraded as well as traded goods, and some extend the portfolio choices to include nonfinancial assets or several financial assets. The models behave differently as the relative speeds of adjustment in the goods and financial markets are varied, although many writers now agree that adjustments in the markets for financial assets may dominate both the short-run and the long-run overall outcomes. Some work has appeared incorporating expectations, although the variety of patterns possible here has made conclusions about expectational effects difficult to codify. The sharply defined outcomes of the austere models have been softened by the introduction of market substitutions and of inhibiting elements such as uncertainty and transactions costs. It has been noted, for example, that direct investment flows as well as trade flows respond to the exchange rate, and this dulls the distinction between the behavior of the capital and trade accounts. Capital flows may be limited by uncertainty or, when they are covered for exchange rate risk, may be self-limiting as a result of the generation of reverse capital flows. They may also be limited by the development of rational expectations about the continuation of exogenous disturbances. Repercussions among international markets dull the impact of initial changes, and governments adapt their policies to experiences induced in an interactive framework. But the central results of the new theory remain intact and relevant.

Among the truths that have become clear about a world with a high degree of capital mobility and flexible exchange rates are: (1) the effect of the government mix of monetary-fiscal policy on the relative excess demands for money and other financial assets strongly influences the way the policies affect the balance of payments and through this the way they ultimately affect demand for domestic output; (2) it cannot be taken for granted that any measure that expands demand in one country will spill over to others through the trade account—as when such transmissions were analyzed with Keynesian multipliers; and (3) fiscal deficits, financed by borrowing and undertaken by a country unilaterally, are almost certainly less effective in expanding that country's output than they were made out to be by traditional closed-economy Keynesian models or open-economy models neglecting capital mobility.[20]

The new theory also bears a disturbing implication that balance of payments deficits may now correspond more closely in time to periods of high unemployment than they did in a period of less flexible exchange rates and lower international capital mobility, if government agencies fail to coordinate their policy instruments appropriately. An automatic fiscal deficit, for example, incurred as a country's unemployment grows, may lead to a current balance of payment deficit which crowds out the effects of the fiscal stimulus if it is not accompanied by an adequately expansive monetary policy. But a concurrence of trade deficits and unemployment is just the milieu in which pressures build up for governments to adopt illiberal international trade policies. When exchange rates were less flexible, and institutions for shuttling funds from one currency denomination to another less developed, there was reason to expect balance of trade deficits to be associated with recoveries from recession (in what came to be called the "nondilemma" cases); in these circumstances the payments deficits could be less readily blamed for domestic market woes. An ironic result of the new world of heightened capital mobility is that, although the flexible exchange rate regime was in part proposed and defended on the ground that it could reduce the demands for protection that were put forward to improve the balance of payments, it may not pay off in this way unless governments are able to avoid unbalanced mixes in their monetary-fiscal policies.[21]

---

20 Ronald I. McKinnon, in exploring a simple open-economy model in which output is a positive function of price, has concluded that fiscal policy is largely ineffective under either fixed or flexible exchange rates. See "The Limited Role of Fiscal Policy in an Open Economy," *Banca Nazionale del Lavoro Quarterly Review*, no. 2 (1976), pp. 95-117.

21 While the dollar has a fixed exchange rate against almost as many countries as it has a flexible rate, the great bulk of its trade and capital flow is conducted across rates that are not fixed. Hence, the economics of a flexible exchange rate regime is generally instructive in understanding the U.S. role in the world economy after 1973. The same is not true of individual continental European countries because of the importance of intra-European trade and the existence of the snake arrangement for a joint float of a number of the currencies. But if the snake is considered as a whole, its members' relationships with the rest of the world are predominantly implemented in a flexible exchange rate milieu. Some developing countries whose currencies are firmly tied to that of their major trading partner continue to operate, of course, under a predominantly fixed exchange rate regime. Nonetheless, since the great bulk of world trade and financial flows

Much has been written since 1973 about vicious and virtuous circles into which countries are allegedly drawn as a result of demand management policies that cause them to inflate more or less than the world average. There is truth in the characterization if the experience of such countries is compared with what might have been the case under fixed exchange rates. Countries that inflate their monetary base more than other countries under flexible rates cannot export their excess money to the rest of the world as they could have if the rates were fixed, and they therefore suffer the full consequences of their easy money policies. Similarly, countries that underinflate their money stock do not attract monetary reserves from abroad, and hence they reap unmitigated effects from their relatively deflationary stance.

Moreover, as noted earlier, unbalanced governmental policies may be treated with more complacency than they deserve because any excess by a government contributes to worldwide financial developments which may combine with excesses elsewhere to create hazardous conditions for particular markets. Under flexible exchange rates, danger flags signaling inflation must especially be hoisted on the soil of those countries whose monetary changes are unrestrained. To illustrate the point, consider a circumstance in which some governments begin to run large budgetary deficits but strictly limit the change in their money supplies, while others control their budgets but allow money to expand excessively. The disturbances cause countries with expanding public debt to export securities and to experience current account deficits vis-à-vis the countries with expansive money supplies. Those countries with current payments deficits will suffer little inflation despite their budgetary deficits and may yield to self-congratulation for their virtuous monetary conservatism. The countries undergoing monetary expansion may also be self-congratulatory because of their budgetary caution and the surplus in their current international account, but they will nonetheless suffer inflation equal to their rate of monetary expansion. The private market, in its search for balanced portfolios, will shift excessive debt, which is internationally mobile, from one group of countries to the other, where there is excessive money that is not internationally mobile, and will limit the global change in the rate of interest. For the world as a whole, the fiscal profligacy of one group will have contributed as much to global inflation as the monetary profligacy of the other, although the inflationary consequences are unequally distributed.

---

is between currencies that do not maintain preannounced exchange rate margins, the discussion of this chapter emphasizes the contemporary economics of a flexible exchange rate regime.

Effects of these government policies can realistically be considered only in the form of changes introduced into an environment of policy expectations. And it is the difficulty of ascertaining the expectational environment at any time that makes the appraisal of actual policy proposals hazardous. Expectations of future policies and conditions are necessarily affected by any change in present policy, and the nature of the change in expectations that is engineered can either dull or intensify the policy's results. When given inflationary or deflationary policies are properly and fully predicted, for example, the policies come to have no significance at all in real terms since all prices adapt to the projected rates of change and leave no policy disturbance. As an example of this, consider a country that experiences a sustained 10 percent rate of expansion in its money and government debt while the rest of the world experiences no change. With a constant level of employment, that country will come to have a 10 percent rate of growth in its price level, a 10 percent annual rate of depreciation in the exchange value of its currency, and, as a result of these rates of change, a 10 percentage point premium in its nominal interest rate over rates abroad. In view of expectations, the real interest rate in the inflating country is then perceived by both domestic and foreign investors to be the same as the real rate abroad. Capital movements in this equilibrium of real variables are limited to changes in overall portfolio size, and portfolios are balanced as if expected price changes were everywhere zero and interest rates were everywhere at the foreigner's level. Demand inflation in the country experiencing the expansion of financial assets no longer affects output decisions in either country or the balance of payments.

It is in this light that one must understand the tendency for capital to move toward, say, Switzerland—a low money growth and low nominal interest rate country in the mid-1970s—from, say, the United Kingdom, a high money growth and high nominal interest rate country. Switzerland's nominal interest rate on three-month deposits in April 1976 was only 1.25 percent while the United Kingdom's money market rate was 9.18. Switzerland's money growth rate for all of 1975, however, had been but 2.2 percent while the United Kingdom's was 15, and the Swiss franc had appreciated against sterling by 11.1 percent. It was only because the Swiss franc was likely to continue appreciating that many investors chose to abandon a more than 9 percent nominal rate of interest for only 1.25 percent.

There is another sense in which divergent demand management policies can magnify policy problems as they are seen by governments, especially in the countries whose currencies are depreciating.

When a country's currency is depreciating, and the depreciation is not anticipated by market participants and does not merely offset internal price changes already achieved, the government of that country may observe a deterioration in its Phillips curve trade-off between inflation and unemployment. The effects are not symmetrical among countries, however, so that the opposite is unlikely to be observed in appreciating countries. The deteriorating trade-off appears because depreciation may raise prices without at the same time giving much stimulus to an enlarged overall output in the depreciating country. Initially, industries that use traded goods as inputs in such a country reduce production as those inputs rise in price, while industries that produce traded goods expand. The contraction of the one group of industries may be less than, equal to, or greater than the expansion of the other, depending on the share of intermediate goods in total imports and the substitutability of domestic products for imports. The net demand directed toward domestic goods by the depreciation (assuming the elasticity conditions for exchange market stability are fulfilled) may well result initially in higher prices rather than output expansion. Consequently, when investors are hesitant, as they have been in industrialized countries in the 1970s, increased transitional unemployment may well accompany rising prices. The combined price and employment effects will then appear in the statistics as an upward and also rightward movement of the Phillips relationship, presenting a heightened policy dilemma for government officials. In countries that see their currencies appreciate, transitional unemployment may occur for somewhat analogous reasons, but since it is associated with falling prices, the unemployment would not be statistically distinguishable from a movement along a traditional Phillips relationship, which is usually thought to be defined by increasing job search costs in periods of falling or deficient demand.[22]

Although these effects probably were prominent in U.S. experience in the mid-1970s, freely fluctuating exchange rates need not

[22] Rudiger Dornbusch and Paul Krugman have noted that a flexible exchange rate may in some cases cause the Phillips curve to have a steeper slope than it otherwise would, because demand expansion policies operate more directly on prices when they lead to currency depreciation than they would if the exchange rate were fixed. ("Flexible Exchange Rates in the Short Run," *Brookings Papers on Economic Activity*, vol. 3 [1976], pp. 527-35.) Robert J. Gordon has recently reported that his price and wage equations for the U.S. economy after 1971 suggest a steeper Phillips curve than before 1971. ("Can the Inflation of the 1970s Be Explained?" *Brookings Papers on Economic Activity*, vol. 1 [1977], pp. 253-77.) The argument in the text above suggests that the currency depreciations of recent years, which tended to compensate for previously misaligned price levels, may have caused observed Phillips curves to shift to the right in depreciating countries as well as to become steeper.

disturb the Phillips curve trade-offs once the rates have achieved a full equilibrium with prices. For the exchange rates will go far toward compensating for differences in money supplies and price levels that divergent policies among countries create, and in this way they will minimize the disturbances that would otherwise be perceived in any one country.

A considerable amount of attention has been focused in recent years on changes in product prices as a part of the process of direct transmission of inflation among nations. The transmission of inflation through external product price increases has been especially emphasized in connection with countries between which the exchange rates are fixed. However, similar considerations apply to domestic price effects of an exchange rate depreciation when the depreciation is not the result of foreign nominal price declines. Imported price increases raise the cost of a country's goods in which tradable goods are inputs, and they raise the demand for the country's exports and its domestic substitutes for imports.[23] The analysis of these effects involves the closeness of substitutability, on the one hand, or complementarity, on the other, between foreign goods and their domestically made counterparts, the relative importance of traded goods in the economy, and the downward flexibility of prices of nontraded goods. In general, the following propositions apply: the larger the tradable goods sector of an economy, and the closer the substitutability of foreign goods for domestic tradables, the more exposed the country will be to increases in traded goods prices. Also, the poorer the substitutability between tradable and nontradable goods, and the stronger are tradable and nontradable complementarities, the more exposed the country will be. And the more inflexible in the downward direction are domestic prices, the less opportunity will the country have to maintain price stability in conjunction with high employment by constancy in its demand policies—which would require nontraded prices to decline to offset price rises in tradable goods.[24]

---

[23] The discussion is sometimes referred to as the Scandinavian approach to inflation transmission because of the attention given to a version of it by Scandinavian economists interested in explaining the experience of the highly indexed Norwegian and Swedish economies. See Odd Aukrust, "Inflation in the Open Economy: A Norwegian Model," in L. B. Krause and W. S. Salant, eds., *Worldwide Inflation: Theory and Recent Experience* (Washington, D.C.: Brookings Institution, 1977), pp. 107-53; and Gösta Edgren, Karl-Olaf Faxén, and Clas-Erik Odhner, "Wages, Growth, and the Distribution of Income," *Swedish Economic Journal*, vol. 71 (September 1969), pp. 133-60.

[24] Sung Kwack and W. D. Nordhaus, using different techniques, have presented estimates, respectively, that a 1 percentage point change in dollar import prices gives rise to a 0.12 and a 0.14 percent increase in the U.S. price level. (Cited in

The impact of external price changes on an economy depends, in addition to the circumstances mentioned, on productivity differentials between sectors of the economy producing traded and nontraded goods, respectively. It has been alleged that productivity is systematically higher in traded than in nontraded goods sectors in countries that experience more rapid growth (because services, which lag technologically, weigh heavily in the nontraded sector).[25] If this is true, one must expect externally enforced price changes to have especially large absolute effects on the overall price levels of especially progressive economies. This is because wages must be similar throughout an economy, and an altered price/wage ratio in the traded goods sector must be accompanied by a larger price/wage adjustment in the lower-productivity nontraded sector in order for profit and output to be sustained in the nontraded sector. It does not seem to have been widely noted, however, that the proportional price change in the nontraded sector need not be greater than the proportional change in the traded sector for equilibrium to be achieved so long as the productivity ratio between the two remains unchanged. Furthermore, Officer has recently questioned the contention that a systematic bias of this sort exists among countries.[26]

Monetarist thinking on international inflation implicitly or explicitly takes as one of its premises the law of one price—the tendency of tradable goods to have the same price in all countries, when measured in a single currency and when allowance is made for trade barriers and transportation costs. Monetarists also are attracted to the premise that the monetary and real sectors of the economy are dichotomous, which is to say that relative prices of goods and services are determined by "real" demand and supply forces and are independent of the value of money. The level of output and employment then tends to a "natural" rate determined by relative prices only. The foreign exchange rate is, in the eyes of this group, best seen as

Sweeney and Willett, "The International Transmission of Inflation.") Sweeney and Willett go on to note that this suggests an "effective size" of the U.S. import sector some two and a half to three times the size of actual imports. It is clear, however, that quantitative work on this matter—a general equilibrium problem that is sensitive to many special conditions—is in its infancy.

25 See Bela Balassa, "The Purchasing Power Parity Doctrine: A Reappraisal," *Journal of Political Economy*, vol. 72 (December 1964), pp. 584-96; Gottfried Haberler, "International Aspects of U.S. Inflation," in Phillip Cagan and others, *A New Look at Inflation* (Washington, D.C.: American Enterprise Institute, 1973); and Ronald I. McKinnon, *Monetary Theory and Controlled Flexibility in the Foreign Exchanges*, Essays in International Finance, no. 84 (International Finance Section, Princeton University, 1971).

26 L. H. Officer, "The Productivity Bias in Purchasing Power Parity: An Econometric Investigation," *IMF Staff Papers*, vol. 33 (November 1976), pp. 545-79.

determined by the relative demand in terms of home currency for the existing stock of a foreign currency. The exchange rates, together with the price levels for goods and services at home and abroad, become the prices which make residents of the world willing to hold the world's assortment of currencies. If the stock of home currency is increased, the value of that money will depreciate against both home goods and foreign money. And, somewhat paradoxically in terms of Keynesian partial equilibrium views, if real economic growth at home exceeds that abroad, thereby increasing the home demand for cash balances, the home currency will appreciate against both home goods and foreign money if the home money supply is not increased.[27]

Contrasts in neomonetarist and older Keynesian results in the international sphere stem in part from the fact that neomonetarist writings employ a general equilibrium approach that implicitly or explicitly brings international capital movements into the analysis while older Keynesian analysis disregarded the international capital account and embodied, in that sense, only partial equilibrium. In a simple Keynesian view of a spending disturbance with fixed exchange rates, for example, an increase in home investment, by stimulating demand and imports, would worsen the balance of payments by causing the balance of payments on current account to deteriorate. In a simple monetarist recital of responses to the same disturbance, the increase in home investment increases income and the demand for money and causes an inflow of reserve money from abroad, which implies a movement toward surplus in the overall balance of payments. The reconciliation of these apparently contrasting views of the balance of payments implications of enlarged spending lies in the behavior of the capital account, which is implicitly assumed not to change (or to change by less than the current account) in the simple Keynesian approach but to move generously toward surplus in the monetarist analysis. The increased home investment constitutes an increased supply of home securities, which the new theory recognizes as causing interest rates to be pressed upward so that capital is attracted from abroad.[28] The contribution of monetarist writers has

---

27 H. G. Johnson, "The Monetary Approach to Balance of Payments Theory," in J. A. Frenkel and H. G. Johnson, eds., *The Monetary Approach to the Balance of Payments* (Toronto: University of Toronto Press, 1976). An excellent critique of several strands of international monetarism can be found in Marina v. N. Whitman, "Global Monetarism and the Monetary Approach to the Balance of Payments," *Brookings Papers on Economic Activity*, vol. 3 (1975), pp. 491-536.

28 Joan Robinson dealt with this matter in "The Foreign Exchanges," in her *Essays in the Theory of Employment* (New York: Macmillan, 1937), but it was usually neglected in multiplier theory.

been to note that the induced capital inflow will typically be greater than the trade deficit; that is, balance of trade changes induced by aggregate spending changes will tend to find more than complete external financing.[29] Hence a country where spending expands may be expected to gain reserves as long as the domestic money supply is held in restraint; the necessary increase in the monetary base is in effect borrowed from abroad.

In a world of fixed exchange rates monetarists expect money to be discharged from countries where it is in excess supply to those where it is in excess demand, and they expect no country for long to experience a price inflation that diverges from the world average. If the stock of international reserve money is fixed, for example, and it is distributed worldwide so that it constitutes a part of each nation's money supply, any one country's measures to expand the national, nonreserve component of its money are offset by reserve losses to the others. Not only is the nation's monetary policy then frustrated—in the sense that no independent increase in its money supply is achievable—but even its efforts to increase the money supply must be brought to a halt when the nation's reserves are dissipated. The one country's effort to inflate becomes an engine of inflation abroad, and it is possible for the originating country's money stock to rise only in the proportion that the world money supply rises. Where one country's currency is used as reserve money by others, of course, that nation can continue an expansion as long as other governments are willing to buy that currency against their own—the phenomenon that took place under the dollar standard of the 1960s.

Some monetarists have emphasized that a devaluation, undertaken from a condition of general equilibrium, has no lasting effects on the balance of payments or, indeed, on anything else except the distribution of the world's monetary reserves. For with the attraction of reserves toward the devaluing country, prices rise there and fall in the revaluing areas, and relative prices both between and within countries remain unchanged. The monetary approach does not imply, however, that an exchange rate alteration cannot hasten an adjustment from a disequilibrium to equilibrium when the adjustment has been slowed by money price inflexibility.

Where exchange rates are flexible, international monetarism must focus on national money supplies and national price experiences. The approach implies that one country's inflation would appear like another's if the latter's inflation were measured by converting its

29 See Mundell, "Capital Mobility and Stabilization Policy under Fixed and Flexible Exchange Rates."

prices and money stock into the former's currency at market exchange rates; the exchange rates would compensate for differences in both money and price growth. To measure a global rate of inflation that properly reflects differential inflation rates, one must take a weighted average of inflation rates across countries. And to obtain a global money measure with which this might be compared, one must use an aggregate of money summed at a fixed exchange rate or, probably better, a weighted average of money stock growth rates in all countries.[30]

In the light of recent theory, it is not clear that countries' balances of payments on current account should show less variation with flexible than with fixed exchange rates. Data indeed show that the current account balances, by one simple measure, were considerably more variable under flexible rates between 1973 and 1976 than under the pegged rates of the 1960s. Calculation of the standard deviation of the annual current account balance about the mean annual balance for each of ten industrialized countries shows that the standard deviation was in every case higher by a factor of two or more in the 1973–1976 period than in the 1960s. Because the 1973–1976 period coincided with a strong deterioration of the current account balances of all these countries in connection with the world oil crisis, the data do not yet tell us much about what can be expected in the future.

Several writers have investigated the degree of divergence of monetary policies and rates of price change among countries in the period of generally flexible exchange rates as compared with a recent period of pegged rates. With or without taking capital mobility into account, theory indicates that governments have more capability to pursue independent monetary, fiscal, and price level policies under flexible than under fixed rates so that one would expect rates of change in monetary and price magnitudes to have diverged across

[30] Arthur Laffer erred in an attempt to explain "world inflation" by "world money growth" in a popular article in which he summed national money stocks at varying exchange rates on the dollar into a dollar value world money time series and then compared this with price indexes that were also converted into dollar terms by an exchange rate factor. ("Global Money, Growth, and Inflation," *Wall Street Journal*, September 3, 1975.) In a strict monetarist view, the result should have paralleled results that would have been obtained by comparing U.S. prices and the U.S. money supply. An effort by the staff at the Chase Manhattan Bank (*Business in Brief*, no. 127, April 1976) involved a similar flaw although the Chase numeraire was the SDR, and that study did not err in adjusting price indexes for exchange rate changes. Some of the issues of measurement and the case for the IMF's geometric mean of national rates of change as an appropriate measure of changes in the world money stock are set out in W. H. L. Day and H. R. Heller, "On the Definition of the World Money Supply," IMF paper, 1976; processed.

TABLE 7

MEAN AND VARIATION IN MONEY SUPPLY CHANGES ACROSS FOURTEEN INDUSTRIAL COUNTRIES, 1961–1977

Period	*Mean of Country Rates of Change in Money Supply*	*Standard Deviation*	*Coefficient of Variation*
1961–1970	7.1	4.419	0.622
1971	11.8	5.848	0.496
1972	10.7	5.113	0.478
1973	10.5	6.184	0.589
1974	6.4	4.983	0.779
1975	8.0	5.731	0.716
1976	12.3	4.665	0.380
1977	9.3	3.805	0.408

SOURCE: Calculated from data in *International Financial Statistics.* Countries included are the United States, Canada, Japan, Austria, Belgium, Denmark, France, Germany, Italy, Netherlands, Norway, Sweden, Switzerland, and United Kingdom.

countries as exchange rates became more flexible. Furthermore, since national monetary changes have an exaggerated impact on internal prices under flexible exchange rates as compared with the impact under fixed rates, one might expect the divergence of price levels under flexible rates to be more pronounced than that of monetary changes. This is just what is found.

Tables 7 and 8 display means, standard deviations, and coefficients of variation for rates of change in the narrowly defined money supply and the consumer price index across fourteen industrialized countries for 1961–1970 and subsequent years. The tables extend calculations that were earlier reported by Robert Heller.[31] From Table 7 it will be seen that the standard deviation of rates of monetary growth among countries was higher in each of the first five years after the end of the Bretton Woods system, beginning in 1971, than during the 1961–1970 period when rates were pegged. In 1977, nevertheless, the standard deviation was less than in the 1961–1970 decade. Furthermore, the coefficient of variation, which takes into account the growth in the group's mean rate of change, was generally smaller in the 1970s than in the 1960s. Money supply changes, therefore, are

[31] "International Reserves and Worldwide Inflation," *IMF Staff Papers* (March 1976), pp. 61-87.

TABLE 8

MEAN AND VARIATION IN CONSUMER PRICES ACROSS FOURTEEN INDUSTRIAL COUNTRIES, 1961–1977

Period	*Mean*	*Standard Deviation*	*Coefficient of Variation*
1961–1970	3.4	1.125	0.331
1971	5.1	1.755	0.344
1972	4.5	1.836	0.408
1973	7.5	1.678	0.224
1974	12.6	4.181	0.332
1975	10.7	4.471	0.418
1976	8.9	3.867	0.433
1977	8.6	4.095	0.475

SOURCE: Calculated from data in *International Financial Statistics*. For countries included, see note to Table 7.

in most years more different under flexible exchange rates but not as different as the mean rate of money growth.

When the divergence is measured by the standard deviation, price changes shown in Table 8 are in every year more divergent after 1970 than before. They are also more divergent when measured by the coefficient of variation in every year but one.

International Coordination of Economic Policies

Efforts to secure a certain degree of coordination in the economic policies of the major industrialized countries are not new. The desire for greater coordination has been part of the rationale for forming each of the existing international organizations related to economic affairs, and it has been the raison d'être of innumerable conferences and high-level meetings. Efforts exercised through the International Monetary Fund, the Bank for International Settlements, and the Organization for Economic Cooperation and Development have been especially important and productive, and the work of the secretariats of those organizations has been outstanding. Yet the level of coordination of policy decisions remains at best loose, and regularized meetings and ad hoc conferences alike tend to consist of informal discussions—sometimes, unfortunately, less than wholly candid—of national approaches to common problems. The historical requirement that national governments be responsible to national constituencies but yet cooperate in the solution of global economic problems will continue to plague the process in the future.

Some gains can be made if consensus is achieved on a more realistic image of the problems. A number of anachronistic views no doubt hinder effective intergovernmental efforts. One is that expansions in economic activity in one country, when there are fixed exchange rates, will only partly spill out overseas. Another is that domestic expansions can be kept entirely at home if the exchange rates are flexible. Both these views suggest a substantial degree of autonomy for domestic policy measures in whatever combination policy makers choose to use them. But both views are faulty—in degree if not in kind—as a result of the recent rapid growth in international interdependence and especially the growth in capital mobility. In particular, with flexible exchange rates sufficient capital mobility can render debt-financed domestic fiscal policy largely impotent, monetary policy possibly potent only at the expense of some demand contraction in other countries, and unbalanced monetary-fiscal policies possibly unexpectedly effective or ineffective when combined with contrastingly unbalanced policies abroad. Corporations with multinational operations shift their financial assets and liabilities to take advantage of changing credit conditions in various national markets, and Eurobanks now bridge the gap between local and international capital markets in a way banks never did before. It is clear that simple coordination of generally expansive or contractive policies among nations is no longer enough.

Rather, what is required is coordination of, or at the very least full sharing of information concerning, the whole policy mix in various countries. One country's fiscal automatic stabilizer may prove either useless or explosive depending on its own accompanying monetary policy and the mix of policies undertaken overseas. Similarly, a country's monetary policy may prove either helpful or destructive to plans of other countries—even when there is an agreed goal of worldwide expansion or contraction—depending on other policies at home and the mix abroad. The challenge to policy coordination is, on both a technical and a diplomatic level, enormously greater now than it was only a few years ago. Governments must be especially wary that their own policies in combination with those of other countries do not result in unintended excesses. The problem is particularly critical in the late 1970s and early 1980s because past international efforts to combat a protracted inflation accompanied by unemployment have synchronized aggregate spending changes in the industrialized countries.

The theory of the balance of payments that incorporates capital movements suggests that countries can still make domestic economic policy in some isolation from other countries if an appropriate policy mix is pursued. In particular, when the world economy is in general equilibrium and other governments pursue unchanged policies, if a government can add to or subtract from domestically held financial assets in just the pattern that matches domestic residents' asset demand at existing prices, no international exchanges of such assets need be induced, and the exchange rate will be left free to balance international transactions on current account. The policy undertaking will have the effectiveness of a policy change made in a closed economy.

If all countries should simultaneously pursue identical policies, regardless of the mix, the policies would again be successful, and the countries could enjoy a common result. The opportunity to proceed in this way, however, is in general incompatible with policy autonomy for individual countries.

The matter is complicated when several countries are changing their policy mix in different ways at the same time. In this case, to achieve autonomy one country must compensate for the incipient imbalances in the policy mix of all the others, where their individual measures are appropriately weighted for the intensity of likely total market response.

The problems of coordination focus on the structure of balances of payments where the international transmission of economic change necessarily takes place. International agreement on balance of payments goals, or agreement that the structure of the balance of payments is to be subjugated to other ends, is critical. The debate over the exchange rate realignment in the early 1970s heightened recognition of the necessity of achieving at least consistency in governments' balance of payments goals. In particular, there was some facing up to the fact that all countries cannot simultaneously have current account surpluses. On the other hand, an attempt to impose current account balance on each country would be disastrous, for it would imply the absence of international investment. Diplomatic efforts in the mid-1970s to secure an appropriate sharing of the worldwide current account deficit vis-à-vis OPEC was perhaps necessary to prevent the onslaught of beggar-my-neighbor commercial policies among deficit countries, which could only have worsened the problem. In the end, however, the efforts seemed to deteriorate into some intolerance of different countries' implicit or explicit decisions to proceed with adjustment at different rates.[32]

A globally optimal matrix of current account surpluses and deficits emerges when private decision makers are free to trade goods and services and claims internationally so as to maximize their individual utilities, as long as such a matrix is not inconsistent with full employment and price stabilization goals. Fortunately, the public demand management policies which do least to disturb any given equilibrium of such private choices are at the same time the most effective for national demand management, and an international set of such policies would be consistent among countries.

Therefore, a mix in each country of monetary and fiscal policies that is designed to minimize induced international exchanges of financial assets appears desirable. To the extent that each country succeeds in such a policy, it will leave its own residents free to balance portfolios on a global basis, it will avoid interference with the policies of other countries, and it will succeed in its own demand management objectives.

This approach implies that governments will change the supply of various maturities of the public debt and the monetary base at approximately equal proportional rates for any small incremental change, with a view to preserving market portfolio balance in at least those financial assets of which the supply is under government control.[33] Where the mix is changed between increments of monetary-fiscal expansion or contraction, the goal would be to minimize the effects of government policies on real interest returns on financial assets.

While the prescription implies the loss of independence for one policy variable in the national arsenal of regulatory instruments, we have seen that independent exercise of monetary and fiscal policies gives rise in any case, through international adjustments, to somewhat unpredictable outcomes. The exchange rate becomes an endogenous variable in the policy system envisioned, and the interest rate and the balance of international lending are unaffected by changes in the government's financial position.

---

[32] See Gottfried Haberler's condemnation of the attack on Germany's surplus in "The International Monetary System after Jamaica and Manila," in William Fellner, ed., *Contemporary Economic Problems, 1977* (Washington, D.C.: American Enterprise Institute, 1977), pp. 239-88.

[33] The interest rate implication of the prescription is that the real rate of interest (that is, the nominal rate of interest less the expected change in the internal purchasing power of the currency) will be unchanged. Any difference in the expected domestic and foreign inflation rates, along with the difference in domestic and foreign nominal interest rates, will be offset by the expected rate of change of the exchange rate.

An internal marriage of monetary and fiscal policy of this sort flouts the tradition of an independent central bank. The growing need for a concerted policy, however, seems to make a genuinely independent central bank increasingly a modern day anachronism.

Measures to Escape Stagflation

Unemployment and inflation that are both high by historical standards have plagued industrial countries for a full decade. Is it possible to point the direction economic policies must take if better times are to follow? Several suggestions have emerged in this chapter.

1. It is important that markets regain some resilience in order that they can, with less delay, accommodate the structural changes that have occurred and the changes that must be expected. Markets must reduce the profits to be contemplated by price setters who consider price increases and thereby accelerate inflation or resist its deceleration. Government regulations designed to protect the positions of particular groups are a prime cause of downward relative price rigidity, and relaxation of the society's propensity to regulate could go far toward improving the adjustment process. Minimum wage legislation that favors the skilled over the unskilled and the experienced over the inexperienced is one of the offenders. But regulations limiting price adjustments in a host of other markets where workable competition is potentially present are also a source of market dysfunction. Perhaps the most salutary change that has a chance of accomplishment in the reasonably near future is a further general reduction of tariff and nontariff protection of domestic producers. Business firms and trade unions facing potential global competition are much less able to resist adjustment and contribute to inflationary price rises that create unemployment than are price setters who are protected from external pressures. National economies stand to gain better access to the world's goods as well as movement toward a reduction in both inflation and unemployment from more liberal trade policies.

2. Anything that can be done toward hastening national consensus in the United States and in other countries on major economic issues will release creative energies. Incentives in a decentralized economy are suppressed whenever property rights and expectations about claims to the fruits of economic activity are brought into question. They are released again when the rules governing rewards (and penalties) are confirmed, providing that the rules are not too much biased against reward associated with the activity.

3. Greater stability in national demand management policies can provide private individuals and firms a better norm against which to lay their own plans. In particular, it is important that the rate of inflation be stabilized, for stops and starts in the rate of price level change often make the best-laid private plans go astray and give rise to subsequent market maladjustment and unemployment. It will be pointed out in subsequent chapters that long-run continuance of the dollar-centered monetary system probably requires a substantial reduction in inflation in the United States. It follows, then, that while demand management in the United States may be used to compensate for variations in private spending, it must be used carefully to avoid inflationary pushes that are costly to slow down. In particular, data are critically needed to help distinguish unemployment caused by supply changes from that caused by demand changes. A rule of thumb to the effect that the rate of growth of aggregate spending (nominal GNP) should never exceed, for more than a two-year period, the average rate of growth of output (real GNP) for the previous decade could be a helpful safeguard. Excessive nominal output growth must be a signal for a reduction in the rate of monetary growth if concern for short-run exigencies is not to result in protracted inflation.

4. Monetary and fiscal policies should be more frequently considered as if they were a single instrument of demand management and, when necessary, they should be adjusted in tandem to minimize the international exchanges of assets which chiefly propagate demand disturbances among countries under flexible exchange rates. While the monetary-fiscal policy mix may be changed in the light of changing domestic and foreign conditions, its change should be carefully coordinated with the anticipated mix in other countries to achieve desired national demand goals.[34] A major gain from the adoption of more flexible exchange rates is that the policies of the leading industrialized countries now require coordination of means rather than of ends. Coordination of the mix of monetary and fiscal policies can leave to the exchange rates such adjustments as are necessary to accommodate differences in overall demand objectives. The new requirement should be politically less strenuous than the old.

[34] In the terminology of planning theory, the merger of monetary and fiscal policy into one financial management tool implies a reduction in the number of policy instruments and in the number of planned targets: the single financial policy instrument becomes aimed at the single target of the rate of inflation. Aggregate employment, the exchange rate, and the structure of the balance of payments become resultants of the aggregate of private decisions and endogenous in the policy model.

6
Gold, SDRs, and Dollars

Undertakings by governments to limit movements in their exchange rates require an internationally acceptable monetary medium. Although for centuries gold served in this role in one way or another, it is clear now that gold is unlikely ever again to dominate decisions in international finance as it did prior to 1971. National currencies, especially dollars, have become the dominant form of international reserve money.

Gold's attractiveness as a monetary medium became steadily tarnished during the past half century because of gold's growing scarcity and because governments wanted freedom to manage spending in their national markets without the constraint that gold convertibility of their currencies implied. The IMF's second amendment goes far toward removing the remaining international legal trappings of the metal by making gold unacceptable for tenders of payments to the Fund and even by banning its use as an international numeraire in any future regime of pegged exchange rates. The amendment, however, leaves unresolved a number of questions, including what is to become of existing monetary gold stocks and the extent to which the Fund's special drawing rights (SDRs) can replace gold.

The SDR, a fiat international reserve medium initiated in 1970 after difficult negotiations, has been thought by many international observers to be the successor to gold in the international order, for at least a number of gold's former functions. But in the absence of agreement to substitute SDRs for the enormous and continuously expanding sum of foreign exchange reserves which now serves governments as a first line of defense for the exchange rates, there has been no simple way to inject SDRs into the monetary system without seeming to add fuel to the world's inflation. Furthermore, the instrument's future in a system of managed exchange rates is severely limited by existing restrictions on the ways SDRs may be acquired and used by governments and by the magnitude of the political commitment that seems essential to make a system based on a supranational fiat money workable. As an accounting unit, SDRs have become a permanent part of the financial scene. But as a reserve medium, they have at present little chance of displacing the currencies of a few industrialized countries.

Concern has frequently been expressed about the inflationary potential for the world of the more than trebling of total official reserve holdings between 1970 and 1978. It is well to remember, however, that those holdings materialized as a result of the petroleum crisis and the foreign exchange market interventions of governments whose currencies were otherwise in short supply. The reserve growth was due to a changed demand for reserves by governments rather than an explosion of supply, and it would not have been avoided had the world been on a gold or an SDR standard so long as authorities were not prohibited from acquiring foreign exchange. In the circumstances, restraints on the process would certainly have been unpopular. The additions to reserves have taken the form of foreign exchange—chiefly dollars—because these acquisitions served what appeared to be desirable ends; they were either acquired by petroleum exporters for investment or by other countries to influence the exchange rates. It is argued below that while the reserve accumulations are a possible future engine of inflation, they are not an imminent one. The problems with further reserve accumulations are connected with the exchange rate and inflationary implications of the acquisition process rather than with the likelihood that money supplies will soon be expanded to achieve the traditional proportion between reserve accumulations and money stocks.

While the outlook for gold as a monetary medium is not bright, gold's monetary implications cannot be disregarded so long as authorities have large investments in the metal. Governments are unlikely again to turn to monetary automaticity based on gold and hence are unlikely to make substantial further bullion investments—despite apprehensions frequently voiced during the reform negotiations. Their occasional sales of gold, nonetheless, will have effects on national and international liquidity that must be considered. Most likely, monetary gold held by IMF members, an amount constituting some 35 to 40 percent of the world's total hoard, will rest uneasily in official vaults for years to come and appear increasingly attractive to statesmen as a means, together with government debt, of financing public expenditures. When sold to the public, such gold will take its place as an industrial and artistic material along with silver, platinum, and other relatively uncommon but useful metals.

How Gold Was Dethroned

Some disaffection with a monetary system ordered upon gold was evidenced in the nineteenth century, especially by advocates of bimetallism. Nonetheless, the decade and a half of prosperity that preceded World War I created an aura of glamour for the international gold standard that inspired officials to rehabilitate it in the 1920s. Disenchantment then set in as a byproduct of the worldwide depression of the 1930s when a number of countries found their money supplies dragged downward through their efforts to maintain external gold convertibility. By the end of World War II the rejection of the dictatorship of economic policies by international movements of the metal was nearly complete. The United Kingdom's disavowal of international gold standard commitments in 1931 and that of the United States in 1933 marked the end of the appeal of monetary automaticity. Countries that did not suspend gold convertibility in that period adopted extensive trade and payments controls. The new economics to which the depression gave birth called for monetary-fiscal management of national demand aggregates by governments. In the IMF charter negotiated in 1943 the advantages of exchange rate stability were made secondary to governments' needs to maintain full employment in that the Fund could not object to a country's decision to alter its exchange rate in cases of fundamental disequilibrium. The final disenchantment with gold on the part of U.S. authorities came in the late 1960s and early 1970s when the U.S. pledge to maintain external gold convertibility once again appeared to restrain policy makers from pursuing a desired course of internal demand management. After a brief trial of curbing balance of payments deterioration by monetary and fiscal restraint in 1969–1970, the government opted in 1971 for monetary independence and abandonment of the mandate for gold convertibility.

An important part of the case against gold in the monetary system rests on the inelasticity of its supply. Since gold's supply does not grow with the world's output and trade and with what many regard as reasonable rates of inflation, it has a chronic tendency to become scarce in world markets. The tendency for governments then to protect their official supplies by conservative demand management policies has been seen as risking unemployment as a result of chronically deficient demand. Escape from gold's perennial scarcity would be possible if gold were recurrently revalued relative to other money taken together, and the original IMF charter provided a mechanism for just such steps. When revaluations can be anticipated, however, the anticipation leads to private hoarding, which accentuates the very scarcity that the parallel revaluations are intended to remove. Furthermore, such purposeful revaluations redistribute wealth in ways that are often unpopular. The unpopularity in Europe and North America of the world's leading gold producers, South Africa and the Soviet Union, for example, enhanced the case against revaluation in the 1950s and 1960s.

Although the inelasticity in the world's physical gold stock is the source of criticism of gold by some, it is the source of its advocacy by others. Those who fear governments' propensities to overinflate point to the desirability of full convertibility of money to gold as a means of restraining monetary expansion. The focus of public policy, however, has been on unemployment more than inflation since World War II, and the desire for freedom for monetary management has prevailed.

In the United States gold coins were called in from circulation and the gold redeemability of paper money was suspended in 1933. Federal Reserve Banks were still required to maintain a 25 percent gold certificate reserve against their note and deposit liabilities. When these requirements threatened to become a constraint on Federal Reserve policies in the 1960s, however, they too, were removed. Similarly, sterling was never freely convertible into gold for either internal or external purposes after 1931.

On the international level, gold had a conspicuous position in the original design of the IMF. Parity values for currencies were fixed in terms of gold or the U.S. dollar at its 1944 gold value; normally 25 percent of each member's original subscription to the Fund and a similar share of subsequent subscription increases were paid in gold; and gold emerged as the only asset that was always usable by a country for the repurchase of its currency from the Fund. Although gold may have derived its strength from its convertibility into U.S. dollars in the years immediately following World War II, it was still perceived to be the monetary system's prime asset.

As was predictable, gold's scarcity value intensified with the passage of time. The value of world trade in nominal terms grew five times as fast as world monetary gold stocks between 1951 and 1964; between a fourth and a third of that growth was due to price changes. Gresham's Law, according to which more abundant money forms drive scarce money forms from circulation, was certain to appear.

The first crack in the edifice was the "gold bubble" of 1960 when the open market price of gold in London advanced beyond the critical level of $35.10 at which official stocks were thought to be available to the market. The price advanced within a few days to $43 an ounce and made world headlines before it was turned back by U.S. gold sales through the Bank of England. The bubble was subsequently characterized as a misunderstanding between the Federal Reserve System and the Bank of England concerning which authority bore the responsibility for maintaining parity between the official and private prices for gold in the London market. In fact, it reflected the beginning of market pressures on the official price that ultimately could not be denied. In 1961–1962 the United States, not wishing to stand gold losses alone, took the leadership in organizing the gold pool, a group of six countries persuaded to share in the provision of gold for sale to private purchasers in order to prevent the free market price from exceeding the official price. But repeated sales of gold were unwelcome to the group, and when strong gold demand appeared once again in February–March 1968, the gold pool countries abandoned the attempt to keep the private and official prices at parity. In the two-tier system that followed, central banks agreed to refrain from open market purchases or sales, and the open market price was free to go its own way. In its initial push, the open market price surged to more than $42 and then, in March 1969, to nearly $44. After a brief return to the official value of $35 at the end of 1969, the price climbed dizzily and reached $193 at the close of 1974. In mid-1979 it traded in the region of $280 while the official price was $42.22.

The abandonment of efforts to keep the private price of gold at par with the official price in 1968 marked a point near the end of gold's use as a monetary metal. Following the March breakup of the gold pool, only one major country in the world had an effective monetary constraint because of gold, and that was the United States, which since 1946 had fulfilled its IMF exchange rate obligations by maintaining convertibility of the dollar into gold for foreign governments and central banks. Three years and five months after the end of the gold pool, the United States too capitulated, and the final rigid link between gold and national currencies disappeared.

The SDR was defined by the first amendment to the IMF charter as equal to one dollar's worth of gold at the 1969 parity, and when it appeared in the early 1970s to be losing its utility as a medium of exchange along with gold, its assigned value had to be changed. It was too valuable, when viewed in terms of gold's open market price, to be spent at its official price to effect international settlements. To preserve the SDR as a medium of exchange, executive directors of the IMF in July 1974 severed its link with gold; its course was at that time defined as that of the value of a basket of specified amounts of sixteen national currencies (see Table 2).

The historic and critical role of gold in monetary affairs arose from its place in a heterogeneous monetary aggregate in which the parts were kept exchangeable at par values. The mandate to assure maintenance of par values of other forms of money with gold was a significant constraint on overexpansion of the supplies of the other moneys because of the inelasticity in gold's supply. But for internal circulations, the mandate to maintain gold convertibility mostly disappeared in the 1930s. And since the breakdown of the Bretton Woods rules in 1971, countries have been free of obligations to maintain parities internationally. Gold has become simply part of an assortment of more or less liquid assets held by governments and international organizations without any pretense of parity. The relative values of foreign exchange, SDRs, and gold, have been subject to change in response to market forces. Is there any reason gold cannot continue to play this role? There is not, and many governments are likely to retain their gold investments indefinitely. In such a role, however, gold is no longer a constraint on the system and is no more than a socially expensive anachronism.

The Jamaica Decisions

A stated objective of the monetary reform negotiations was to reduce the role of gold and reserve currencies in the monetary system and make the SDR the system's principal reserve asset. But as shown in Chapter 2, the arduous negotiations succeeded only in removing some of the legacy of gold's legitimacy without either reducing the role of reserve currencies or effectively promoting the SDR.

While historically the demonetization of gold has proceeded through steps that increasingly concentrated the metal in the hands of higher monetary authorities, the IMF reforms reverse this trend. In the past, gold coins in circulation gave way to the concentration of bullion in national treasuries and central banks especially in the period between the World Wars; then the IMF's quota requirements led to further centralization of gold in an international organization. The Jamaica decisions, however, provide for restitution of one-sixth of the Fund's gold to governments of member countries and sale of another one-sixth on the open market. The open market sale is not necessarily inconsistent with demonetization since, in the end, if gold is not to be reserved for monetary functions it should be available for alternative uses. Furthermore, even restitution need not be inconsistent with the goals of demonetizing gold if countries refrain from creating base money in their national currencies against their new gold acquisitions. Still, restitution allows member countries to obtain, in exchange for their own currencies and at official prices, a reserve asset with a market value in excess of its official price; and they obtain the asset without any sacrifice of reserve tranches in the Fund, which they treat as automatically available liquidity. It is therefore scarcely deniable that some governments will be likely, in time, to follow more inflationary policies than they might have otherwise and in that way monetize their gold gains. Furthermore, the final demonetization by sale of the metal on open markets is unlikely to proceed as rapidly through the layer of national monetary authorities as it might have through a single international organization. In this, too, the Jamaica agreement concerning restitution was in fact a step backward from the stated intent to reduce gold's monetary position.

The open market sale of 25 million ounces of Fund gold for the new trust fund reflects, of course, the combined interests expressed in the negotiations toward reducing the monetary importance of gold, on the one hand, and toward obtaining additional aid for the poorest countries, on the other. The decision to distribute approximately one-third of this amount to lower-income countries—but not necessarily those with the lowest income—on the basis of their shares in total IMF quotas compromised the objective frequently mentioned in the reform discussions to help the very poorest. Ironically, the twin objectives of the sale of gold for the trust fund evoked conflicting hopes about prices the Fund might obtain at its gold sales. To minimize the monetary role of gold, some hoped the Fund's sales would result in a sharp decline in gold's market value. But to maximize aid to beneficiaries of the trust fund, other observers hoped for a maximum gold sales price.

Gold sales began on June 2, 1976. During the first two years of the four-year program to dispose of one-third of the Fund's gold, 12.5 million fine ounces were sold to the public—banks and gold dealers—in twenty-one auctions, and 12.26 million ounces were distributed to governments of member countries of the Fund at the former official price of SDR35 per ounce. Average prices realized at the auctions ranged from a low of $109.40 on September 15, 1976 to $170.40 on May 3, 1978. Profits of the sales, which went to the trust fund, came to $1.3 billion as of May 1978. Low-interest loans totaling $375 million had been made at that time to thirty-five eligible member countries, and in August another $676 million to forty-three countries was approved.

Governments of countries which produce no gold were hardly a factor in the world gold market between 1975 and 1978. Small amounts of gold were acquired by France in connection with the trust fund's early public gold sales, and the United States and India have executed small sales of gold from their own resources. Italy used gold, at an unofficial price, as collateral for a loan from Germany, and France adopted a quarterly reevaluation of official gold stocks to make them reflect changes in market prices. Most countries, however, have carried their gold stocks on their books at official values and have been neither buyers nor sellers. The Group of Ten agreement negotiated in 1975 concerning the avoidance of official gold acquisitions was quietly allowed to lapse in 1978.

IMF open market gold sales have had a small and transitory deflationary effect on world liquidity during a period of strident inflation. The sales, in most cases for dollars, have removed national money from circulation and have reduced commercial bank reserves; in the degree that trust fund holdings were redeposited with central banks, however, the net reserve positions of those banks were not changed. Distribution of the proceeds of the sales through trust fund activities restored the money to global circulation and rebuilt commercial bank reserves with, of course, an altered international distribution. But in the interval during which trust fund loans were being processed, and to the degree that trust assets were not wholly disbursed, the gold sale process was deflationary. Unfortunately, the potential for some deflationary effect was much more than neutralized during 1976–1977 by central bank activities to provide adequate monetary growth for employment expansion.

Gold sales by the United States and India similarly had temporary monetary effects. The initial U.S. sale occurred in 1975, in connection with the restoration to U.S. residents of the privilege of holding gold, when the Treasury sold on the open market 753,000 troy ounces of gold from its stock of 276 million ounces, a sale of less than 0.3 percent of the stock. In May 1978 a program of semiannual sales of 300,000-ounce amounts was begun, and in August the announced volume of sales was stepped up. The Reserve Bank of India's still smaller sales began in the spring of 1978. As a result of these sales money was withdrawn from circulation but then restored by government spending.[1] The lasting effects in each case, therefore, were only small reductions in the amount of government debt that would otherwise have been outstanding.

The Future of Gold in the Monetary System

Should gold's attenuated role as a monetary medium be ended, and if so, how? There seems little doubt that any effort to restore gold's role in the monetary system at a fixed value would be a mistake. Localized disturbances in the world economy are not sufficiently easily dissipated among nations, or even among regions within nations, through labor and other factor mobility to permit a single monetary and fiscal policy for the world. And without harmonized policies for aggregate demand management among countries, exchange rates fixed through any common denominator such as gold cannot be sustained. But unless it is to serve as an integrating element in the congeries of reserves, gold is a dear resource to set aside for the purpose of merely expressing an international claim. Accounting entries do as well, and there is no reason that the precious metal should not be released for industrial purposes where its special noncorrosive, electrical, reflective, and aesthetic properties can be enjoyed. While it is not essential that gold be reallocated for nonmonetary purposes, therefore, such a step would be productive.

A meaningful plea for a thoroughgoing return to gold can be made on the ground that only a firm link of money stocks to a commodity not easily reproduced can control inflation. If it were credible that governments would in fact subordinate their propensities for monetary expansion to a convertibility pledge, this case for gold could be very attractive despite the monetary inflexibility it would imply. Since it has been discarded decisively over a fifty-year period, however, the idea of gold convertibility as an inflation control no longer inspires confidence. Only public rejection of the ideas that have been used to justify excessive monetary growth seems likely in the 1980s to be an effective inflation control.

The final demonetization of the gold in national reserves seems unlikely to happen soon, either directly as a result of national gold sales, or indirectly as a result of centralization of bullion holdings in an IMF substitution account and subsequent sale. Governments will avoid decisions leading to large-scale liquidations of their gold, in part

---

[1] See Albert E. Burger, "Monetary Effects of the Treasury Sale of Gold," Federal Reserve Bank of St. Louis *Review* (January 1975), pp. 18-22.

because overt breaks with monetary traditions could be politically risky in a milieu of already declining public trust in money. Certainly most central banks will reflect a reluctance to sell off gold against anything but an external currency, although the United States has sold gold against dollars on the ground that a sale against foreign currencies would only lead prospective gold buyers to sell dollars to obtain the needed exchange. There are also unlikely to be large bullion purchases, for gold is a speculative commodity investment no longer suited to the responsibilities of treasuries and central banks. In particular, the unlikelihood that the United States will be in the foreseeable future a buyer of gold at a fixed exchange rate must give pause to other governments that might consider acquiring gold. The reserve changes of interest to authorities in each country will be those that have consequences for their own currency's exchange rate against other currencies. For these reasons it seems right to expect that gold will stay at the bottom of the pile of reserve assets for most nations for some time, and that from that position it will little influence governments' policies. When treasuries desire to slow growth in government indebtedness without diminishing government expenditures or raising taxes, open market sales in external currencies will occur. But meanwhile gold no longer constitutes a threat to the fabric of international monetary relations.

The Design of the SDR

The inauguration of the special drawing right in the International Monetary Fund in 1970 was an event of historic significance. Never before had nations agreed to the issuance of an internationally acceptable fiduciary money by an international organization. The achievement was not reached without travail, and what were thought to be its risks were carefully, perhaps too carefully, hedged. The negotiations were motivated primarily by the United States and the United Kingdom, which urged a new source of reserve growth to supplement or replace continued growth in foreign exchange reserves. Negotiations were resisted, however, by governments of several Western European nations which believed reserves were already overly abundant because of inadequate monetary discipline on the part of the reserve currency countries.

France, in particular, argued over several years that additional reserves were unnecessary and that any additional reserve money created by fiat should at the most be considered only a supplement to gold. French representatives at one time gave mild support to a credit reserve unit (CRU) which would have been issued to countries in proportion to their gold holdings and spent only in settlements containing fixed proportions of gold and CRUs. Generally, the French took the view that if any reserves were created they should be recognized as additional credits by surplus countries to deficit countries. In consequence, they should be free from control by the IMF, where the influence of the United States, a major deficit country, was strong, and they should earn interest for those who accepted them in financial settlements. France was a country with a surplus and was in the process of converting the larger part of its international reserves into gold.

The United States argued the case for additional reserves on the ground that continued accumulation of dollars by other countries would sooner or later jeopardize confidence in the dollar's gold convertibility, while adjustment of the U.S. balance of payments to an overall surplus would cut off the only practical source of reserve growth available to the world community under existing arrangements.

In the end, plans were laid for the creation of special drawing rights in the IMF, so called to distinguish them from the ordinary drawing rights of members.[2] The central issues of the negotiations then became the extent of the need for additional reserves, the terms on which they would be made available to countries and used if they were brought into being, and, in particular, how they might be initially distributed among countries.[3]

The problem of need was finally finessed by calling the negotiations "contingency planning" and the reserves to be created "contingency reserves." SDRs would be brought into being only when there would be substantial agreement among governments concerning their usefulness. According to the amendment, SDR allocations or cancellations are planned over basic periods usually of five years' duration. Six months before the beginning of each period the managing director of the IMF must report to the executive directors whether he has found broad support for a specific proposal for an allocation or cancellation. If he has, and if approval is given by the executive directors,

---

[2] Joseph Gold, the IMF's literate counsel, has written a charming essay on the naming of the world's new international money, acknowledging the unattractiveness of the present appellation and commenting on the merits and demerits of some alternatives. See his "Special Drawing Rights: Renaming the Infant Asset," *IMF Staff Papers*, vol. 23 (July 1976), pp. 295-311.

[3] The long negotiations leading to the SDR amendment, along with other aspects of the Fund's history, are handsomely chronicled in both Margaret Garritsen de Vries, *The International Monetary Fund, 1966-1971: The System under Stress*, 2 vols. (Washington, D.C.: IMF, 1976); and Robert Solomon, *The International Monetary System, 1945-1976* (New York: Harper and Row, 1977).

the proposal goes to the Board of Governors where the motion must carry by 85 percent of the votes weighted in proportion to members' quotas. The formula leaves the United States a veto, since this country's vote in such matters is, even after the 1978 quota increases, weighted approximately 21.5 percent of the total, and it also gives to the Common Market countries a veto if they vote in unison. If the United Kingdom votes in conjunction with two or more larger members of the Commonwealth, it can negate an allocation, as can developing countries taken together, and various other combinations of large and small countries. Indeed, the countries that feared excessive reserve creation succeeded in negotiating very conservative requirements for SDR allocation.

Surplus countries in the late 1960s insisted that those who would become spenders of the new reserve money should pay interest on their outstanding disbursements and agree to repurchase them. Surplus countries furthermore demanded a limit on their individual obligations to provide their own currencies against the new claims. By contrast, those who wanted a new reserve instrument pure and simple sought an asset that would be generally acceptable by participating governments and without the expectation of interest or reconstitution. The positions were reminiscent of those taken by surplus and deficit countries at the time the IMF's original charter was negotiated, with the difference that by the late 1960s the roles played by continental European countries and the United States were reversed.

In the end, a reconstitution rule was imposed, interest payable from those who reduced their SDR holdings below their cumulative allocations to those who increased their holdings was required, and each country's obligation to accept SDRs against its own currency was limited to three times the country's cumulative SDR allocation. The reconstitution rule that emerged does not require a country to repurchase the entirety of any SDRs that it spends, but it requires every country to hold in each moving five-year period, calculated quarter by quarter, SDR balances that are on the average not less than 30 percent of the country's cumulative allocations of SDRs.

Countries pay interest on their SDR allocations but earn interest on their holdings so that to the extent their SDR holdings exceed their allocations (they have provided their own currencies against SDRs) countries have net interest earnings. Since July 1974 the SDR interest rate, along with the Fund's rate of remuneration to countries whose currencies have been drawn to less than 75 percent of quota in the general account, has been linked to a weighted average of short-term market interest rates in the United States, the United Kingdom, the Federal Republic of Germany, France, and Japan. In particular, in late 1977 the rate was established quarterly at three-fifths the level of the weighted average of market rates in those countries.[4]

Because some countries must repurchase SDRs at various times and others might experience accumulations approaching the obligation limit, the IMF exercises guidance over the flow of SDRs, periodically publishing a list of countries designated to receive them. SDRs are transferred only on the books of the IMF and are held only by the authorities of participating IMF members.[5] To prevent countries from fleeing from a reserve currency into SDRs, a country, in order to spend its SDR holdings, must demonstrate to the Fund a balance of payments need, although with Fund approval, transactions by agreement among participating countries have always been possible, and the second amendment now liberalizes these opportunities.

Perhaps the most difficult aspect of SDRs to negotiate was the question of how allocations would be distributed among participating governments. France argued early in the discussions that the group receiving new reserve units should be limited to those whose creditworthiness was well established and then that any new reserve medium should be distributed in proportion to gold holdings. Robert Roosa of the United States, after leaving his post as under secretary of the Treasury for monetary affairs, proposed that they should be distributed to countries to the degree that those countries' currencies were used in making international settlements—what he called a self-qualifying criterion.[6] The void between these two positions, which clearly reflected differences in national interests, was wide. In the final draft of the amendment the proposal of the Fund's managing director was accepted to the effect that all Fund members who choose to participate would be invited to share in allocations, when voted, in proportion to their quotas in the Fund.[7]

As indicated in Chapter 2, the matter of the distribution of SDRs among countries was nonetheless not put to rest with the adoption of the first amendment to the IMF charter. Instead, growing demands

---

[4] Between July 1975 and July 1978 the interest rate varied between 3.75 and 4.0 percent. See IMF, *Annual Report* (1978), p. 73.

[5] The Bank for International Settlements was designated an agency also authorized to hold SDRs in 1976.

[6] Robert V. Roosa, *Monetary Reform for the World Economy* (New York: Harper and Row, 1965).

[7] In fact, eight members of the Fund—six Arab countries, Ethiopia, and Singapore—originally opted out of participation in the SDR arrangements. As the second general allocation was being scheduled for the beginning of 1979, however, several more countries became participants, leaving only one IMF member outside the arrangement.

for attention to their problems by developing countries—demands that took the form of calls for a New International Economic Order in resolutions of the U.N. General Assembly and other bodies in 1974–1975—came to include prominently a proposal that SDR allocations be distributed so as to favor the poorest countries. Developing country spokesmen pointed out that allocations according to IMF quotas favored richer countries and were contrary to stated objectives concerning the poor. By creating a link between international economic assistance and SDR allocations they hoped to funnel at least a limited amount of aid to poor countries without repeated recourse to political processes in the aid-providing countries. The providers, however, saw this link as a scheme to deprive them of control of part of a foreign assistance program that had both domestic and international political implications, and also as a threat to the creditworthiness of a fiduciary asset that had as yet no track record. Discussion of the SDR-aid link took place in a technical group of the Committee of Twenty[8] but bore no fruit in the final stages of negotiation of the comprehensive second amendment.

SDRs Today

The second amendment has in fact changed the SDR's position little. The procedure for allocation and cancellation emerged from the deliberations unchanged, and the limit on obligations of members to accept SDRs, the requirement for limited reconstitution of SDR balances, charges for SDR usage, and rules for designation all remain in effect.[9] The amendment does liberalize opportunities for SDR participants to purchase currencies from other participants by agreement without the necessity of authorization by the Fund (Article 19), and it reduces the IMF weighted voting majorities required for the further liberalization of SDR rules. The SDR replaces gold in most of the latter's former functions in IMF operations. The SDR may, for example, be used by SDR participating countries to pay part of their subscriptions at the time of increases in their IMF quotas and to pay charges for use of Fund resources. It may also be used by the Fund to purchase currencies for the replenishment of Fund currency stocks and for distributions to members of net income or portions of the

[8] See *International Monetary Reform: Documents of the Committee of Twenty*, pp. 95-111.

[9] But, as noted in the Epilogue below, the fraction of cumulative allocations that participating countries must reconstitute over moving five-year periods was reduced from 30 to 15 percent in 1979.

general reserve. Furthermore, the SDR becomes permanently the unit of measure for the Fund's accounts.[10] But the SDR remains a small element in the total of international reserves and a credit instrument that is not freely usable even after it has been earned in commerce.

SDRs in existence in April 1978 amounted to SDR9,314.8 million, with a dollar value of $11,421 million, of which SDR1,371 million was held by the general account of the Fund. This cumulative allocation was the product of equal allocations in each of the three years of the first basic period, 1970–1972. The second basic period, a five-year interval beginning on January 1, 1973, ended without additional allocations. SDR holdings by countries in August 1978 constituted only 4.0 percent of their total reserves, whereas at the close of the first basic period (December 1972) they had amounted to 5.8 percent. The net users of SDRs up to April 30, 1978, were chiefly the nonindustrial countries, whose holdings were SDR1,276 million less than their cumulative allocations. The industrialized countries recorded at that time a net use of only SDR95 million. The balance of SDR1,371 was acquired by the Fund's general account. An SDR19.6 billion increase in allocations during a three-year third basic period was authorized by the Board of Governors in December 1978 subject to member ratification. (See Epilogue.)

The case made in 1977–1978 for additional SDR allocations was that if SDRs are to progress toward a central role in the international monetary system their relative importance in international reserves had to be increased. The argument, however, had a hollow ring. The broad case for the SDR from the beginning rested on the allegation that if it occupied a central role, international reserves could be more rationally managed—by expansion when there was shortage and by contraction when there was excess supply, with global inflation a prime piece of evidence of the presence of excess supply. There is no case for adding SDRs to the international reserve stock merely to maintain or increase the SDRs relative position in the stock while the stock is also being fed by government acquisitions of foreign exchange. The task is to slow the rate of non-SDR reserve creation rather than to add an SDR increment to it if indeed the SDR ratio is an appropriate matter for concern.

In the monetary reform negotiations, considerable attention was given to possibilities for a substitution facility in the Fund through

---

[10] Details of the changes are discussed in *Proposed Second Amendment to the Articles of Agreement of the International Monetary Fund: A Report by the Executive Directors to the Board of Governors* (Washington: IMF, March 1976). For the SDR's valuation, see Table 2.

which member countries would replace some or all of their existing foreign exchange reserves with SDRs. The Committee of Twenty's technical group on global liquidity and consolidation reported that "the establishment of a Substitution Account would not present major technical problems."[11] Holders of reserve currencies who deposited the currencies in the account would receive SDR allocations for them. It was further suggested that, in order to permit reserve currency countries to earn SDRs and to redeem their own currencies from Fund holdings without reducing world reserves, these countries might be allocated SDRs as their balance of payments surpluses caused their external liabilities to fall below some predetermined level. Interest would be paid to countries on the SDRs they acquired by substitution, and this interest would be financed by the IMF's passing through the interest it earned on assets acquired in the exchange.

Country representatives in the negotiations, however, expressed awareness of some costs members might experience as a result of substituting SDRs for foreign exchange reserves. It was clear that they were being asked to give up forms of reserves which could be freely spent and invested for SDRs which might continue to be encumbered with the need requirement and with limitations on countries' obligations to accept. In addition, representatives of some developing countries noted that their foreign exchange reserves, when placed on deposit in commercial banks, enabled them to secure credit lines that were a multiple of these balances, but that SDRs, so long as they were not privately held, could not serve this role. In a similar vein, it was pointed out that currency reserves on deposit in Eurobanks probably enabled some multiple expansion of reserves, for better or for worse, which SDRs could not. There were concerns as to whether the substitution would be mandatory or voluntary for individual countries, partial or complete, all at once or executed by stages, and whether it would apply to existing balances only or also to balances that might be acquired in the future.

Academic discussion of a substitution facility arose in the 1960s in part as a result of concern about the "overhang" of allegedly excess dollars in official holdings. The perennial fear was that a flight from the dollar to gold or other currencies would strain the par value system to the breaking point. It could in the process destroy some of the claims serving as international reserves and the available means of creating reserves. The problem to be solved was perceived as a tendency toward an excess supply of reserves caused by continued balance

[11] *International Monetary Reform: Documents of the Committee of Twenty*, p. 169.

of payments deficits on the part of the leading reserve currency country. The task, then, was to sop up the existing excess and to shift the system toward a reserve medium which would have a controllable supply and which would be convertible only as needed for legitimate payments.

Even as negotiations on a substitution facility proceeded, however, the problem changed. Reserve accumulation accelerated not as a result of an unwanted supply but in response to demand. It seems clear that severe restraints on reserve growth would have been unpopular with countries with balance of payments deficits, on the one hand, or with surpluses, on the other, in the 1974–1977 period. The large-scale accumulators of reserves were (1) oil-exporting countries which, after 1973, were unable to absorb annually goods and services equal to the value of their foreign exchange earnings, and (2) other countries, notably Germany, Switzerland, and Japan, which developed overall balance of payments surpluses and desired to slow the rate of appreciation of their currencies. In the circumstances of worldwide inflation, countries with balance of payments deficits, including the United States, were often not unhappy to avoid some of the inflationary pressures which depreciation of their currencies would have induced, and hence they welcomed, to a degree, surplus countries' accumulation of their currencies or of the currencies to which they were tied in bloc arrangements.

Reserve accumulation in dollars thus grew out of the mutual concern in many countries for the pattern of exchange rates. The acquisition of reserves in the form of dollars resulted from the dollar's characteristics as an intervention medium as much or more than from its characteristics as a reserve medium, and this generalization applies to the oil-exporting as well as to the non-oil-exporting reserve gainers, in the sense that the oil exporters cared about the dollar's exchange value. This fact must be kept in mind in consideration of the future role of SDRs and of reserve holdings generally.

Possible Form of an SDR-Centered System

Plans for a substitution facility are not dead. Indeed, the second amendment to the IMF charter commits members to the objective of making the SDR the "principal reserve asset of the international monetary system," and a substitution facility is, in the minds of many, a central part of that commitment. The SDR, however, is not a monetary instrument whose value is assured by the instrument's acceptability in a wide range of transactions. Promotion of the use of the instrument, even as a reserve asset, therefore requires governments to assume additional specific obligations. What is the form of these obligations? And how might an SDR-centered system function? What might such a system achieve? To approach these questions, the framework of a possible SDR-centered system must be considered.

First, it seems clear that SDRs added to the system to promote the SDR role should indeed be injected by means of a substitution facility in which the SDRs replace reserves now held by monetary authorities. For although the association between reserve holdings and inflationary finance is not a close one, an injection of reserves without substitution would for many countries create reserve holdings sufficiently excessive to induce or permit their governments to follow more inflationary policies than they would otherwise have followed. It seems fair to assume that SDRs would be substituted for a portion of the gross reserves of participating countries rather than for net reserves (official external liquid assets less specified official external debts), although certain official liquid liabilities might be offset against liquid assets. Gross reserves, as reported for most countries, are the funds available without further undertakings for net official short-term support to the foreign exchange market. For some countries, reserves calculated net of intermediate-term foreign debt would be negative.

Second, the substitution must be thought of as irreversible if the advantages of possessing a homogeneous reserve asset are to be achieved. This implies a continuation of the requirement by the IMF that a country have "need" to exchange SDRs for a currency before that country can use its SDRs for this purpose, or else, as suggested below, countries would have to accept a commitment to maintain a share of their reserves in SDR form.

Third, to ensure the maintenance of the SDR's value, participating countries' commitments to provide "usable" currency in exchange for SDRs would have to apply to a multiple of SDRs allocated by substitution as well as to a multiple of those allocated in the usual way. The process of transferring SDRs either by designation or by agreement could continue unchanged.

Fourth, an interest rate equal to the market rate obtainable on assets that are equally as attractive as the SDR would have to be paid on the SDRs allocated through the substitution facility in order to compensate recipients for the interest they would forgo on their foreign exchange holdings. That is, the SDR allocation through the substitution facility would have to be treated, for purposes of interest, the same as the SDRs that countries now hold, while charges to countries on the SDRs they obtained through substitution would be inappropriate. As mentioned above, the IMF would presumably finance interest payments on the additional SDR allocation with interest earnings on the foreign exchange assets it would itself acquire through substitution. Such a procedure for substitution and interest transfers, however, suggests that the IMF might remain for some time the holder and manager of the claims it acquired on governments and banks. Insofar as the claims were against governments, they could be funded into long-term obligations; then the global deflationary effect of, say, U.S. balance of payments surpluses and U.S. government amortization of the IMF-held obligations with earned SDRs could be offset by further SDR allocations. Dollar obligations of banks, especially of Eurobanks, which the IMF might acquire through substitution, would create special problems, for any funding of these short-term deposit claims into longer-term maturities would give the banks leeway for creating new liquidity for governments and for the public. A careful balancing by the IMF of withdrawals of its deposits from banks and lengthening of its deposit maturities might then be necessary to minimize the effects of the substitution operation on the world's money markets.

Last, decisions would have to be reached concerning the treatment of governments' new acquisitions of foreign exchange following the once-for-all substitution. The Fund's proposal on this point in 1975 provides one approach. In a speech in Frankfurt, Germany, the managing director suggested that governments might want to explore an arrangement under which IMF members would hold no less than specified proportions of their total reserves in the form of SDRs.[12] SDRs in such an arrangement would presumably serve to limit reserve creation through foreign exchange acquisitions by central banks in the same way that required deposits at central banks now serve to limit money creation by commercial banks in most developed countries. With a minimum reserve ratio for SDRs in effect, it seems clear that countries acquiring foreign exchange through exchange market intervention would have to be able to insist that other countries, presumably designated by the IMF, *sell* SDRs to them against currencies, if limitations on SDR supply are to be made more than simply a constraint on the intervention activities of the less inflationary countries. This point is discussed further below.

[12] The text of Johannes Witteveen's address to the Conference Board in Frankfurt, Germany, is published in *IMF Survey* (October 28, 1975).

The Rationale for an SDR System

Three arguments probably constitute the main case favoring an SDR-centered system over the present dollar-centered system. These arguments are considered in turn.

The first is that an SDR-centered system will, by consolidating reserves into a more homogeneous package of assets, limit the destabilizing shifts among assets that occur when governments can hold alternative reserve assets which undergo changes in relative values. As long as the minimum SDR share required in each country's reserves is less than 100 percent, of course, some degree of choice over the remainder of the gross reserve portfolio remains. And governments would remain free to speculate with owned or borrowed reserves insofar as the assets acquired in such transactions fell outside the definition of foreign exchange reserves that was adopted for the plan. The question remains how the IMF itself would manage the portfolio of short-term assets it would acquire from participating governments. Indeed it is unclear that the IMF could safeguard the value of that part of its portfolio held by banks without making many of the same adjustments central banks would have made. Nevertheless, an SDR system would somewhat limit government choices. It would also create for individual governments a number of serious problems.

Governments are understandably reluctant to give up their freedom to choose the composition of their reserve assets. The SDR system which has been outlined demands that they make a once-for-all conversion of reserves into SDRs that are perhaps usable only under a designation procedure subject to international scrutiny. Governments might be concerned about the usability of their SDRs to finance, say, military and paramilitary activities—including covert activities—in support of national security objectives. Governments will also want to assess the outlook for the valuation that will be assigned the SDR in the periodic reconsiderations of the valuation formula. On another front, if the rule requiring a country to reconstitute a share of its SDR holdings over moving five-year periods should be applied to SDRs obtained by substitution, the value of countries' present reserve stocks would be damaged. It will therefore not be easy to negotiate the details that will make an SDR-centered system workable and also acceptable to its participants.

A second goal frequently mentioned in favor of an SDR-centered system is that the SDR should provide governments with a more stable reserve asset than individual currencies (or gold) have demonstrated in the past decade. To make the SDR such an asset was the justification for defining it, in 1974, as a weighted average of currencies of the sixteen countries, each of which accounted for 1 percent or more of world trade. A similar objective has of course inspired the design of the European unit of account (EUA) as the numeraire for settlements among governments in the narrow exchange rate margins arrangement in Europe, and the objective has inspired numerous artificial currencies for the denomination of private debts.

While the objective is especially attractive to governments which feel they have been caught holding a losing portfolio, it has not always been clear even to those same governments that the inflexible SDR bundle is more promising than bundles of assets they might hold as a result of careful and flexible asset management. Failure of the OPEC countries, after repeated formal considerations of the matter, to shift their numeraire for petroleum prices from the dollar to the SDR is a case in point. The fact is that countries can generally gain as much stability in value for their reserve holdings as the SDR can give them, whenever they choose to take it, by suitable diversification of their reserve portfolios among currencies. And if governments fear diversification because of its effects on the exchange rates, they must also feel some concern for the management that the IMF would bring to the currency holdings it would acquire in a substitution facility.

In any case, interest rates obtainable on assets in various currencies may be expected over long periods to reflect tendencies for those currencies to depreciate or appreciate in foreign exchange value as well as in internal purchasing power value. Thus, short-term losses that may appear to governments to be the result of poor portfolio choice may in the long run be reasonably well hedged. Recognition of this point makes diversification less imperative than it might otherwise seem.

Finally, with respect to the goal of obtaining a stable-valued reserve asset, if governments or private parties demand a "cocktail" currency, banks will surely supply the need that is not otherwise satisfied. Among the accounting units for the denomination of bond issues and commercial debts that have made their appearance in the private markets in recent years are EUAs, ECUs, Eurcos, Arcrus, B-units (Barclay's Bank), and IFUs.[13] And with a demand for deposits in any of these or similar units, there can be little doubt that banks will offer deposit facilities. Indeed, two large banks, one in New York and one in Germany, announced in 1978 a willingness to accept deposits as well as to make loans in SDRs.

[13] These functional money units are discussed further in Chapter 8 below.

A third case for an SDR-centered system of international reserves, and one that is preeminent in the minds of many, is to slow the worldwide inflationary process by bringing the supply of international reserve media under control. If SDRs held at the IMF were the only usable reserve, it is easy to imagine that the supply of international reserves could be restrained, and then, with a suitable limit on the supply of international reserve money, that global inflation could be curbed.

As shown below, however, the linkage between gross reserve holdings and national monetary policies is weak. Countries with strong currencies acquire reserves to protect employment and income in their international trade-related industries, and countries with weak currencies often spend their reserves and borrow more abroad in order to export their inflations. A limitation on foreign exchange reserves in relation to SDRs represents in the first instance a limitation on reserve acquisition in countries with strong currencies rather than a limitation on spending on the part of countries that tend to tolerate inflation. To ensure that the limitation on global stocks of SDRs puts pressure on countries where inflation is most rampant, countries with strong currencies might insist on the privilege of demanding SDRs from countries with weaker currencies. The IMF would then have to develop a set of rules designating countries which must *sell* SDRs analogous to the rules which at present designate SDR buyers.

It is perhaps interesting to explore how an SDR-centered system containing these conditions might operate in comparison with a dollar-centered system.

Operations of SDR- and Dollar-Centered Systems

The systems differ in a number of ways but seem to differ primarily in the international distribution of the inflation and disinflation that weak and strong currency countries respectively succeed in exporting. As long as countries hold some of their reserves in dollar form, as long as the dollar remains the principal intervention currency, and as long as there are effective international money and capital markets, U.S. monetary policy remains a key element in the inflationary or deflationary performance of both systems.

A Dollar-Centered System. A dollar-centered system is defined as one in which the dollar is used as the principal reserve asset and intervention currency by all countries, and in which U.S. authorities largely refrain from open market purchases and sales of foreign exchange.

Exchange market interventions are undertaken only by others and to limit exchange rate movements. S-countries (surplus countries), which tend to follow less inflationary monetary policies than does the United States, are distinguished from D-countries (deficit countries), which tend to follow more inflationary policies than the United States. Much of the discussion of this and the next few subsections runs in terms of the position of S-countries and D-countries relative to the United States and its currency which serves as the pivot of the system.

In a dollar-centered system the S-countries have an option, unconstrained by international rules other than those implied by surveillance, to intervene in the foreign exchange market by purchasing dollars, thereby importing some of the rest of the world's inflation, or to allow their currencies to appreciate. S-countries seem to value this option. Each D-country, conversely, has an option of letting its currency depreciate, on the one hand, or of exporting some of its homemade inflation, on the other—the latter option being dependent, of course, on the existence of owned or borrowable dollars. The United States, as a nonintervenor, does not have these options. It does, however, receive or export inflationary stimuli vis-à-vis the rest of the world in the degree that other countries, taken together and in net terms, purchase or sell its currency. When other countries buy dollars, they strengthen the dollar and in some degree help finance U.S. payments abroad; in strengthening the dollar, they reduce inflationary pressures in the United States. When, on the other hand, other countries sell dollars, the sales cause the dollar to depreciate, and the action accelerates inflation in the United States.

An SDR-Centered System. In an SDR-centered system, the options and results for the three groups are somewhat changed. If this system is initiated with all participating countries in fact holding the minimum required fraction—say, half—of their reserves in SDRs, D-countries wishing to prevent their currencies from depreciating may intervene with owned or borrowed dollars without drawing on their SDRs, thereby seeing their reserve ratios either remain unchanged (if the intervention dollars are borrowed abroad) or rise (if the intervention dollars come from the country's existing holdings). When a D-country so intervenes, the dollar is depreciated against S-currencies, and the D-country's inflation is imported in some degree by the United States and by all countries whose currencies are pegged on the dollar. The inflation which the D-country exports is in fact imported by the United States in just the same degree as would have occurred under a dollar-centered system. Now in fact that outcome is unchanged even if the D-country finances part of its intervention with SDRs. For then the S-countries, designated to receive SDRs, are likely to purchase them against dollars, and it will be those countries' SDR reserve ratios that will rise. The dollar, nonetheless, will depreciate against S-country currencies all the same.

When an S-country intervenes to support its currency, however, the outcome for the United States is not the same as in a dollar-centered system. An S-country acquisition of dollars through open market purchase with S-country currency must be accompanied by a purchase of SDRs if the S-country does not possess excess SDR reserves. D-countries will presumably be among those the IMF will designate as SDR sellers. But the D-countries losing SDRs must then also sell off dollars in exchange for their own currencies in order to maintain their reserve ratios, if they are not holding excess SDRs. The dollar will then have been appreciated against S-currencies by S-countries' dollar purchases and will have been depreciated against D-currencies by D-countries' dollar sales. The asymmetry between the effects of an S-country intervention and a D-country intervention compared with results in a dollar system arises because there is a minimum ratio specified for SDR-dollar reserve holdings but not a maximum. Countries acquiring dollars must acquire SDRs (unless they use the dollars to repay loans, and chronic S-countries are not the large international borrowers), whereas countries losing dollars need not dispose of SDRs.

Comparisons. These operational differences in the two systems lead to several comparisons.

The international sharing of inflation. The position of the United States is not the same in the two systems. In the dollar system, D-country intervention depreciates the dollar against S-currencies, and S-country intervention appreciates the dollar against S-currencies; D-country inflation is shared by the United States when D-countries intervene, and S-country stability is shared by the United States when those countries intervene.

In the SDR system, on the other hand, while D-country intervention has the same inflationary effects on the United States as under the dollar system, S-country intervention yields the United States only a part of the S-country stability that would occur under a dollar system. S-countries under an SDR system import less inflation with their interventions, and the United States imports less stability.

Countries' options to intervene. There seem to be few differences in the constraints the two monetary systems put on the opportunities of D-countries to intervene in their exchange markets, as long as the countries have access to an international dollar capital market. D-countries can intervene in an SDR system without use of their SDRs or without concern for the future of their SDR-currency reserve ratios as long as they can obtain through international borrowing the dollars they want for foreign exchange market sale. Indeed, SDR holdings are unnecessary to them, except insofar as the holdings bolster the countries' external credit. S-countries likewise retain their prerogative to intervene as long as they can demand SDRs from D-countries in amounts to match the necessary ratio of their SDR to their dollar holdings. Only if the exhaustion of SDR stocks outside the S-countries finally prevents S-countries from acquiring additional SDRs do the strong currency countries encounter a constraint on their ability to intervene. Such a circumstance would, of course, thrust more of the global inflationary pressure back on the softer currency areas and on the dollar bloc as a whole.

In the end, the case for a minimal SDR requirement in reserves seems to rest on possible improvements in the adjustment mechanism between dollar surplus areas and the rest of the world. But only if it ultimately throws inflationary pressures back on inflationary-minded governments, leading them to follow less inflationary policies, will the arrangement be a constraint on global monetary expansion.

The U.S. as monetary authority. It follows that in the SDR system, as in the dollar system, global inflationary forces remain substantially dependent on U.S. monetary decisions. Countries with softer currencies than the dollar can in either system export their inflation to the dollar bloc as long as dollar credit is available to them.

If, in a dollar-centered system, the United States tightens its monetary policy, the cost of external borrowing to D-countries for intervention is increased, and some global deflationary pressure is achieved. At the same time, the United States, as the pivot of the system, moves closer to the S-country group, increasing the number of D-countries and their average inflation relative to the United States and decreasing the number of S-countries and their relative deflation. D-countries as a group will consequently have larger deficits with the United States but smaller deficits vis-à-vis the declining group of S-countries, and the D-country sale of dollars for S-currencies will diminish. But since S-country purchase of dollars is likely also to diminish, the net effect of intervention on the value of the dollar, and hence on the U.S. importation of inflation, might be small.

In an SDR system, a restrictive U.S. monetary policy has similar effects. In increasing the cost of dollars to D-countries wishing to avoid depreciation, a restrictive U.S. policy would restrain inflation. And again, the policy would have little effect on the amount of inflation or deflation the U.S. imports from others.

Perhaps most significant in this argument is that an expansive monetary policy in the United States is capable of contributing to expansive policies in the world under both an SDR- and a dollar-centered system. Dollar availability to deficit countries permits them to export inflation to the United States even if not to countries with stronger currencies than the dollar. A fractional gross reserve SDR system with the dollar as the world's intervention currency does not, therefore, seem to relieve the United States of responsibility for an important part in world monetary policy.

The SDR as an Asset That Could Be Held by the Public

It has often been suggested that the SDR might be changed so that it could be held by the general public.[14] If public use of the SDR were achieved, the asset's use as a reserve medium could then be more in keeping with the spirit of a regime of managed exchange rate flexibility. But very serious additional problems would arise.

In general circulation, the SDR could not, for example, continue to be valued as a currency bundle unless it were convertible on demand into that bundle or the bundle's market value equivalent. This means that the IMF or other agencies would have to engage in market interventions to maintain the standard. Since, however, the SDR would then have to be supplied to meet market demand, its supply could not be regulated as a means of restraining world inflationary tendencies even if that technique were otherwise feasible. The pace of expansion of supplies of the national moneys which defined it would determine the pace of expansion of the SDR's supply.

If, alternatively, the SDR were not pegged against one or more other currencies, its value would be a matter of its own market supply and demand. And it cannot be taken for granted that the supply of SDRs could be determined by a simple allocation process since it would have to be expected that financial intermediaries would accept deposits and make loans in SDR terms and in the process multiply the outstanding liquid SDR claims. Controlling the supply of SDRs

[14] A recent statement of the proposal is K. Alec Chrystal, *International Money and the SDR*, Essays in International Finance, no. 128 (International Finance Section, Princeton University, June 1978).

would be characterized by all the problems that now characterize control of the supply of dollars on a global basis. The regulation of supply might be left to the actions of national monetary authorities, but such a system would then be little different from present arrangements. For the IMF to manage the supply of SDRs, it would presumably have to be armed with the powers of a central bank to remove SDRs from circulation when SDR creation of short-term credit seemed excessive and to inject them when private market SDR creation seemed inadequate. In such a circumstance, the political process through which IMF monetary decisions were reached would become of enormous importance. Even if these problems were resolved, one would still have to assess whether the introduction of one more monetary authority into an already confusing array of such authorities was desirable.

A limited form of private participation in SDR transfers was discussed in the technical group on intervention and settlement of the Committee of Twenty.[15] In it, commercial banks operating in a par value exchange rate regime would be authorized by their central banks to purchase and sell SDRs at prescribed margins around par as long as SDRs were transferred only among central banks. Such an arrangement would allow SDRs to serve as the means of international settlement at the margins of the band of permitted exchange rate movements with the interventions executed by the banks in arbitraging transactions, just as such interventions were under an international gold standard regime. Since claims against the IMF in SDRs would never be held by banks or other unofficial entities, SDRs purchased and sold for transfer among central banks would be less likely to become the basis for private SDR credit expansion. The scheme is workable under a par value system although it appears to introduce little change from the system in effect before August 1971 beyond putting the initiative for intervention in the hands of private banks instead of in the hands of the monetary authorities. The arrangement has little meaning for a regime without prescribed intervention margins.

The outlook for extending the use of the SDR as a reserve asset in the present system, therefore, is not bright. Its function as a unit of account, however, is increasingly well established and a useful adjunct to the floating currency arrangements.

---

[15] See *International Monetary Reform: Documents of the Committee of Twenty*, p. 123.

The SDR as Unit of Account

As a unit of account, the SDR has been made the numeraire of all IMF accounts where its basket definition mitigates the effects of changing national currency values on the Fund records. It is also the value unit against which several countries peg their exchange rates. It has come to be used as the standard for value quotations in a number of private contracts, including Suez Canal tolls and numerous bond issues, and it has been seriously considered as a price numeraire by groups such as OPEC and the International Air Transport Association (IATA). A few banks, already engaged in making SDR-denominated loans, have expressed willingness to accept SDR-denominated deposits. Other conglomerate currency units have, of course, appeared for special usages, but the SDR, as an internationally recognized unit with a purchasing power that changes less through time than any of its currency components, seems likely to be part of the foreseeable scene.

Foreign Exchange Reserves

Between 1969 and 1978 the international reserves reported by IMF member countries increased from SDR79 billion to SDR264 billion, an increase of three and a third times. Of the total SDR185 billion reserve increase, SDR169 was in the form of foreign exchange, and the remainder was in the form of SDRs themselves and increases in reserve positions in the Fund. Official gold holdings declined more than SDR4 billion. The foreign exchange acquisitions by monetary authorities before 1973—some SDR54 billion—were largely due to efforts by some industrialized countries to restrain appreciations of their currencies in the foreign exchange markets. Between 1973 and 1977, however, the major gains—approximately SDR50 billion—were made by the oil exporters. In 1977 and 1978 a group of industrial countries and non-oil-exporting developing countries, this time chiefly the United Kingdom, Japan, and Germany, again accounted for most of the reserve gains as a result of exchange market intervention—the three countries accounted for SDR24 billion of the total SDR42 billion reported.

The foreign exchange accumulation by the central banks of non-oil-exporting countries fostered inflation by adding directly to global money supplies, except to the extent that the foreign exchange purchases were accompanied by specific offsetting monetary operations.[16] Where oil was marketed through government monopolies, reserve accumulation by oil exporters did not automatically give rise to monetary expansion—a matter which leads some writers to argue that these official holdings should not be treated like other additions to official reserves. Nonetheless, in these countries, too, government deficit expenditures in the local economies, financed by central bank credit, led to sharp exportable inflation.

The traditional view of the link between reserve increases and inflation—that reserve availability permits countries to follow expansionary monetary and fiscal policies that would otherwise have been impossible without exchange rate depreciation—is of limited usefulness in the present context.[17] In particular, this view should not lead one to look for increases in the aggregate of national money stocks in some historically prescribed proportion to aggregate reserve increases or to look especially to the reserve-accumulating countries for the next round of inflation. For increments to the world's reserve stock now occur because governments least inclined to inflation, or countries where absorption is otherwise limited, choose to acquire and hold currencies of international settlement rather than see the international currencies depreciate—especially against the currency

[16] An illustration of the transactions involved begins with a country with a balance of payments surplus whose central bank purchases foreign exchange on the open market to inhibit appreciation of its currency. The first effect of the intervention is an injection of central bank money into the domestic economy—"high-powered money" that can serve as the basis for further liquidity transformation by commercial banks. The foreigner's money, or a vehicle currency, has, however, been temporarily removed from worldwide circulation. If, nonetheless, the central bank invests the currency it has acquired—say, dollars—in a money market abroad, as is customary, the circulation of that currency is restored while a less liquid asset, perhaps a Treasury bill, is removed from private hands. At that point, the surplus country has in effect accepted payment for its export balance in terms of a dollar Treasury bill—a foreign promise to pay—and the country's central bank has monetized the Treasury bill by purchasing it, and in that way it has added to global liquidity. This no doubt completes a typical sequence of events. If the central bank subsequently neutralizes the effects of its reserve acquisition by a domestic open market sale of securities (perhaps those of its own government), the monetary consequences of the activities are reversed. Some foreign residents, perhaps U.S. residents, will at this point have given up a promise to pay (a Treasury bill), and domestic residents in the surplus country will have acquired a promise to pay (the bond of their government). The surplus country's central bank's role is then only that of an intermediary, and neither the stock of financial assets nor the liquidity of the assets will have changed on a global basis. Unfortunately, offsetting of the monetary consequences of foreign exchange market interventions has been, on the whole, inadequate.

[17] This view characterizes H. Robert Heller's association of reserve expansion with inflation in "International Reserves and Worldwide Inflation," *IMF Staff Papers* (March 1976), pp. 61-87.

of the intervenor. In the recent period of reserve expansion, international loans have permitted a number of countries that would otherwise have had overall balance of payments deficits, including the United States, to avoid disinflation and also currency depreciation. These countries spent the liquid assets they acquired abroad as they borrowed them. Countries that then accumulated and held the reserves tended to experience inflation in the process and were put in a position to permit still more inflation. Yet to the extent that Germany and Japan—major accumulators of reserves among the industrialized countries—are unlikely to take the lead in demand-expansive policies in the near future and that some oil-exporting countries will convert their reserves to goods and services at a limited pace, the reserves created to date do not constitute a threat of early inflationary monetary expansion that is a multiple of the reserve growth. Ratios of reserves to global money supplies are likely to be higher in the future than in the past.[18]

A substantial literature has developed in recent years concerning optimal reserve levels for countries and for the world. A comparison of the cost to a country of holding assets in internationally liquid form (rather than as real capital) with the cost of being without liquid reserves (having to adjust) is usually the basis for such studies.[19] None of these approaches explains very well, however, the massive voluntary reserve accumulations of recent years. It appears that a measure of optimal reserves for a country has neither good predictive value nor normative content unless it takes into account the country's internal income distribution objectives that become reflected in the country's exchange rate policies.

In subsequent chapters the theme recurs that both inflation control and the maintenance of a liberal trading system depend on governments' exercising restraint in their efforts directly and indirectly to manage the exchange rates. The surplus country foreign exchange accumulations that have been considered in this chapter

[18] For a similar position, see Gottfried Haberler, "How Important is Control over International Reserves?" in Robert A. Mundell and Jacques J. Polak, *The New International Monetary System* (New York: Columbia University Press, 1978).

[19] See, for example, H. Robert Heller, "Optimal International Reserves," *Economic Journal*, vol. 76 (June 1966), pp. 296-311; Peter B. Clark, "Optimum International Reserves and the Speed of Adjustment," *Journal of Political Economy*, vol. 78 (March 1970), pp. 356-76; F. Steb Hipple, *The Disturbances Approach to the Demand for International Reserves*, Princeton Studies in International Finance, no. 35 (International Finance Section, Princeton University, 1974); and H. G. Grubel, "The Demand for International Reserves: A Critical Review of the Literature," *Journal of Economic Literature*, vol. 9 (December 1971), pp. 1148-66.

are one instrument for such management, and deficit country foreign exchange liquidation and borrowing are of course others. Indeed, since 1973 a trickle of private financing of balance of payments deficits has turned into a torrent. This flood of international credit, in which the large banks have played a critical intermediary role, is the subject of the next chapter.

7
The Flood of International Credit

The worldwide inflation of the 1970s has been made possible by an enormous expansion of credit within and between nations. The international loans have facilitated the maintenance of high growth rates in a number of developing countries and have provided many countries a period in which to adjust their economies to the circumstances of quadrupled petroleum prices. The loans also, however, have contributed to the inflation by providing balance of payments financing at given exchange rates, permitting the excess demands of a deficit country to spill into foreign markets, and they have accentuated price distortions that exchange rate adjustments would have eliminated. This chapter concentrates on the relationship between the loans and inflation.

One matter to be considered is an allegation that the Eurobanks —engaged in borrowing and lending currencies external to the countries of their residence—have made a unique contribution to inflation through generating liquidity that has not been adequately taken into account in any nation's monetary policies. It will be of interest to see if the development of Eurobanking can be blamed, on such grounds, for the exceptional virulence inflation has exhibited.

Also considered will be the growth of IMF lending activities in recent years, a large part of which has been related to the need for financing the petroleum-related trade imbalances. In a world that has turned to managed exchange rate flexibility one would expect a decline in the IMF's balance of payments financing role. It will emerge from this chapter and the next that there is in fact one exception to this generalization, and that is where financial markets are too underdeveloped to play their appropriate part in buffering predictably reversible balance of payments disturbances. The exception, however, should not be allowed to cloud the general rule.

The dramatically increased engagement of the large banks in the United States and Europe in international lending since the mid-1960s has raised apprehensions that those institutions have taken credit risks that put them in danger of failing in epidemic fashion and of dragging the economy of the Western world with them. The position of the banks in this regard needs to be considered to get a feel for the risks to which society is exposed.

Some views that emerge from this chapter are that while the financing of economic development is vital and must be cultivated, financing to maintain an inflationary rate of growth in world aggregate demand and unduly to sustain petroleum-related and other payments imbalances should not be sought. It is therefore important to sort out the purposes that international lending should be serving. While all loans are in some degree fungible so that control of their specific purposes does not necessarily control the ways in which funds are finally used, influence on the purposes for which external funds are made available can have some value. On the level of lending by international organizations, one can conclude that more multilateral official financing should be directed into the World Bank and other agencies dedicated to developmental funding as opposed to the IMF where the primary concern is the financing of balance of payments deficits. In private lending, the regulation of loans by purpose is less feasible because of the multinationalization of banking in the Eurocurrency market. Here, however, one can still say that restraint by the U.S. Federal Reserve authorities of Federal Reserve credit, the controllable component of the chief currency of international settlement, can be an effective restraint on the size of world dollar portfolios. It is therefore of value as an inflation restraint for the world as a whole as well as for the United States in particular. Restraint by the Federal Reserve is also imperative to ensure that the United States is not victimized by future flight from the dollar.

Eurobanks and the Inflation

Before the late 1950s, Eurobanking—the practice of accepting deposits and making loans in a currency external to the residence of the bank—was virtually unknown.[1] A supply of dollars that could be

[1] Two recent helpful studies of the Eurocurrency market are E. Wayne Clendenning, *The Euro-dollar Market* (London: Oxford University Press, 1970); and Ronald I. McKinnon, *The Eurocurrency Market*, Essays in International Finance, no. 125 (International Finance Section, Princeton University, December 1977).

used by European banks in this way seems to have arisen as a result of the search by holders of dollars for a placement which would make funds yield a return greater than that permitted in the United States by the Federal Reserve's Regulation Q. The supply was accentuated by the desire on the part of eastern European governments to hold liquid international assets in dollar denomination in Western Europe for security reasons. As a demand for the funds was found in financing trade and development, other governments, banks, and multinational corporations found the unregulated Eurobank interest rates attractive and shifted their deposits from U.S. to offshore banks. Eurobanking burgeoned when the British and American governments took steps, for balance of payment reasons, to limit the international lending of their currencies by their own residents. British constraints on external sterling loans in the 1960s caused British banks to expand their operations in dollars and then in other external currencies. And the U.S. capital export controls—the interest equalization tax on new issues of longer-term securities, the ceilings on foreign direct investment flows, and the Federal Reserve System's controls on overseas lending by banks—contributed to both the demand for and supply of dollar deposits in Europe. Foreign branches and subsidiaries of U.S. corporations turned to offshore sources of finance, often London branches of the New York banks, and at the same time these and other foreign holders of U.S. deposits were induced by Eurobank interest rates and the importance of cementing new banking connections to shift deposits abroad. Banks in the United States found their overseas branches convenient and profitable placements for funds and, on occasions, vital sources of funds.

The gross size of liabilities of banks denominated in external currency in major European countries, the Bahamas, Bahrain, Cayman Islands, Panama, Canada, Japan, Hong Kong, and Singapore, as estimated by Morgan Guaranty Trust Company, grew from essentially nothing at the beginning of the 1960s to $110 billion at the end of 1970 and to $660 billion by the end of 1977. Excluding interbank deposits, the net size of the market, according to Morgan Guaranty Trust, was in December 1977 $380 billion, an amount exceeding the narrowly defined U.S. money supply.[2] Nearly 80 percent of those deposits are in dollars, and all are time deposits of short to intermediate maturity. Only large deposits are accepted. Approximately two-thirds of the liabilities reported by London banks to the Bank

[2] Each country reports total external currency liabilities to nonresident depositors. See Morgan Guaranty Trust Company of New York, *World Financial Markets*, and also Bank for International Settlements, *Annual Reports*.

of England in November 1977 had maturities less than three months, and another fourth had maturities between three months and one year. The market for Eurocurrencies can be thought of as a worldwide wholesale market for nearly liquid international claims, denominated in a few internationally acceptable currencies.

An aspect of Eurocurrency markets that attracted much attention in the late 1960s and early 1970s was the degree to which such banking activities were multiplying credit, possibly outside the surveillance of any of the national monetary authorities, and thereby fostering worldwide inflation. In an attack on the view that the reported growth in outstanding Eurodollar deposits had to be explained in terms of deficits in the U.S. balance of payments or other reallocations of an existing stock of dollars, Milton Friedman pointed out in 1967 that some proportion of recorded Eurodollars was certainly the product of nothing more than the "stroke of the bookkeeper's pen."[3] Friedman and some others saw Eurodeposits as arising from a process of credit multiplication not unlike that for a relatively closed banking system in a single national economy. In this view, one bank's loans provide another bank's reserves and deposits until the system's liabilities become several times the assets constituting the system's primary reserve medium. The view that the Eurobanks were creating bank deposits led naturally to additional suspicions that here was a money creation process outside the jurisdiction, and perhaps even the consciousness, of the world's monetary authorities. Many observers agreed when Arthur Laffer proposed that the growth in the global money stock had to be seen as the growth of nationally reported money stocks *plus* the growth in Eurocurrencies.[4]

One effort to understand the Eurocurrency markets consisted of efforts to calculate the multiple of dollar deposits created by Eurobanks on the basis of the banks' dollar holdings, or increments to their holdings, in the United States.[5] Results varied widely, but it is probably fair to say that as a result of such studies additional

[3] Milton Friedman, "The Euro-Dollar Market: Some First Principles," *Morgan Guaranty Survey*, October 1967.

[4] Arthur Laffer, "Global Money and Inflation," *Wall Street Journal*, September 23, 1975.

[5] See, for example, Michele Fratianni and Paolo Savona, "International Liquidity: An Analytical and Empirical Interpretation," and Rainer S. Masera, "Deposit Creation, Multiplication and the Eurodollar Market," in Guido Carli and others, *A Debate on the Eurodollar Market*, Quaderni di Ricerche, no. 11 (Rome: Ente per gli Studi Monetare, Bancare e Finanziari Luigi Einaudi, 1972); also John Hewson and Eisuke Sakakibara, "The Eurodollar Deposit Multiplier: A Portfolio Approach," *IMF Staff Papers* (July 1974).

weight has been given to the view that increments to the stock of U.S. dollar deposits held by Eurobanks are unlikely to result in large increments to net Eurobank dollar liabilities. Loans made by Eurobanks do not need to return to the same or other Eurobanks where they can be loaned again—that is, there is substantial leakage from the Eurobanking sector of the money markets. In addition, any decline in Eurodollar interest rates resulting from a transfer of deposits from U.S. banks to Eurobanks induces some offsetting outflow of the Eurodollar market's potential credit base.[6] Increasingly, the banks dealing in Eurocurrencies have been recognized as simply a sector of the worldwide financial market, highly sensitive to relative credit conditions in other sectors and capable of only a small amount of the system independence that might characterize a more closed banking arrangement.[7]

Careful analysis has indicated, too, that only a small fraction of the size of the Eurodollar market can constitute claims that are not counted in one or another country's money supply statistics. Hence, caution is required in contending that growth in Eurodollars is to be added to growth in national money supplies to obtain proper estimates of world monetary growth.[8] Eurodollar deposits held by governments and central banks, for example, are not to be counted as money supply in the hands of the public, and Eurodollar deposits that have arisen from shifts of U.S. deposits to Eurobanks and from conversions of other currencies into dollars for Eurobank deposit have a counterpart banking claim in the country whose currency was converted. The chief process through which Eurocurrency liabilities to nongovernments and nonbanks have been created without giving rise to corresponding claims in other currencies consists of cases in which Eurobanks have made loans to nonresident nonbanks in a currency external to the country of the borrower. Additions to the

[6] John Hewson and Eisuke Sakakibara, *The Eurocurrency Markets and Their Implications: A "New" View of International Monetary Problems and Monetary Reform* (Lexington: D.C. Heath, 1975).

[7] Fratianni and Savona obtained multiplier estimates as low as 1.87 and as high as 7.68 for total Eurodollar deposits relative to the Eurobank system's total international monetary base when different proxies for the monetary base were used. Their multipliers, however, were not the incremental multiplier, which Fred Klopstock (*The Euro-Dollar Market: Some Unresolved Issues*, Essays in International Finance, no. 65 [International Finance Section, Princeton University, March 1968]) thought to be near unity and possibly less. The Hewson and Sakakibara multipliers, which recognized interest rate leakages, were smaller, ranging from 0.63 to 1.61.

[8] In fact, all European countries regularly reporting data to the BIS include external currency *holdings* of their residents in their broader monetary aggregates but not in the narrowly defined money supply.

world's stock of short-term claims from this source have been estimated at $50 billion as of 1974–1975 by Helmut W. Mayer, of the Bank for International Settlements, and at about $31 billion by Richard J. Sweeney and Thomas D. Willett, formerly of the U.S. Treasury.[9] While these sums are large, they are hardly alarming when one considers that the Eurocurrency deposits consist of time deposits in large denominations which then must be thought of as a component of one of the more broadly defined global monetary aggregates like M_4. They probably are not at this time more than 2 to 3 percent of such an aggregate.

Still another aspect of the contribution of Eurocurrencies to inflation concerns the amount of the maturity transformation in which the Eurobanks have engaged.[10] As indicated in Chapter 5, financial intermediaries help enhance spending by their role in transforming the public's claims on the more distant future into claims of short maturity. In creating liquidity, they increase the spendability of the community's wealth. The Eurobanks, however, have not engaged in a great deal of maturity transformation. Rather, presumably to ensure their own safety, they have sought as much as possible to match the maturities as well as the currency denominations of their claims with their liabilities. Table 9 shows that 68 percent of London bank external currency deposits in November 1977 were very short term (less than three month's maturity) but that 53 percent of bank claims were also very short term. At the other end, 23 percent of the banks' claims were intermediate term (one year or more) but 6 percent of the deposit liabilities were also of intermediate maturity. Thus, not more than 15 to 17 percent of the Eurobank assets and liabilities included in that report had been transformed from a maturity of more than one year to a maturity of less than three months.

These matters suggest that the activities in the Eurocurrency markets have not contributed to the decade-long worldwide inflationary process very differently than have the lending activities that have taken place through other institutional arrangements. International lending through all channels has contributed to inflation by

[9] Helmut W. Mayer, "The Net Size of the Euro-currency Market, and Its Relation to the World Money Supply" (Bank for International Settlements, Monetary and Economic Department, February 1976; processed); and Richard J. Sweeney and Thomas D. Willett, "Eurodollars, Petrodollars and World Liquidity and Inflation," in *Stabilization of the Domestic and International Economy*, Carnegie-Rochester Conference Series on Public Policy, vol. 5, a supplement to *Journal of Monetary Economics* (New York: North Holland, 1977), pp. 277-311.

[10] The argument of this paragraph follows Jürg A. Niehans and John Hewson, "The Eurodollar Market and Monetary Theory," *Journal of Money, Credit, and Banking*, February 1976, pp. 1-27.

TABLE 9

RELATIVE MATURITIES OF EUROBANK CLAIMS AND LIABILITIES
1974–1977
(percent)

	1974		*1975*		*1976*		*1977*	
Maturities	Liabilities	claims	Liabilities	claims	Liabilities	claims	Liabilities	claims
Less than three months	71	59	65	54	68	55	68	53
Three months to less than one year	22	21	28	23	25	22	26	24
One year and more	7	21	7	24	7	24	6	23

NOTE: Columns may not add up to 100 percent because of rounding.
SOURCE: Calculated from Bank of England *Quarterly Bulletin*, November date balances.

recycling currencies of international settlement from surplus to deficit countries, by adding more liquidity to the positions of borrowers than was being denied ultimate lenders, and by permitting the multiplication of national currencies, perhaps especially in countries with balance of payments deficits, to a degree that might not otherwise have been possible. The Eurobanks were not unique. They were only one sector in an increasingly integrated worldwide money and capital market.

An important factor in the growth of the Eurocurrency market was the freedom of the banks from regulation of their external currency activities. Exempted from reserve requirements, deposit insurance premiums, interest rate ceilings, and other costly regulations on externally denominated liabilities, the Eurobanks have had a competitive edge in their dollar loan and deposit activities over U.S.-domiciled banks and over other countries' banks in the business denominated in those countries' respective home currencies. The Eurobanks have been able to attract deposits with premium interest rates while remaining highly competitive in their lending rates. Had not the U.S. banks been able to participate in the market through their overseas branches, and had banks in other countries not been able to participate through their home offices as well as their branches, banks in many countries would undoubtedly have pleaded for protection from the unregulated competition. As it is, the pleas for Eurobank regulation have come not from the banking community but from observers concerned that excessive Eurocurrency credit creation may lead to failure by some of the banks and that Eurocurrency credit has been and will be inflationary.[11]

It is widely agreed that regulation of banking in external currency will not be an easy matter since the physical location of such banks is largely immaterial to the conduct of their business. New York banks, for example, exploit their branches not only in London but in the Bahamas, in the Cayman Islands, and elsewhere in order to escape the burden of U.S. regulations and taxes. European banks similarly employ their overseas branches. The U.K. government has up to now resisted pleas that Eurocurrency banking in London—the heart of the market—be regulated on the ground that British regulations would only drive the business elsewhere. Clearly, only a nearly universal agreement among countries concerning regulations could make new rules effective if market participants found the rules onerous.

[11] See, for example, Guido Carli, "The Eurodollar Market and its Control," in Carli, *A Debate on the Eurodollar Market*, pp. 5-20.

In view of the matters considered above, efforts to regulate Eurobanking activities through specific restrictions do not appear to be a very productive use of the time of monetary experts at the end of the 1970s. Securing and maintaining the cooperation among competitive nation states necessary to make controls effective is probably impossible. Furthermore, to date, there is little evidence that the Eurobanks have played a large role in inflation other than the important role of financial intermediaries, collecting funds from points in the world where they are in excess supply and placing them where they are in excess demand. The rapidity with which funds can be withdrawn from any bank in a period of speculation or uncertainty, together with the absence of any guarantee that there is a lender of last resort for the market, seems to have inhibited the banks from lending long and borrowing short. When in 1974 the flood of OPEC funds seeking short-term deposits had to be matched against borrower demands for longer-term loans, short dollar interest rates fell relative to long until the maturity transformation required of the banks became modest.

The Eurobank loans have facilitated the continuance of expansive monetary policies by governments of borrowing countries and have sustained exchange rate relationships that would otherwise not have been viable. Still, Eurobanks are not alone in this activity; indeed, Eurobanking materialized out of earlier governmental efforts to control loan flows in domestic currencies from leading national monetary centers, efforts subsequently abandoned.

Control of inflation requires effective regulation of the money supplies for which national governments are responsible. Specific lending of dollars and other currencies of international settlement for balance of payments purposes can and should be discouraged. But quantitative rather than qualitative credit restraint in both the United States and other countries is in the end necessary.

Credit restraint by the U.S. Federal Reserve System can be especially effective in a dollar-centered world and is called for on both international and domestic grounds. Probably only restraint in U.S. money supply growth can be an effective constraint at this time on worldwide dollar intermediation. Furthermore, in the background is always the fact that unless U.S. credit restraint is successful in preventing chronic dollar depreciation, flight from the dollar by the currency's holders will accelerate the depreciation, bring the dollar-centered system to an end, and impose traumatic inflation on the United States. This sobering line of thought is considered further in Chapter 9.

Balance of Payments Financing by the IMF

The private financial market has not been the sole source of financing for payments imbalances in the early and middle 1970s. The International Monetary Fund, national governments, and even the institutions devoted to developmental finance have also played a part. The IMF has extended both its own resources, a measure which expands the worldwide monetary base, and borrowed resources, a measure which may or may not have net monetary consequences.

In the short three years between April 1974 and April 1977, member countries' outstanding drawings on the IMF's resources quadrupled from less than $4 billion to more than $16 billion. Approximately $6.9 billion of this more than $12 billion of net drawings on the Fund were made under the oil facility established in 1974 to ease the financing of international payments imbalances arising from increases in world petroleum prices. The remainder was due largely to use of the compensatory financing facility in 1976–1977 and to members' drawings on their credit tranches in the Fund.

The oil facility was originally to be financed largely by IMF borrowings from oil-exporting countries, but in the end it was financed largely by borrowings from Canada and countries in Western Europe. The sales to Fund members of the currencies the Fund borrowed are repurchased as each member's balance of payments need ends, and in any case within seven years. The users of the facility pay interest charges near what market rates were at the time the loans were initiated, and these payments are matched by similar Fund interest payments on its borrowings. In effect, the Fund interposed its own credit between that of borrowing countries and those who were lenders. The 1974 facility was extended with new financing through 1975, but lending under the program came to an end in May 1976.[12]

[12] Because lenders were governments and central banks, any part of the funds provided by them to the IMF that arose from additions to central bank liabilities or the drawing down of claims by one central bank on another represented the creation of a monetary base suitable for supporting further commercial bank credit in the currency provided. When borrowing governments then sold the proceeds of the loans in foreign exchange markets, however, equivalent amounts of monetary base were destroyed in the currencies of those countries. In the degree that governments spent the proceeds of the loans without selling them in exchange markets, the loans created monetary base for the world. When loans to the IMF were financed by member government borrowing in private capital markets, the implementation of the oil facility in the Fund did not contribute directly to monetary expansion but may have contributed to public debt outstanding. In view of the various possible monetary consequences, it seems a fair presumption that the oil facility made only a limited direct contribution to global money supplies. Nevertheless, it was inflationary insofar as it made

Total use of Fund resources other than the oil facility grew between April 1974 and April 1977 from just over $3.5 billion outstanding to $9.5 billion. All this growth took place in use of the compensatory financing facility and in credit tranche drawings by members, aggregate use of gold tranche drawings declining slightly in the period. Use of the compensatory facility, which is outside the credit tranches of member drawing rights in the Fund, increased markedly in 1976 and 1977, partly as a result of the falling off of commodity prices and partly as a result of the liberalization of access to this facility.[13]

The increase in Fund quotas from $29.2 to $39 billion in conjunction with the comprehensive amendment to the Fund charter and the increase that is expected as a result of the seventh general review of quotas completed in 1978 will, of course, make possible further extensions of the Fund's activities. In addition, in 1977 the managing director of the IMF, Johannes Witteveen, took the lead in seeking some $17 billion of still further credits to the IMF from balance of payments surplus countries to restore the Fund's supplies of certain currencies and to provide leeway for additional balance of payments financing. By mid-1977 this effort had been scaled down to the neighborhood of $10 billion but was declared to be viable on the basis of pledges received. The supplementary credit facility—popularly called the Witteveen facility—was a repetition of the intermediary role for the Fund that was pioneered with the oil facility. It was again viewed as temporary and as operating by the establishment of lines of credit for those countries approved to draw on it under suitable conditions. Market-related interest rates were again to be paid by the Fund to those from whom it borrowed and to be charged to those who used the facility.

The reduced role for balance of payments financing that seems called for in a world with flexible exchange rates calls into question

---

international settlement currencies available to countries in balance of payments deficit and thereby made possible the continuation of demand expansion programs that could not otherwise have been sustained in those countries with given exchange rates.

[13] From 1966 members had been permitted to draw up to 25 percent of quota under the facility in one year and up to 50 percent altogether without impairing ordinary drawing rights; from December 1975 those ceilings were respectively raised to 50 and 75 percent, and the calculation of the export shortfall was simplified so as to shorten the wait before a borrower's eligibility could be established. Member use of the Fund's compensatory facility, the buffer stock facility, the extended fund facility, and ordinary drawing rights all added directly to the world's money supply and its monetary base when the drawings were not sold against the domestic currencies of the drawers.

these extensions of IMF capability. The extensions have been justified largely on the ground that the overall petroleum-related deficit was unresponsive to exchange rate changes. Thus, the short-run policy alternatives would be either aggregate demand curtailment by petroleum-importing countries, on the one hand, or import restrictions that could spread in a chain reaction, on the other, if financing were not available. While this view was probably an appropriate one for 1974 and 1975, it was less attractive by 1977–1978. By then, pressure on countries to complete their adjustment to the changed unit prices of petroleum seemed called for.

It is certainly clear, for example, that the size of the oil-related global balance of payments disequilibrium has always been influenced by the amount of multilateral financing available. Not only has the financing made possible a delay in adjustments in oil-importing countries, but it has also made possible some of the oil price increases announced by the petroleum-selling cartel. If buyers were faced with more effective constraints on the external financing of their balance of payments deficits, oil exporters would have to choose among greater bilateral financing of their export surpluses, more competitive pricing in a limited market, and production cutbacks. While some oil exporters would presumably give strong weight to production cutbacks in their response to a less ebullient international credit market, others would elect to increase price competition and bilateral financing as part of their policy mix. The latter responses would be helpful elements in an overall adjustment.

The discussion of need for balance of payments financing should in particular not be confused with nations' need for foreign aid. For poor countries as well as rich can and should over reasonable periods limit their current account deficits to the flows of developmental capital available to them. In general, foreign aid is best administered by the agencies designed for raising and apportioning development finance and not by agencies designed for temporary balance of payments financing.

These observations, coupled with the conclusion of Chapter 3 that official interventions to prevent movements of the exchange rates should rarely if ever be protracted, suggest that extensions of official international resources for balance of payments financing should in the future be looked upon skeptically. The continuation of expansive financing risks unnecessary protraction of worldwide inflationary forces and also perpetuation of the petroleum-related world trade disequilibrium.

An exception to which attention will be given in the next chapter is the case of some compensatory financing of balance of payments deficits because of temporary shortfalls of export earnings in developing countries. Here the underdeveloped state of local financial markets may impede flows of private short-term funds that in other countries play a role in stabilizing the exchange rate. This imperfection of market institutions opens a role that in other circumstances would be inappropriate for IMF financing.

The Risk Exposure of International Banks

Outstanding international loans of banks in eleven industrial countries, including U.S. banks and their overseas branches, increased more than fourfold, from $61 billion to $261 billion, between 1970 and 1975. The lending rate continued to expand in 1976 and 1977. The U.S. banks and their branches have retained a share in this loan aggregate that is just under 40 percent.[14] This enormous credit expansion, combined with credit growth in banks' domestic markets, has raised questions about the exposure of the banking system to risks of creditor default and about whether the expansion can continue and what the consequences might be of a slowdown in the expansion rate. The fact that developing countries which are not oil exporters obtained some $60 billion of bank credit between 1970 and the end of 1976 has, in the minds of many, added to the apprehension with which the buildup has been viewed. It has been easy to recall the specter of the international banking crisis of 1931 when a bank failure in Vienna spread fears to Western Europe and then to North America that finally led to widespread bank closings in a number of countries. In the discussion that follows the internationalization of the loan portfolios of the large banks is first considered and then attention is given to the significance of a slowing in the growth of the international credits.

Are Banks Overexpanded? The inflationary environment of the 1970s in which banks took advantage of growing stocks of reserve money to extend loans and make investments reduced for a time the ratio of bank net worth to assets—a traditional measure of the security bank stockholders provide to bank depositors. In the United States, that ratio declined from 7.1 percent in 1969 to 6.5 percent in June 1974 before improving to the neighborhood of 7.3 percent in Septem-

[14] *IMF Survey*, August 16, 1976, p. 242.

ber 1977. The decline in 1974–1975 in this and other balance sheet ratios thought to indicate bank safety was highlighted by a spate of bank failures that was out of line with the low failure rate of a prior thirty-year period. The fifteen U.S. banks that failed, or were forced to merge with larger banks, between September 1974 and November 1975 included the largest bank ever to fail in U.S. history, the Franklin National Bank of New York with assets of $3.6 billion. The failure of prominent banks in Europe, of which the largest was the I. D. Herstatt Bank of Cologne, and the known involvement of U.S. and British banks in the continental banks that failed heightened the concern. Scandals in the Chiasso branch of the Swiss Credit Bank in 1977 extended the feeling that the banks had perhaps become unsafe.

While it cannot be said that banks are out of the woods in the rebuilding of their creditworthiness, there has been improvement in their capital positions. U.S. banks have bulwarked depositor security since 1972 by raising an average of $3.1 billion of additional capital per annum through stock issues, reinvested earnings, and borrowing in terms subordinated to the rights of depositors. Equity and subordinated debt of insured U.S. banks grew by 67.5 percent between June 1973 and September 1977, while deposits grew only 56.7 percent. In strengthening their capital positions, banks have depended heavily on the reinvestment of profits and on debt financing in order to avoid diluting ownership and control, especially in view of the depressed state of the equity market. Since the 1960s they have been permitted to treat subordinated debt as part of capital. Although admittedly debt is inferior to equity as a security pledge to depositors, for debt requires that fixed interest and amortization charges be met if the bank is to remain solvent while equity capital does not, the use of subordinated debt has made possible the strengthening of some banks' liquidity positions.

In all countries official regulations aim at limiting bank risk. In the United States, for example, the maximum loan a bank can make to one customer is restricted to a fraction of the bank's capital. Banks are restricted from buying corporate stock; their real estate loans are restricted; and they are regularly examined for the quality of their assets and their management. The prohibition of payment of interest on demand deposits and the ceilings on interest on time deposits are intended to reduce banks' incentives to acquire high risk assets.

In recent years, some U.S. regulations have been eased in the interest of greater flexibility in bank portfolio management. Interest rate ceilings were removed on deposits of $100,000 or more, causing leading banks to turn increasingly to the use of large denomination certificates of deposit for funds. Such funds must be considered more volatile for a given bank than a large number of smaller deposits because they come and go in large blocks, because they exceed the maximum for which there is deposit insurance, and because they are professionally managed by depositors who are likely to be more knowledgeable and quicker to respond to changes in bank and credit market conditions than small depositors would be. Limits on lending to single customers were raised for many banks in the 1960s; national banks were given more freedom in making real estate loans; the ability of national banks to invest in general obligation bonds of state and municipal governments was eased; and, as indicated above, national banks were permitted to count subordinated long-term debt as part of the capital that sets limits on individual and real estate loans.[15]

Whether the present circumstances of bank regulation and bank capital provide the optimal mix of balance sheet safeguards and portfolio flexibility for the United States is difficult to say. What is important is to recall that depositor safety in the system as a whole is, in the end, provided by the willingness and ability of the central bank to monetize commercial bank assets in an emergency, rather than by the particular asset and liability structures of individual banks. Few legal restrictions any longer impair the ability of the U.S. Federal Reserve Banks to loan federal funds to commercial banks against assets that would otherwise be illiquid. And as long as the lender of last resort is willing to lend, the desire of depositors to convert their bank deposits into Federal Reserve Notes need not be frustrated. In the international community, indeterminacy about the role of the lender of last resort raises some problems with respect to international banking that are not inherently critical for domestic banking.

Is the Internationalization of Credit Dangerous? The extent of the involvement of large U.S. banks in international lending received a great deal of publicity after 1974. The announcement that more than half of Chase Manhattan Bank's loans were outstanding to foreign, rather than domestic, borrowers was treated by news media with some alarm. Citicorp of New York revealed in its annual report for 1975 that 58 percent of its fourth quarter 1975 average loans

[15] See R. Alton Gilbert, "Bank Failures and Public Policy," Federal Reserve Bank of St. Louis *Review*, November 1975, pp. 1-6.

were outstanding to foreign borrowers while 29 percent of total loans were foreign currency denominated. It also indicated that more than two-thirds of the bank holding company's earnings came from outside the United States. The firm then devoted a substantial portion of its report to discussion of its control of the quality of its foreign loans. Confidence of the public in these developments was not enhanced when it was revealed by the *Washington Post* in 1976 that both Chase Manhattan and Citibank, along with some other very large banks, were on the comptroller of the currency's list of "problem" banks getting especially close surveillance, although it subsequently became clear that the banks' problems were related more to domestic than to international activities.

The large money market center banks were not the only ones increasingly involved in international lending, although they dominated the field. Whereas in 1967 only 15 U.S. banks had overseas branches, by 1975 that number was 126, and the number of branches had grown from 295 to 762.[16] A number of the larger banks in the Midwest, South, Southwest, and Far West of the United States were reaching out to share in a lucrative market.

There is reason to believe that the internationalization of the operations of large banks in Europe, North America, and Asia has not been accompanied by a deterioration in the stability of the international banking structure. For one thing, the risk of complete default by borrowers is somewhat reduced because no more than fifty banks in the United States and an equal number in Europe hold the majority of the international loans to nonbanks, and cooperation among lenders and borrowers to minimize default risks and to arrange necessary debt rescheduling is now in some degree institutionalized. Furthermore, it may be better recognized today than it was in the 1930s that markets must be open to the products of debtor countries if the latter are to earn the foreign exchange they need to make debt service payments. In any event, the internationalization of the loan portfolios of individual banks has permitted diversification in those portfolios that purely domestic operations would not allow.

A study of loan loss ratios for domestic and international loans of ten large U.S. banks, 1962–1971, found that the banks' losses as a percentage of loans were lower for foreign than for domestic loans. It also concluded that the loss ratio on the foreign loans was less variable and hence presumably more predictable than the domestic

[16] Andrew Brimmer, "International Finance and the Management of Bank Failures," paper presented at annual meeting of American Economic Association, Atlantic City, N.J., December 1976.

ratio.[17] A study of the 1974–1975 loan experience of 780 U.S. banks engaged in domestic lending and 110 engaged in foreign lending showed similar results. Net charge-offs for losses on domestic loans came out to be 0.36 and 0.74 percent of the total of domestic loans for the years 1974 and 1975, respectively, and only 0.08 and 0.15 percent for foreign loans.[18]

The banks have also gone through a process of learning to live with flexible exchange rates. Whereas the spectacular 1974 failures of the Franklin Bank in New York and the Herstatt Bank in Germany involved heavy losses in foreign exchange trading, and other banks reported large foreign exchange losses in that year, much greater caution has marked bank activity since that time. Open positions permitted to foreign exchange traders have probably been reduced at all banks, and greater attention is given to country and currency exposure in overall bank portfolios. While the Herstatt Bank had made a brief and, for a time, widely envied reputation for success in uncovered foreign exchange activities, the lesson of its collapse was not lost on the banking community.

It is worth remembering, too, that the international loans of banks do not necessarily represent bank exposure to foreign exchange rate risk. Citicorp, for example, in its 1975 annual report pointed out that "over half of our loans abroad involve lending within a country to a borrower in his own currency. . . . The local currency asset is generally offset by a locally acquired liability in the same currency, limiting exposure to normal credit factors."

Concern with risks peculiar to international borrowing and lending has led the bank supervisory agencies in the United States—the Office of the Comptroller of the Currency, the Federal Deposit Insurance Corporation, and the Board of Governors of the Federal Reserve System—to instigate, beginning in 1978, a semiannual "Country Exposure Report" for banks in order to increase information on foreign lending on a country-by-country basis. The agencies have also cooperated in the development of procedures to strengthen supervision of the international aspects of banking.[19] The Bank for International Settlements and the World Bank have made especially great strides toward improving current information on the debtor-creditor status of nations, debt service schedules, and lending terms and conditions.

[17] Fred B. Ruckdeschel, "Risk in Foreign and Domestic Lending Activities of U.S. Banks," Board of Governors of the Federal Reserve System, International Finance Discussion Papers, no. 66, July 30, 1975.

[18] Robert Morris Associates, reported in *IMF Survey*, August 16, 1976, p. 245.

[19] Federal Reserve Bank of New York *Quarterly Review*, vol. 3, Spring 1978, pp. 1-7.

Still somewhat enigmatic, nonetheless, is the matter of the responsibility of national central banks in a web of financial relationships that has increasingly been built out of assets and liabilities denominated in external currencies. In recent years, the largest international loans have been syndicated among banks of several lending nations, perhaps sometimes in the currency of none of them, and with the participation of banks which are in turn jointly controlled by banks of several nationalities. The minicrisis of 1974 raised questions as to which central bank or banks had supervisory and lender of last resort responsibilities in the institutional relationships of such character. In particular, was it clear who was responsible for the internationally owned joint venture banks and how the central banks were to deal with liabilities in external currencies? On September 9, 1974, central bankers of the major industrial nations, meeting in Basle, issued a statement which included the following:

> The Governors . . . had an exchange of views on the problem of the lender of last resort in the Euromarkets. They recognized that it would not be practical to lay down in advance detailed rules and procedures for the provision of temporary liquidity. But they were satisfied that means are available for that purpose and will be used if and when necessary.[20]

Subsequently, in testimony before the Senate Permanent Investigations Subcommittee, Governor Henry Wallich of the Federal Reserve Board, said: "The Federal Reserve is prepared, as a lender of last resort, to advance sufficient funds, suitably collateralized, to assure the continued operation of any solvent and soundly managed member bank which may be experiencing temporary liquidity difficulties associated with the abrupt withdrawal of petrodollar—or any other—deposits."[21] It is presumably agreed that in the event of crisis, each country's central bank will stand behind its own banks and the overseas branches of those banks. This leaves liquidity problems to be handled in the way such problems become reflected on the books and in the activities of parent banks. National central banks have responsibility for monetizing the external currency assets as well as the home currency assets of the banks in their respective jurisdictions. This could require a high degree of inter-central bank coordination and particularly a willingness by Federal Reserve authorities to fund Eurodollar assets. The central bank bilateral swap lines would presumably be called on

---

[20] Statement by Governor Henry C. Wallich before the Subcommittee on Investigations, Committee on Operations, U.S. Senate, October 11, 1974; published in *Federal Reserve Bulletin*, vol. 60 (October 1974), p. 760.

[21] Ibid.

here. Other problems, such as those that might arise from the emergency imposition by one or more countries of foreign exchange controls, are also left to be handled as best they can be by central bank cooperation.

Since the stability of the banking structure, on a worldwide as well as country-by-country basis, ultimately depends on the capabilities of the providers of national currencies to monetize the non-liquid assets of banks, the nature of the response the central banks collectively would make to a crisis situation is of the essence. The authority structure within which a suitable response would be designed is less than wholly satisfactory, and the capability of the central banks taken severally, rather than collectively, to respond adequately is open to question. Still, the smallness of the liquidity transformation in which the Eurobanks have engaged limits the external currency risk to which any country is exposed. Furthermore, each central bank has enormous power to provide liquidity to the system in its own currency, and the inter-central bank working relationships are good. These factors are the safeguards for the present global banking system.

Is the Debt of Developing Countries Inferior? Much of the public apprehension concerning the international involvement of U.S. banks has stemmed from the extent of bank lending to developing countries. U.S. bank claims on residents of non-oil-producing developing countries, other than branch bank claims in the country and the currency of the branch operations, reached $40 billion at the close of 1977. Are these claims more subject to default than other bank assets?

First, it must be recognized that large-scale lending by U.S. banks to developing countries did not originate with the petroleum crisis, although it accelerated following the beginning of that period. Before the mid-1960s, lending to developing areas was modest, largely taking the form of trade credit and the financing of raw material development. In the mid-1960s, U.S. multinational corporations, induced to expand their external operations in part by the overvaluation of the dollar, financed their operations through their usual U.S. banking ties, and when the U.S. capital export controls came into force, the firms turned to foreign banks and the overseas branches of their home banks. The U.S. firms were attracted to countries with conservatively managed economies and either low wages or rapidly growing markets or both. After 1973, borrowing by official agencies in developing countries accelerated.

Further, to put the developing country debt in perspective, it is important to remember that the growth of the debt and its service charges partly reflects inflation. While the overall debt of non-oil developing countries more than doubled between 1972 and 1975, from about $75 billion to $180 billion, the dollar prices of developing country imports and exports nearly doubled also. When the nominal debt is deflated by export prices, the "real" debt is shown to increase by only about one-fifth. Furthermore, dollar values of these countries' exports and their combined gross national products grew at about the same rate as their external debt so that the burden of the debt for developing countries, when the countries are taken collectively, did not increase much.

The situation with respect to individual countries, of course, differs. Total service charges on externally held public debt, as a proportion of exports, for example, varied from as low as 0.6 percent for The Gambia to as high as 45.9 percent for Uruguay in 1975. And in the ten countries in which the U.S. stake is especially high, the ratio varied from 2.6 percent in Thailand to 28.9 percent in Chile.[22] Debt service ratios will change in future years as a result of the maturity structure of individual country debt and repayment schedules and changes in export earnings. Some observers expect it to rise, on the average, through 1980. Renewed inflation or deflation in commodity prices, however, could change all that.

About two-thirds of overall non-oil developing country debt at the end of 1976 was public debt, or private debt with a public guarantee, and had a maturity period greater than one year. The proportion of U.S. bank loans with intermediate to long maturity to developing countries, however, was somewhat less than this.

Complete default on any large international loan has been avoided in the late 1960s and 1970s in spite of worldwide recessions and the global payments imbalance related to petroleum. One ingredient in the successful experience has been the continued high supply of loanable funds. Lenders have, for example, normally rescheduled debts that became unsustainable.

The forum for negotiating the rescheduling of publicly held or publicly guaranteed debt involving several governments has usually been a "creditors' club" or the World Bank. Some forty renegotiations of public debt involving eleven debtor countries occurred in twenty-one years, 1956–1977. The form of the negotiations ensures

---

22 Developing country debt to U.S. banks is highly concentrated in a few countries: Mexico and Brazil, together, account for half of it, and eight other countries—Argentina, Chile, Colombia, Peru, Korea, the Philippines, Taiwan, and Thailand—account for a large part of the remainder. Debt service charge ratios are reported in World Bank, *Annual Report*, 1977, table 6, pp. 112-13.

equal treatment among creditor governments. With the exception of numerous reschedulings for India and Pakistan, which were handled through the World Bank, a creditors' club such as the "Paris Club"—one usually chaired by the French Ministry of Finance—has been convened on the application of the debtor after that country has worked out a suitable relationship with the IMF. Typically, debt relief has been conditioned on new debtor performance standards which were then monitored by the IMF. Both debtors and creditors have salvaged something in these renegotiations.[23] Rescheduling of a number of debts to private creditors has paralleled these official negotiations.

When viewed in this context, the debt of developing countries does not yet seem to be cause for alarm. Overall it has grown only a little faster than other main economic magnitudes, and it is hedged with reasonable security. While individual debtor countries may encounter problems, and failure in some countries could create difficulties for some large U.S. or foreign banks, only an extended and widespread recession in industrialized countries would be likely to precipitate extensive defaults. Such an event would certainly stimulate support activities to lending banks by their central banks, regardless of the structure of commercial bank assets, so that reschedulings would likely take the place of outright borrower defaults, and bank depositors would in the large be assured of liquidity.

The Continuing Expansion. The rate of international borrowing continued to grow in 1977 although the growth was slowing compared with 1975 and 1976. Table 10 shows that total borrowing through foreign and international bonds and publicized Eurocurrency credits was of the order of $67.2 billion in 1977, as compared with $63.1 billion in 1976 and $43.4 billion in 1975.

One way of envisioning the whole lending phenomenon is as a vast banking portfolio adjustment process. Banks of the industrialized countries have extended their loans and deposits on a global basis as they have been permitted to do so by the growth in the respective monetary bases of the currencies being loaned. The rise in the ratio of international to domestic loans that accompanied the expansion has represented a major step toward integration of the world's money and capital markets, a process unlikely to cease unless it is set back

[23] See testimony of Under Secretary of State for Economic Affairs Richard N. Cooper before the Subcommittee on International Finance of the Senate Committee on Banking, Housing and Urban Affairs, August 29, 1977, distributed by Department of State, Bureau of Public Affairs, Washington, D.C.

Table 10

BORROWING IN INTERNATIONAL CAPITAL MARKETS, 1974–1977, BY CATEGORY OF BORROWING COUNTRY
(billions of U.S. dollars or equivalent)

	1974	*1975*	*1976*	*1977*
Total foreign borrowing (international bonds and Eurocurrency credits)	40.6	43.4	63.1	67.2
Category of borrowing country				
Developed	23.6	21.4	31.5	32.5
Developing	10.0	13.2	19.5	23.8
Centrally planned	1.2	2.8	2.4	2.6
International organization	5.4	5.4	8.6	7.2
Other	0.4	0.6	1.0	1.2

SOURCE: Data for 1974 and 1975 are as reported in *IMF Survey*, June 6, 1977, Supplement on International Lending. Data for 1976 and 1977 are from *Borrowing in International Capital Markets*, Fourth Quarter, 1977, World Bank Document EC-181-/774, p. 1.

by a series of significant borrower defaults. As the largest money center banks attain the balance they desire between internal and external loans and tend to limit the growth in their external loans to that of their total assets, other banks will step forward to extend the internationalization process in response to attractive foreign-domestic earnings differentials. There is, unfortunately, as yet no slackening in the rate of growth of the monetary base in U.S. dollars.

A slowdown, however, is eminently to be desired. If it occurs, will it precipitate problems such as defaults on outstanding international indebtedness? By no means necessarily so. It has been argued earlier that there is no reason why the petroleum-related balance of payments deficits should not be adjusted rather rapidly now, reducing the need for balance of payments financing. Some countries that have overextended themselves, of course, may become applicants for reschedulings, particularly if there is a decline in the prices of their chief export commodities. Major exporters of copper—Chile, Zaire, Zambia, and Peru—for example, required reschedulings after a 1974–1975 precipitate fall in the world copper price. With a broad commodity price decline, the problem could certainly become more general, necessitating some central bank rescue efforts. But it is significant that developing country debt is concentrated in countries that have relatively strong and diversified economies. These countries also have strong reasons for maintaining their creditworthiness.

At the Paris meetings of the Conference on International Economic Cooperation, 1975–1977, representatives of developing countries pressed hard for steps toward generalized debt forgiveness as a contribution by industrialized countries to a New International Economic Order. The industrialized countries, on the other hand, especially the United States, wisely resisted the plea,not only on self-serving grounds but also on grounds that it would constitute an inappropriate allocation of assistance among both recipient and donor countries and that it would impair the credit of countries that deserve access to the private capital markets in the years immediately ahead. Debt forgiveness and reschedulings should be considered only on a country-by-country basis and only when there is no good alternative.

Summary

The flood of international credit in the 1970s has helped make possible a global inflation of unprecedented magnitude. The private financial markets have by and large functioned in a predictable and efficient way despite official efforts on some occasions to suppress them. Although the recent extraordinary growth in international lending by the largest banks as they have diversified their loan portfolios on a multinational scale may not continue, whatever gap they leave is likely to be filled by other banks which take their turn at international diversification. Only reduction in the growth in the monetary base of the currencies of international settlement, limiting the rate at which overall bank expansion can take place, is likely to slow the extension of bank credit significantly on a worldwide basis. Control of the supply of dollars is especially critical in order to preserve the value of the chief reserve and vehicle currency and to prevent an escalation of dollar depreciation. Should central banks, such as the Federal Reserve authorities in the United States, succeed in enforcing a slowing of the growth in bank reserves and currency in circulation, tendencies for international loans to slow should not then be offset by increased balance of payments lending by official agencies. While slowing the financing of payments deficits will not ensure a reduction in world inflation, it will at least ensure that inflation is more confined inside the countries that generate it by national monetary growth. By intensifying the problem at its source, reduced international financing may then induce corrective measures. International lending should be predicated on opportunities for meaningful capital formation rather than on the state of a borrower's balance of payments. The lending should also be financed without excessive liquidity creation on a global basis; that is, the liquidity of lenders should be reduced in the degree that the liquidity of borrowers is augmented. "Real" lending, of course, need not be impaired by a decline in the growth of nominal credit since the inflation rate in terms of the loanable currency may also subside. These criteria suggest that in forthcoming years the role of the IMF in financing should be limited. An exception is the desirability of some compensatory financing of temporary shortfalls of export earnings by developing countries where inchoate financial markets limit flows of private funds which would otherwise buffer short-run pressures on the exchange rates.

This and other special problems characterizing developing countries and regional blocs are considered in the following chapter.

8
The System and Special Groups of Countries

While increased flexibility in the exchange rates has worked well for many countries, some countries have special problems with flexibility, whether that flexibility affects primarily their own exchange rates or the rates of others. Developing countries, in particular, have expressed concern with the system of floating, but they are not alone. After the introduction of wider bands for rate flexibility, countries of the European Economic Community promptly created the snake, a narrow margins arrangement; and although the membership of that group has fluctuated since 1972, a core of central and northern European countries has appeared to find continuing advantages in it. Other countries have tied their currencies to that of a major trading partner or to some index of currencies, as described in Chapter 1. In addition, various financing arrangements outside the IMF have emerged to serve special needs. Some countries, for example, including most of the industrialized countries and also specialized groups in Africa, Latin America, and Asia, have formalized reciprocal obligations with selected partners in connection with balance of payments financing, usually through central bank lines of credit. And several groups of countries have carefully considered the possible advantages of reserve pooling. This chapter surveys some of these special arrangements and the reasons for them.

The Developing Countries

Recent years have brought increasing awareness of the great heterogeneity in the problems and prospects facing different developing countries. Still, the spokesmen for such countries have with remarkable unanimity been critical of the move to greater exchange rate flexibility, especially flexibility among the currencies of the more industrialized countries. Clearly the new international monetary arrangements touch on several problems which these countries share.

First, a great number of developing countries experience an unusual degree of instability in their export earnings. This is because the range of each such country's exports is typically small and specialized in minerals or agricultural products that are sold in competitive world markets and that experience high price volatility. Developing countries therefore seek international monetary rules that might tend to stabilize (and raise) world market prices for their products.

Second, developing countries have been nearly unanimous in calling for greater stability in internal relative prices. Freely flexible exchange rates between their own and other currencies generate changes between the internal prices of traded and nontraded goods which disturb the planning process and internal political relationships and which allegedly induce little resource reallocation because of the low adaptive ability of the underdeveloped economies. Furthermore, leaders in these countries contend that their institutions for transferring business pricing risks among parties are not sufficiently developed to obtain maximum offsets and to place remaining risk with those having least risk aversion, so that business risks associated with exchange rate movements are especially burdensome. Perhaps even more important, the developing countries have deplored any substantial flexibility among the rates of the countries that are their major trading partners. A rate swing—between the currency of a country which is a major export market and that of one which is a major import supplier, for example—can shift a given developing country's terms of trade significantly. In addition, developing countries feel that their exports and imports are more concentrated by destination and by source than those of more developed countries which have greater product diversification in both production and consumption.[1]

Third, the developing countries have a common interest in open markets in the industrialized world. Many of them have acknowledged that a monetary system that can keep current account imbalances under control in the industrialized countries is an important means of reducing political pressures for import protection there. On these

---

[1] H. Robert Heller has found that five national characteristics, consisting of openness of the economy to trade, smallness of the economy, degree of commodity concentration of exports, degree of integration of local with foreign financial markets, and similarity of home and foreign inflation rates, are rather good predictors of whether countries float or peg their exchange rates. See "Choosing an Exchange Rate System," *Finance and Development* (June 1977), pp. 23-26.

grounds, therefore, they find a certain amount of exchange rate flexibility useful.

Fourth, they have a common interest in increasing the flow of capital and technology from richer to poorer countries. Official aid programs have shown themselves sensitive to the state of the balance of payments of the aid-providing country. Since it is easier to gain support for a program that has already begun than it is to create a new program, developing countries have, on these grounds, too, sensed the desirability of an effective balance of payments adjustment process. Most of all, however, in the international monetary reform negotiations developing countries aimed at obtaining arrangements that involve further capital transfer commitments. Toward this end, they negotiated vigorously to obtain a link between creation of new reserve money in the form of SDRs and transfers to the poorer nations and to obtain aid through other means such as the demonetization of gold and the parallel reduction in internationally held gold stocks.

Finally, there is the outsiders' syndrome. Poorer countries share a sense of being politically and economically unimportant—outside the decision circle and vulnerable to policy decisions that do not fully take account of their interests. They have combined their strength in recent years to obtain greater voting power and broader representation in the International Monetary Fund as well as in the U.N. General Assembly and other international organizations.

Instability of Export Earnings. The instability of primary product prices was well illustrated in the 1972–1977 period. Cacao prices in New York, for example, soared 559 percent, from 31 cents per pound to $2.05 between 1972 and November 1977. Coffee prices (New York) rose from 50.40 cents per pound to $2.46, a gain of 388 percent. Rice (Bangkok) jumped from $147.12 per metric ton in 1972 to $617.08 early in 1974 and then fell by more than half to $264.50 in mid-1977. The New York import price of sugar similarly jumped five times between 1972 and the end of 1974 but then returned to near its 1972 level by the end of 1977. Among the metals, the price of copper in London increased two and a half times between 1972 and the second quarter of 1974, but by the end of 1977 was again near its 1972 average. Tin, meanwhile, rose from $1.71 per pound (London) in 1972 to nearly $4.16, then fell nearly a third to $2.84 in late 1975 before beginning a steady rise that carried it to $5.81

at the close of 1977.[2] Such large dollar price changes implied large changes in dollar foreign exchange earnings for the countries exporting those goods (and of course equally large changes in dollar import costs for the countries which are net importers), although the changes were softened in most countries by some movement of their own exchange rates against the dollar.

Since the 1920s, governments of countries exporting primary products have attempted to gain greater export price stability through international agreements on commodity prices and supplies. Before World War II those agreements were typically cartel-like arrangements among producer countries to restrict supplies reaching the markets with a view to raising as well as stabilizing prices. In the 1940s and 1950s, however, interest developed at the United Nations Food and Agriculture Organization, at the United Nations Secretariat, and at national capitals in favor of commodity agreements that would involve both consuming and producing countries. This approach found a place in chapter 6 of the ill-fated Havana Charter for an International Trade Organization and provided the rationale for subsequent agreements concerning wheat, tin, and coffee and for study groups for various other commodities.

Programs for a New International Economic Order espoused by representatives of developing countries in the U.N. General Assembly and other international gatherings after 1973 inevitably approached price stabilization via commodity agreements for a list of primary products. At the Conference on International Economic Cooperation in Paris, 1975–77, the United States and other industrialized countries finally accepted in principle the creation of a common fund, to which both consumer and producer countries would contribute, to finance buffer stock operations in a list of primary commodities to be determined. Buffer stock operations, which aim to purchase excess supplies of commodities when markets are glutted and to release supplies when markets are tight, are less objectionable than attempts to attain price stability by production restraint or by fixed prices on assured transactions among consuming and producing nations.[3] At least buffer stocks undertake to transfer goods from periods of greater to less abundance, but they, too, are open to serious objection. Their rationale is based on the assumption of alternating periods of shortage and glut, while prices in fact also experience substantial

2 Prices cited for 1972 are the annual average. Data are from IMF *International Financial Statistics*.

3 J. Carter Murphy, "Bulk Purchase International Commodity Agreements," *Journal of Political Economy*, vol. 64, no. 6 (December 1956), pp. 507-19.

trends. It is exceedingly difficult to distinguish cyclical from trend price movements at any point, and failure to do so may result in committing all the buffer stock's resources either to cash or to commodities, thus ending the facility's ability to enter the market on more than one side. Often in the past, producer pressures have resulted in excessive buffer fund support of the market until the fund's resources were entirely committed to commodities. Then, with the cessation of support, the market suffered sharp price declines and had to endure the slow working off of the excessive stockpile, so that in the end little stability was achieved. In recent years the unexpected virulence of inflation has had the opposite effect, transforming buffer stock resources into cash. Estimates based on the actual prices and demand-supply conditions for tin and copper suggest that a buffer fund of perhaps $7 billion would have been necessary to have kept price movements of those two commodities within ±15 percent per year during the 1956–1973 period.[4] Against this large sum, the $3–6 billion mentioned at the Conference on International Economic Cooperation for a common fund to stabilize prices of up to eighteen commodities appears very small. An inadequate fund, however, risks not lasting through a protracted swing or a concerted swing of many commodity prices at once.

It must be remembered that private speculation buffers free market price movements to the extent that the movements can be anticipated and to the extent that storage of stocks will yield an expected rate of return on capital equal to the expected value of capital's alternative uses. It is not clear that it is in the interest of developing nations to see substantial amounts of global capital committed for a purpose that does not meet a market efficiency test.

A more appropriate approach than buffer stocks to the problems of primary commodity exporting countries is the IMF's compensatory finance facility which provides balance of payments financing to countries experiencing deficits because of shortfalls in commodity export earnings. This approach leaves prices free to perform their role of accelerating production and limiting consumption in times

[4] G. Smith and G. Schink, "International Tin Agreement: A Reassessment," Discussion Paper no. 75/18, OASIA Research, U.S. Treasury; M. Desai, "An Econometric Model of the World Tin Economy," *Econometrica*, vol. 34 (January 1966), pp. 105-34; Gordon Smith, "An Economic Evaluation of International Buffer Stocks for Copper," U.S. State Department, Bureau of Intelligence and Research Contract 1722-62008 (August 1965); and Mordechai Kreinin and J. Michael Finger, "A New International Economic Order? A Critical Survey of the Issues," *Journal of World Trade Law*, vol. 10 (November-December 1976), pp. 493-512.

of scarcity and accelerating consumption and limiting production in times of abundance while it permits primary producing countries to experience greater stability of consumption and investment through time. Members of the IMF may now draw on the Fund for up to 75 percent of their quotas under the compensatory financing facility without impairing their eligibility for ordinary general account drawings. The STABEX facility in the Lomé Convention linking forty-six developing nations to the European Economic Community is a similar arrangement for compensatory financing. The amounts available for this purpose remain too small, however, in view of the magnitude of potential financing needs and the underdevelopment of financial markets in primary producing countries that inhibits movements of private buffering funds.

Alternatively, flexibility in the exchange rate of a country specializing in only a few primary products can help stabilize that country's balance of payments and prices in terms of its own currency. Expanding world demand for the country's exports in this circumstance causes its currency to appreciate, dampening the domestic currency measure of the foreign earnings and spreading the enjoyment of the earnings over a wide spectrum of domestic consumers through lowered domestic currency prices of imports. Similarly, declining world demand is cushioned in domestic currency terms by currency depreciation which supports the local currency price of both exports and imports. While exchange rate flexibility does not reduce the impact of external events on the country's import capability in real terms, it can make nominal incomes and prices in the domestic currency more stable through time, and it does spread the effects of the changes more thinly across many domestic interest groups.

Even when the decline in external earnings is caused by adverse domestic supply conditions, such as can be caused by the weather in the case of agricultural commodities, movements of the exchange rate can contribute to the mitigation of some internal problems. If the external demand is price elastic so that the reduced export supply results in reduced foreign exchange earnings, home currency depreciation supports producers' incomes in that currency while it rations the short supply of foreign exchange among consumers. If, of course, external demand is price inelastic so that the short crop turns out to be a boon to producers, currency appreciation will mitigate the producer's gain by causing them to share it with consumers in their own country.

International monetary arrangements, therefore, can alleviate some effects on primary product exporting countries of variations in world market prices. It cannot eliminate the sources of disturbance in supply which are due to changes in the physical or social environment, and it may not reduce the magnitude and rapidity of external demand changes. But it can dilute the effects of such disturbances by spreading the burden through time and over various market participants. Provisions for compensatory finance, in particular, can tide countries over transitory balance of payments problems without delaying too much necessary long-term adjustments. And some flexibility in primary producing country exchange rates can soften the blows and spread the risks in domestic currency terms.

Need for Stability in Relative Prices. Exchange rate changes necessarily affect relative prices as compared with what prices would have been without the exchange rate adjustment, but they do not necessarily upset existing price relationships. To the extent that an exchange rate between any two countries merely compensates for price changes resulting from disparate inflationary conditions between them, the exchange rate adjustment tends to sustain existing price relationships. Nonetheless, developing countries have expressed aversion to the effects of exchange rate movements on relative prices and apparently see them as effects which are more disturbing than accommodating. The problems the exchange rates may pose for relative prices can best be divided into two categories: those that arise from movements in a country's own exchange rate vis-à-vis the rest of the world, and those that arise from movements in the rates between other countries.

Stability in own exchange rate. Movements in the exchange rate of any country where that country is small relative to world markets have the effect of raising and lowering the prices of internationally traded goods, relative to the prices of nontraded goods, in terms of the country's own currency, other things being the same. Because world prices are little affected by the country's adjustment process, the internal prices of the goods the country exports and imports move essentially with the exchange rate; prices of nontraded goods are affected only as a result of secondary adjustments. The change in prices of traded relative to nontraded goods creates inducements for resources to be used more for exports and import replacements, when the change is a currency depreciation, and for resources to be turned away from these uses when the change is an appreciation. These inducements are appropriate for the elimination of payments imbalances. Spokesmen for developing countries contend, however, that limited adjustment capabilities in poor countries inhibit the effectiveness of such incentives and argue that the price changes result chiefly in redistribution of income and wealth. Where many factions are contending for increased shares in a small national product, such redistribution may be a threat to political stability. Furthermore, it is charged that the price changes increase the difficulty of preparing and executing national and regional plans for economic development. In addition, the absence of forward exchange market facilities for shifting the risk of exchange rate movements to professional risk bearers (speculators) is cited as an argument for pegging the rate.

While a large sector within a typical developing country may be "primitive" in character, in that it has only slight interconnections with the cash-oriented economy, the commercial sector of such a country is often quite modern. And in the cash-economy sector of such a country, it is by no means clear that resources are less mobile in response to price inducements than they are in the more developed regions of the world, except that developing countries may be more riddled with oligopoly and that market positions there may be more protected by government regulation than is the case in developed countries. Flexible exchange rates might therefore serve as guides to resource allocation in developing as well as in developed countries were it not for a propensity in developing country governments to regulate and perhaps a propensity among officials there to protect the interests of political allies more than elsewhere.

According to a parallel argument, developing countries are smaller than the optimal size for currency areas because the commercially oriented sector of the economy is very open to international trade. When a large proportion of an area's product is either exported or imported, a depreciation of its currency vis-à-vis the outside world raises most prices internally relative to the prices of the few nontraded goods. The smallness of the nontraded sector ensures that little resource reallocation is induced even while the price level as a whole undergoes substantial dislocation. A part of the theory of optimal currency areas suggests that economies in such circumstances will do well to link their currencies, through the exchange rate, to the currencies of their major trading partners.[5] Recent attention to the monetary approach to the balance of payments, however, suggests an offset to this argument. Emphasizing that an exchange rate change affects the purchasing power of the existing money supply and hence total purchases in real terms, the monetary approach implies that

[5] See Ronald I. McKinnon, "Optimum Currency Areas," *American Economic Review*, vol. 53 (September 1963), pp. 717-24.

in very open economies small changes in the exchange rate should be sufficient to eliminate the real excess demand or supply for money which is pressuring the balance of payments. Hence, open economies may need to experience smaller exchange rate variations through time than more closed economies. The case for an open economy's becoming part of a larger common currency area is therefore weakened.

In connection with the argument that forward exchange markets are essential to efficient risk management and that such markets are usually absent in developing countries, it must be noted that purchase and sale of exchange for forward delivery is not the only way in which international traders can secure a hedge against exchange rate risk. Exchange rate risk arises for international traders and investors when any commitment to pay or receive foreign currency is not offset by a similarly timed commitment to receive or pay, respectively. But any creditworthy commitment may serve as the offset or hedge. A commitment to import with payment to be made in the future, for example, can be offset by a loan to abroad consisting of a spot purchase of the required exchange and its investment in the foreign money market. Or a commitment to export against future payment in foreign exchange can be offset by an arrangement to borrow money abroad for conversion to the domestic currency at the outset of the export commitment. Since, where unrestricted forward exchange markets exist, interest arbitraging activities will tend to make the forward rate stand at a premium or discount, relative to the spot rate, equal to the interest rate differential between the two currency markets, hedging by the placement of credit abroad or at home need not be more expensive to the trader than would be the use of a well-organized forward exchange market for the same purpose. Movements of the *foreign* currency price of a commodity between the time of commitment to sell and the time of payment, of course, can be hedged in the futures markets for commodities that exist in world marketing centers. Only the exchange rate risk is unique to the supplier in the developing country when his position is compared with that of a supplier in a marketing center country. No free market, of course, provides security against risks of government interventions which override existing private contracts, and where frequent changes in government exchange market regulations burden private trade, the governments are to blame. These considerations suggest that the absence of forward exchange market facilities in developing countries need not be a factor in the selection of a fixed or flexible foreign exchange rate. Indeed, forward exchange market facilities are underdeveloped in a number of industrialized countries—among them, Sweden, Italy, and Japan—without being obvious handicaps to trade.

More important to the case against flexible exchange rates for developing countries than the absence of a forward exchange market is the underdeveloped state of their money markets as a whole. For without the presence of a market of some depth in which funds can be put for short-term earnings, the market does not generate the international movements of speculative and interest arbitraging funds that in other countries provide day-to-day and month-to-month stability in the exchange rates. Experience with flexible exchange rates among developed countries has heightened appreciation of the importance of private short-term capital movements in buffering short-term shocks in trading and investing conditions. Neither trade nor direct investment decisions respond immediately to changes in exchange market conditions. Were buffering funds unavailable, exchange rates among developed countries would certainly be more volatile than they are. Short-term credit instruments of high quality and organized markets for such instruments are inchoate in many developing countries and this lack of institutional facilities implies that a substitute for private buffering funds is desirable. This is the case for some official financing of exchange market disequilibriums in such countries.[6]

Official interventions to stabilize the exchange rate of a developing country, however, need not aim at fixing the rate. A policy of relaxing stabilizing operations in accordance with the persistence of market pressures, or of fixing the exchange rate with respect to a moving index—some form of self-adjusting peg—would be preferable to long-term fixity or to occasional discrete adjustment in the pegged rate. Brazil's "trotting peg"[7] illustrates a useful approach.

Stability in exchange rates between other countries' currencies. When there is an exchange rate swing between countries which are, respectively, import suppliers and export buyers of a developing country's products, the developing country's international terms of trade are affected, except insofar as the exchange rate adjustment merely reflects differential price level movements among the external countries. This risk was not present in the regime of fixed exchange rates, and it reflects the fact that developing countries were among

[6] This point is made by W. Arthur Lewis, in his Per Jacobsson Lecture, "The Less Developed Countries and Stable Exchange Rates," Washington, D.C., 1977. A summary of the lecture is given in *IMF Survey*, November 7, 1977, pp. 348-49.

[7] See Juergen B. Donges, *Brazil's Trotting Peg: A New Approach to Greater Exchange Rate Flexibility in Less Developed Countries* (Washington, D.C.: American Enterprise Institute, 1971).

the beneficiaries of the public subsidy in industrialized countries to risk bearing described in Chapter 3 as long as the industrialized countries intervened with publicly owned assets to buffer movements in their exchange rates. The withdrawal of such assured support to the exchange rates by many industrialized countries has thrust back on the developing countries that part of the exchange rate risk the latter countries previously were spared. Perhaps, in this sense, it should not be surprising that the action has drawn protest, although it must be noted that residents of developed as well as developing countries share in the new distribution of risk. To the extent that demand policies can be harmonized within and among industrialized countries in the way described in Chapter 5, swings in the exchange rates of those countries that are unrelated to purchasing power parity can be reduced, and the consequent risks to the developing countries will be made smaller. There is, however, no escaping the absorption of some risk that was previously borne elsewhere.

Need for Capital and Technology Transfers. Among the universal sentiments shared by developing countries is the hope for increased transfers of capital and technology from richer countries to poorer. The common stand of developing countries in negotiations on international monetary reform have reflected this sentiment. In the monetary negotiations of 1972–1976, for example, much of the attention of developing countries centered on linking SDR allocations to IMF member country needs. Developing countries saw in the SDR allocation process a means to increase their claims on more developed countries and have funds made available without the risk of recourse to legislative actions in the aid-providing countries; on the other hand, developed countries saw the demand for the link as a means by which aid-receiving countries would evade donor country scrutiny and as a threat to appropriate restraint in the creation of SDRs. While some European countries at times favored a partial abrogation of the rule for allocating SDRs among IMF members in proportion to member quotas, the United States and still other European governments maintained an adamant defense of the rule. For the time being, the matter has been made largely moot by global inflation and the multiplication of official reserves in the form of foreign exchange.

The review in Chapter 2 of the monetary negotiations of 1972–1976 noted the pressures brought to bear by developing countries, especially in the final stages of the talks, toward obtaining increased access to official international credit apart from the plea for the link.

The increases in IMF quotas, the liberalization of the compensatory finance and buffer stock financing facilities, the temporary oil and Witteveen facilities, the trust fund from sale of IMF gold, the joint IMF–World Bank Development Committee, and expanded World Bank activities were all responses to this pressure.

While it may legitimately be argued that multilateral facilities for capital and technology transfer remain puny in the face of global community needs, questions should be raised at this time as to whether the original division of functions between the IMF and the World Bank was appropriate and whether it should continue to be respected. The IMF's multiplication of facilities to meet special needs of developing countries have pushed it far into the development field; and the World Bank's willingness to consider the broad balance of payments implications of particular investment programs and projects have introduced it to balance of payments financing. Is it important that their roles in developmental financing, on the one hand, and balance of payments financing, on the other, be sharply drawn? A reasonable answer to the question suggests no cause to be dogmatic in the role assignments. On the other hand, in view of the importance of distinguishing developmental from balance of payments financing for the purpose of keeping the latter small, as argued in Chapters 6 and 7, institutionalization of the distinction is helpful. Furthermore, the charter of the IMF and the nature of its resources do not equip it to be an effective provider of developmental capital. Similarly, the terms under which the World Bank institutions function, and, in particular, the program and project orientation of the staff organization in the Bank-affiliated institutions, do not make these agencies the strongest possible policemen of profligate national economic policies. The smallness of IMF resources relative to potential global balance of payments financing demands, while usually cited as a handicap of that organization, is also a source of its strength since it necessitates careful rationing by the IMF of its funds and hence close attention to the policy conditions it imposes on its borrowers. Recent efforts to enlarge the pool of IMF resources, for example through the Witteveen facility, have been justified on the ground that only if the Fund has something substantial to lend can it successfully negotiate tough conditions on its borrowers. With this in mind, leaders of the private financial community have broadly supported Fund enlargement. In thus passing the buck of demanding stringent conditions, however, private lenders in effect extend the IMF's leverage even without an extension of its lending authority. To the extent that token IMF participation becomes a condition for a member's continued access to private credit, the IMF's proper role is achieved without its being supplied with further fuel for international inflation. In view of these considerations, it appears that the global economic system is best served if the traditional division of functions between the Fund and the Bank is preserved. Furthermore, the financial resources of the World Bank deserve to be enlarged while those of the Fund at this time do not. Some enlargement of the compensatory financing facility in the Fund is a possible exception to this proposition.

The oil crisis that erupted in 1973 forced many countries to turn to the credit facilities of the private market and to find there resources never before envisioned. The funds made available through this avenue may have been a factor in the reduction of militancy in the ranks of developing countries between the early and later 1970s, not only because the resources enabled some borrowers to cope reasonably painlessly with severe external problems but also because it dramatized the rewards available to those who follow a reasonable economic course. The plea for blanket debt forgiveness for developing countries voiced loudly at the opening of the Conference on International Economic Policy meetings in Paris, 1975–1977, drifted into oblivion in part because so many developing countries saw their creditworthiness in the private international capital market to be an asset too valuable to jeopardize. These developments represent the power of private markets at its best.

In this connection, greater flexibility in the exchange rates of the industrialized countries has an important advantage for the developing countries. The currency misalignments of the late 1960s bred controls over access to the capital markets of the deficit countries, most of all those of the United States and the United Kingdom, while inducing only limited liberalizations by the surplus countries. While efforts were made in both the United States and the United Kingdom to minimize the impact of the capital export controls on flows to developing countries, and while the rapid expansion of the less controlled Eurocurrency and Eurobond markets was partly a market response to the controls, the message must be clear that persistent balance of payments problems in the industrialized countries are not the friend of open capital markets and expansiveness in foreign aid. Awareness of the need for effective balance of payments adjustment processes must increase the tolerance of developing countries for a more flexible exchange rate system.

Need for Markets Open to Trade. In the same way that overvaluation of currencies with pegged exchange rates led in the 1960s to the imposition or maintenance of controls on movements of capital abroad, the overvaluations stimulated trade protectionism. Sentiments favoring protection of domestic markets from the competition of imported goods seriously threatened the traditional liberal trade stance of the United States at the opening of the decade of the 1970s, and such sentiments have not readily disappeared. Evidence continues to mount, meanwhile, that those developing countries that have oriented their growth policies toward trade have been more successful than those which have emphasized import restraint and autarky.[8] Developing countries, therefore, have a critical stake in the maintenance of world markets that are open to their exports. This consideration also must make these countries view greater flexibility in the exchange rates with some equanimity.

Some danger seems to have appeared in the system that excessive swings or excessive delays in the movement of the exchange rates, enforced by capital transfers responding to lagged information, can still arouse protectionist sentiments. As emphasized in the next chapter, it is important that governments bid for time in their responses to such protectionist pressures in order to give the exchange rates an opportunity to do their work.

The Outsider's Syndrome. The concern of residents of developing countries that their interests may go unattended in international political-economic decisions has almost certainly not been allayed by the majorities those countries have been able to muster in the U.N. General Assembly or by the increment to their combined voting strength in the International Monetary Fund. Small countries suspect, with good reason, that as quickly as they gain genuine influence in one forum, the critical decision making will shift to another. The structure of international monetary arrangements has not much to do with this problem, although the problem is of great importance. Increased recourse to market forces in monetary arrangements, nevertheless, can reduce somewhat the domain over which political decisions are required, and in that sense it reduces the cost of being an outsider. In much the same way that markets generally serve the

[8] The National Bureau of Economic Research series of nine volumes on Foreign Trade Regimes and Economic Development is perhaps the best available documentation of this theme. Jagdish Bhagwati and Anne O. Krueger are general editors of the series, which has recently been concluded with a survey volume by Professor Krueger, *Liberalization Attempts and Consequences* (New York: National Bureau of Economic Research, 1978).

interests of consumers as a class and minorities as political groups better than does the political process within national economies, the automaticity and absence of discrimination that are the hallmarks of well-functioning markets no doubt serve developing countries better than can an international framework of planning in which both the means and the goals are arrived at through official negotiations. Flexible exchange rates are, in this broad perspective, supportive of developing country welfare.

Blocs and Special Arrangements

Special trading and payments arrangements have proliferated in the international economy in recent years. Eighteen different, but sometimes overlapping, trade groupings, each of which provided a degree of preferential treatment for the mutual trade of participating countries, had been formed by developing countries by 1977.[9] In addition, the nine members of the European Economic Community and the seven members of the European Free Trade Association constitute a vast preferential trading area in Europe, and the EEC's link to fifty-two African, Caribbean, and Pacific developing countries through the 1975 Lomé Convention extends the influence of that trading area to the far corners of the globe. In eastern Europe the Council for Mutual Economic Assistance links the economies of Communist countries. Many of these trading arrangements are accompanied by facilities for clearing some payments imbalances among members and by institutionalized arrangements for intermediate-term reciprocal balance of payments financing. Most groupings have a regional orientation with cooperation in development as their goal. This chapter concludes with a brief discussion of prospects and problems of some of these facilities.

The European Economic Community. The Rome Treaty of 1958, which set the countries of Western Europe on the course toward a customs union, removed commercial policy from the arsenal of instruments those governments could use to meet balance of payments pressures and raised in the minds of many observers the belief that more flexible exchange rates would in time become necessary for maintaining intra-Community balance of payments equilibrium. In

[9] A helpful survey by Mark Allen is published in *IMF Survey*, July 4, 1977, pp. 211-13. That entire issue is devoted to trade matters and includes surveys of European arrangements by Sena Eken, East-West trade by Mark Allen, and the Tokyo Round of trade negotiations by Roy Baban.

1970, nonetheless, a committee under the chairmanship of Pierre Werner of Luxembourg proposed steps which, it was hoped, would lead by 1980 to an economic and monetary union in which the exchange rates among currencies of member countries would be rigidly fixed. Under the pressure of common hostility toward the U.S. monetary measures of 1971 and fears that the widened exchange rate margins negotiated at the December 1971 Smithsonian meeting would wreck the delicate structure of negotiated EEC agricultural prices, the six original Community members decided in the spring of 1972 to implement the Werner plan. In April the margin for exchange rate variation around each of the cross parities between members was limited to ±2.25 percent, and it was anticipated that subsequent reductions of this margin would follow. The narrowed margins among the exchange rates of the participating countries contrasted with ±4.5 percent margins agreed to the previous December, resulting from margins of ±2.25 percent for each currency on the dollar. Those countries then in the process of acceding to the Common Market—Britain, Ireland, and Denmark—joined the original six in the arrangement, and Norway and Sweden, while outside the EEC, also decided to participate. Switzerland unilaterally and informally associated its currency with those of the group for a time.

The snake began to wither soon after its birth, for the maintenance of fixed exchange rates depends upon a harmonization of aggregate demand policies which is difficult to achieve in democracies when there is little international labor mobility and when national labor market disturbances are uncoordinated.[10] The British, with the Irish, defected within weeks, in June 1972; Denmark withdrew about the same time but rejoined in October; Italy withdrew in January 1973; France left in January 1974, and, having rejoined, left again in March 1976; and Sweden resigned in August 1977. The Swiss early terminated their effort to stay in line with the group. The remaining body of the snake was kept alive by realignments of the deutsche mark on the other currencies in 1973, 1975, and 1977, but the membership had been reduced, by the end of the latter year, to Germany, Belgium, the Netherlands, Luxembourg, Denmark, and Norway. Strains within this group continued. In general, the persistently conservative monetary policies of Germany could not be matched by the other participants in the scheme, and as time went on, one country after another elected to sacrifice snake membership or

[10] Polly Reynolds Allen, *Organization and Administration of a Monetary Union*, Studies in International Finance, no. 38 (International Finance Section, Princeton University, 1976).

devalue in order to regain freedom to inflate domestic demand. The theory of optimum currency areas suggests that the small countries of northern Europe, which trade intensively with the relatively large German economy, have something to gain by fixing their exchange rates on the currency of their dominant trade partner. The sustained appreciation of the deutsche mark against outside currencies, however, has continued to create problems of internal stagnation and external deficit for those who have remained in the system.

One of the serious casualties to flexible exchange rates in Europe was the common agricultural policy of the Common Market, once intended to permit unfettered trade in agricultural products among members at prices supported through a marketwide intervention scheme. Flexible exchange rates resulted in the use of variable levies and subsidies on intramarket agricultural trade as well as on the trade with external areas. These problems with the common agricultural policy, along with common concerns over chronic appreciations of their currencies against the dollar have kept alive a dream of intra-EEC fixed exchange rates. Disagreement over demand policies, energy, and a host of other matters, however, are a block to progress. New efforts to mass reserves to be used for intra-Community exchange stabilization activities were announced in the summer of 1978, and a European Monetary System was inaugurated in April 1979.[11] The future of such an undertaking is not bright in view of past failures.

Much has been learned about techniques of exchange market intervention from this experience of a joint float by countries with well-developed financial markets. In the initial arrangement, in which each snake currency was to be kept within ±2.25 percent bounds of the central rate on each other snake currency, dollar intervention was to be avoided except when one of the members' currencies reached the dollar intervention point (the side of the tunnel); intervention within the snake was in members' currencies. Although a first approach was that intervention should be the responsibility of the country whose currency was at its ceiling, rather than that of the country whose currency was at its floor value, it soon became clear that limiting the intervention to purchases of foreign currencies without sales had an inflationary bias unless the purchasing government promptly took action to remove its purchases from the money base of the other country, say, by transferring the amount

[11] See Epilogue.

to a deposit account in the issuing country's central bank.[12] Subsequently, interventions were undertaken by the authorities of both strong and weak currencies. Clearance between monetary authorities was required before intervention was undertaken inside the ± 2.25 percent bounds in order to prevent conflicting simultaneous actions and in order to facilitate policy coordination. Claims on other snake countries acquired by the intervention actions of countries with strong currencies, and liabilities acquired by countries with weak currencies, were denominated in European monetary units of account—a unit composed of a prescribed basket of member currencies—and cleared through the European Monetary Cooperation Fund. Settlement was made monthly. In an initial compromise, settlements were made with bundles of assets so constituted that the foreign exchange component of the bundle did not exceed the ratio in which foreign exchange reserves stood to the sum of the debtor country's reserves including gold, SDRs, and reserve position in the Fund; more recently, settlements have been made in dollars. Settlement can be postponed for up to three months, but cumulative liabilities may not exceed agreed quotas, and an interest charge equal to the average of the official discount rates of participating countries must be paid on outstanding balances.

The use of dollars for intervention and for settlement by countries participating in the arrangement for narrow margins may have been fostered by the understanding reached by participants in 1972 that intervention inside the band in other members' currencies would take place only by mutual agreement; intervention against the dollar, by contrast, required no clearance. Furthermore, central bank balances in the currencies of participating countries were kept small through the effort of some countries to discourage external use of their currencies. Dollar purchases by one snake member, nevertheless, when not offset by dollar sales by another, affected the dollar values of all snake currencies, since intercurrency arbitrage kept the cross rates of the currencies in line. It is not surprising, therefore, that dissension arose among members because of lack of consensus about when and by whom dollar interventions were appropriate.[13]

---

12 Ronald I. McKinnon, "On Securing a Common Monetary Policy in Europe," *Banca Nazionale del Lavoro Quarterly Review* (March 1973), pp. 3-21.

13 These problems have been explored by Joanne Salop, "Dollar Intervention within the Snake," *IMF Staff Papers* (March 1977), pp. 64-76, and by Helmut W. Mayer, *The Anatomy of Official Exchange-rate Intervention Systems*, Essays in International Finance, no. 104 (International Finance Section, Princeton University, May 1974).

A novel proposal for a fundamental reform of intervention practices in the snake was put forward by William H. L. Day, who urged limiting all intervention actions to the forward exchange markets.[14] Day claimed for his proposal that it would remove the need for financing and settlements between countries and that it would permit the liberalization of international capital movements because the use of exchange controls to curb speculation could also be limited to the forward market. The suggestion that intervention activities be shifted from the spot to the forward exchange market has been explored on many occasions.[15] The technical complexity of the multiperiod interlinks between spot and forward transactions and the variety of variables influencing exchange market decisions, however, have allowed the discussion to be flawed. The Day proposal, too, has some problems.

One problem is that, although government intervention in the forward market can limit the spot market impact of even sustained balance of payments pressures when exchange markets are free of controls, the achievement will not greatly reduce the buildup of balances that require intergovernmental settlements. Where the original disturbance requires private transactors to enter subsequent markets to repatriate or cover their positions, government forward intervention, which must also be cleared out by subsequent government operations, will not require accelerating intervention activities and will not accumulate outstanding balances. But if an exchange market disturbance gives rise to a private buildup of foreign exchange claims, only a government buildup will offset it. It seems unlikely that the magnitude of unsettled balances among snake currencies will be much reduced if intervention is introduced only into the forward market.

Furthermore, Day's proposal is flawed by his sympathy for the use of exchange controls in the forward markets. He asserts that if controls are employed only in the forward markets, they can be used

[14] W. H. L. Day, "A Reform of the European Currency Snake," *IMF Staff Papers*, vol. 23 (November 1976), pp. 580-97.

[15] See, for example, A. E. Jasay, "Forward Exchange: The Case for Intervention," *Lloyd's Bank Review*, vol. 50 (October 1958), pp. 35-45; J. Spraos, "Speculation, Arbitrage, and Sterling," *Economic Journal*, vol. 69 (March 1959), pp. 1-21; J.H. Auten, "Counterspeculation and the Forward Exchange Market," *Journal of Political Economy*, vol. 69 (February 1961), pp. 49-55; Peter B. Kenen, "Trade, Speculation, and the Forward Exchange Rate," in Robert E. Baldwin and others, *Trade, Growth and the Balance of Payments*, Essays in Honor of Gottfried Haberler (Chicago: Rand McNally, 1965), pp. 143-69; Frank McCormick, "Capital Flows and Government Forward Market Operations under the Crawling Peg," *Journal of Monetary Economics*, vol. 2 (July 1976), pp. 333-50; and Frank McCormick, "A Multiperiod Theory of Forward Exchange," *Journal of International Economics*, vol. 7 (August 1977), pp. 269-82.

to suppress speculation without damage to stability in the spot exchange rate. Exchange controls in either market, however, will suppress interest arbitrage, the transactions which link the exchange rate of one market to that of the other. A covered interest arbitrage transaction involves simultaneous and offsetting purchases and sales in the spot and forward markets, and in the forward market a speculator often provides the matching side to an arbitrager's purchase or sale. Exchange controls in the forward market or the threat of such controls will suppress covered interest arbitrage as effectively as exchange controls in the spot market by threatening the enforceability of private contracts. But without the interest arbitraging flow, the spot exchange rate will go its own way from the forward rate, and spot rate stability will have been lost.

There are no tricks in exchange market interventions that will avoid fundamental problems. And in a regime of fixed exchange rates, most of the fundamental problems stem from differences in demand management policies in the countries involved.

Other currency arrangements. Concern with the extent to which tariff schedules in industrialized countries escalate duties in accordance with the degree to which products are processed has led leaders in many developing countries to believe that, if their secondary and tertiary industries are to develop in a framework of anything larger than national markets, their countries will have to "take in each other's washing." The prosperity achieved in Europe as the EEC and the European Free Trade Area materialized gave additional support to the idea. Plans for preferential trade among developing countries consequently proliferated in the 1960s and 1970s. The oldest such grouping is the Latin American Free Trade Association (LAFTA), consisting of ten South American countries and Mexico and dating from 1960. It was followed by the Central American Common Market (CACM), the Caribbean Free Trade Association (now the Caribbean Community), the East Caribbean Common Market, and the Andean Pact. In 1975 the Latin American Economic System (SELA for the Spanish name) was formed with all Western Hemisphere countries except the United States, Canada, and the Bahamas as members. In Asia, seven countries, spread geographically from Korea to India, signed the Bangkok Agreement in 1975, and at the subregional level there are the Regional Cooperation for Development (RCD) group—Iran, Pakistan, and Turkey—and the Association of South East Asian Nations (ASEAN) consisting of Indonesia, Malaysia, the Philippines, Singapore, and Thailand. In Africa, there are the

West African Economic Community (CEAO for the French name), the Mano River Union, the Economic Community of West African States (ECOWAS), the Central African Customs and Economic Union (UDEAC in French), and the Economic Community of the Great Lakes Countries (CEPGL in French). In 1974 a proposal for a comprehensive African Economic Community was adopted by the Organization of African Unity. Finally, an Arab Common Market links a number of the non-oil-exporting Arab countries, and a Gulf Common Market has been proposed among Bahrain, Kuwait, Qatar, and Saudi Arabia.

Only a few of these trade groups have experienced any dramatic increase in intermember trade. This is because many developing countries have exportable surpluses in only a few goods, and this capacity is tailored to satisfy markets in the more industrialized countries rather than the markets of neighboring developing countries. Only with the slow process of capital accumulation and social and technological transformation will the countries forming preferential trading areas develop industries much affected by their new tariff structures. In many trade groups transportation facilities among members are inferior to those with their traditional overseas markets, in spite of the proximity of the members to each other.

Disappointment with immediate results from trade preferences, together with recollection of the successes of the European Payments Union in stimulating intra-European trade in the reconstruction era following World War II, has led to a spate of plans for regional and subregional payments arrangements to supplement preferential trade. The Economic Commission for Asia and the Far East (ECAFE), the Pearson Commission, and the United Nations Conference on Trade and Development (UNCTAD), have been among the endorsers of such arrangements.[16] Members of the Central American Common Market have established a clearing arrangement among themselves and also a Monetary Stabilization Fund. The Latin American Free Trade Association and the Regional Cooperation for Development group in Asia operate clearing arrangements. Two monetary unions exist in Africa —the West African Monetary Union and the Equatorial and Central African Monetary Union—and proposals have been adopted for an Arab Monetary Fund. Plans for a clearing arrangement and a multi-

[16] See UNCTAD, "Payments Arrangements among the Developing Countries for Trade Expansion," *Report of the Group of Experts*, TD/B/80/Rev. 1 (Geneva, 1966); Pearson Commission, "Partners in Development," *Report of the Commission on International Development* (New York: Praeger, 1969); ECAFE, *Feasibility Study on the Establishment of an Asian Reserve Bank*, Trade/TLP/ARB(1)1 and Trade/TLP/ARB(1)1 Add. 1 (Bangkok, 1972); and United Nations, *Trade and Monetary Cooperation in Asia and the Far East* (New York, 1971).

lateral reserve center in Asia were promulgated by ECAFE in 1971–1972 without great success.

The various arrangements that have emerged can be classified into three types.[17] Clearing arrangements provide for multilateral clearing of intragroup payments imbalances with accounts in an agreed upon unit and with frequent settlements in convertible external currencies. Payments unions provide for intermediate-term credit in addition to the clearing facility. And reserve pooling provides for a more thoroughgoing monetary integration among participants, with partial or complete pooling of external reserves. Most of the arrangements in existence are simple clearing agreements. All anticipate that the participating countries will be intervening in the exchange markets to maintain more or less fixed exchange rates.

The case for clearing arrangements among developing countries typically has three parts. One proceeds from an assumption that the currencies of developing countries tend to be overvalued relative to industrial country currencies more than they are against each other. Where this is true, groups of developing countries could relax payments as well as trade restrictions on intragroup transactions more than they could on transactions with other countries. Such preferential treatment of intragroup trade was the rationale for the European Payments Union of the 1950s. The second part is that a clearing facility could economize on the holdings of external reserves by the members since, with clearing, external reserves held for intragroup settlements could allegedly be reduced. The third part contends that clearing could be executed at lower cost per value unit cleared because of savings on external currency transactions costs.

Each of these arguments is open to skepticism, as Michalopoulos has noted.[18] The view that overvaluation of developing country currencies provides opportunities for gains from liberalization of preferential payments[19] is inappropriate for developing countries whose currencies are not particularly overvalued, or are equally overvalued vis-à-vis all trade partners. Except as a second-best solution, dis-

---

[17] Useful descriptions of the arrangements can be found in Constantine Michalopoulos, *Payments Arrangements for Less Developed Countries: The Role of Foreign Assistance*, Essays in International Finance, no. 102 (International Finance Section, Princeton University, November 1973); and UNCTAD, "Payments Arrangements among the Developing Countries for Trade Expansion," *Report of the Group of Experts*.

[18] Michalopoulos, *Payments Arrangements for Less Developed Countries*.

[19] Jaroslav Vanek supported this view in "Payments Unions among the Less Developed Countries and Their Economic Integration," *Journal of Common Market Studies*, vol. 5 (1966), pp. 187-91.

criminatory reductions of payments restrictions do not lead to more efficient trade and production; rather they lead to some diversion of trade from more to less efficient suppliers and to some distortion of consumer choices from optimal available patterns. Removal of the currency overvaluation by exchange rate adjustment is usually a more effective way of proceeding. An argument for greater flexibility in the exchange rates of developing countries has been made earlier in this chapter. Discriminatory reduction of the payments restrictions which defend an overvalued currency are generally a poor substitute for a move toward exchange market equilibrium.[20]

The hope that clearing unions may reduce the needs of developing countries for external reserve balances is probably an illusion. Although intraregional settlements are typically a small fraction of the total settlements that developing countries must make, as long as a clearing arrangement requires frequent settlement of uncleared balances, external reserves must be maintained for this purpose. When substantial credit lines are available to finance intraregional imbalances, as are proposed in payments union schemes, it is quite another matter. But this possibility is considered later.

Furthermore, savings on the transactions costs in external reserves for intraregional settlements are probably nonexistent. Working balances of demand bank deposits held by central banks of developing countries in international banking centers serve, of course, as clearing funds, and it is unlikely that clearing facilities could be provided at less cost in the banks of developing countries. If, indeed, the clearing of payments for regional trade—either among individual traders or among commercial or central banks—could be executed at lower cost at a regional level than in the international clearing centers such as New York and London, the international banks or the regional ones would surely use a regional mechanism.

The clearing arrangements that exist in the Asian Regional Cooperation for Development group, in the Latin American Free Trade Area, and in the Central American Common Market, therefore, have

[20] While it may be argued that the case for payments preferences parallels that for trade preferences, it should be remembered that an overvalued currency discourages external investment in a region as well as exports to that region; furthermore, the case for preferential commercial policies among developing countries is on shaky ground. Developing countries would probably do better to engage forthrightly in trade negotiations with developed countries for reciprocal relaxation of trade barriers than to follow policies of protectionism and preferential trading. See, for example, Kreinin and Finger, "A New International Economic Order?" and Robert E. Baldwin and Tracy Murray, "MFN Tariff Reductions and Developing Country Benefits under the GSP," *Economic Journal*, vol. 87 (March 1977), pp. 30-46.

probably not themselves made any substantial contribution to economic development.

Payments unions, which provide for substantial lines of credit to member countries with balance of payments deficits, are quite another matter because they do provide real capital to some members of the group. Payments unions among developing countries are, however, rare. The Arab Monetary Fund, chartered in May 1976, is the only plan in operation at the time of this writing. In that instance, twenty-one members of the League of Arab States have each pledged a subscription with over half the total coming from oil states, and drawing rights on the total fund of SDR750 million are proportional to subscriptions. Members may draw up to twice their subscription in any one year and up to four times the subscription in total. Credits may be outstanding for up to seven years.

Payments unions in which the creditor nation or group of nations has neither the right to say no nor the right to insist on conditions for the use of credit usually founder because of expectations that there will be asymmetrical use of the facility. Countries which run persistent balance of payments deficits within the group become chronic debtors to the union and use capital that might otherwise have been employed by the surplus nations. Anticipation of such an outcome makes the countries expecting to experience surpluses reluctant to participate. When outside initial capital can be provided to the scheme, the credit provided to deficit countries need not be wholly at the expense of the surplus countries, and the latter may then be more willing to participate. In this case, however, the question becomes simply whether this use of scarce developmental capital, provided perhaps by the more developed countries, is the most productive use that can be made of it. It is hardly obvious that the commitment of capital to financing intraregional payments balances which may emerge in selected payments union areas is an optimal allocation of that scarce resource. Any incentives it might provide for countries to dismantle payments restrictions in a discriminatory way seem unlikely, as a general rule, to accelerate the developmental process as much as the direct employment of the capital in productive projects.

In some respects the most demanding arrangements for payments among developing countries that have been discussed in recent years are the proposals for pooling external reserves. It is claimed that by taking advantage of negative covariance in the balance of payments positions of participating countries, pooling can make possible the reduction of required reserve holdings; external surpluses of some group members in each period help finance the external deficits of others. Countries, however, which run external balance of payments surpluses do not desire to share their reserves with their neighbors unless they can expect to be repaid in kind so that the continuation of such a process requires that each member, within an appropriate time horizon, balance its pool use. In practice, reserve sharing involves careful and continuous coordination of the economic policies of the group, and only nations with a profound cultural affinity for each other are good candidates for a successful partnership. Among developing countries in a single region, on the other hand, commonalities in export and import composition often result in the countries' experiencing balance of payments surpluses and deficits together so that little saving results from reserve pooling.[21]

The monetary unions in the French franc area of Africa provide the chief experience with reserve pooling. Both the West African Monetary Union and the Equatorial and Central African Monetary Union use the Communauté Financière Africaine franc as currency, which is convertible at a fixed rate (CFA1 = FF 0.02) into the French franc. Each union has its own central bank and its own reserves on deposit at the French Treasury. France guarantees convertibility of the CFA franc into French francs and also provides overdraft facilities. Freedom from exchange restrictions applies to transactions throughout France, Monaco, the French overseas territories, and the CFA area (technically, the "Operations Account" area). It appears that the CFA area is more an extension of monetary arrangements that existed prior to independence for these former French colonies than an arrangement for obtaining reserve economies through pooling. The Banque Centrale des Etats de l'Afrique de l'Ouest, the central bank for the West African Monetary Union, for example, is reported to have maintained excessive balances with the French Treasury.[22]

Functional Monetary Units

In a provocative essay on "artificial" currency units—units of account created for specific purposes such as the denomination of the maturity value of a bond issue or for definition of the par value of a country's currency—Joseph Aschheim and Y. S. Park have pointed out that

[21] Praiphol Koomsup, of Thailand, for example, has shown that the standard deviation of unpooled reserve changes of ASEAN nations, 1966-1973, was less than 4 percent different from the standard deviation of changes in hypothetically pooled reserves. "Reserve Pooling in the ASEAN Region," Thammasat University Faculty of Economics Discussion Paper Series, no. 51 (Bangkok, March 1976; processed).

[22] Michalopoulos, *Payments Arrangements for Less Developed Countries*, p. 16.

currency areas need not be defined geographically. The domain of a currency may be a function rather than a geographical area.[23]

Whereas the IMF's SDR serves not only as a unit of account but as a medium of exchange—for settlements among central banks—private artificial units, such as the private EUA, the ECU, the Eurco, the Arcru, the B-unit, and the IFU, designed by banks, have up to now been used primarily as accounting units for the denomination of bond issues or commercial accounts. If banks agree to accept deposits and make loans in any currency unit, however, and if a market for the unit develops, it could become a private means of payment.

The artificial currency units, typically constituted of baskets of national currencies, serve as units of account that are more stable in purchasing power value through time than at least some individual currencies. And various units serve the needs of those who are participating in different functions. Thus the B-unit (Barclay's Bank) serves as a unit for commercial transactions among western industrial traders, while the Arcru is designed to serve the needs of Arab investors. The private EUA is intended to be attractive to European investors, while the IFU is designed for a broader investment market. Several countries have pegged the external values of their currencies to weighted indexes of the currencies of their trading partners. Aschheim and Park contend that this growing pluralism in money units is a practical response to the variety of contemporary needs, which includes national currencies to be used in intracountry transactions and various nonnational units to be used in particular international transactions. The new units reflect the ingenuity that can be stimulated by market incentives.

---

[23] Joseph Aschheim and Y. S. Park, *Artificial Currency Units: The Formation of Functional Currency Areas,* Essays in International Finance, no. 114 (International Finance Section, Princeton University, April 1976).

9
The Way Ahead

The persistent economic growth and increasing interdependence among non-Communist nations characterizing the first third of a century after World War II were abetted in part by periods of reasonable price stability in industrialized countries and stubbornly won progress toward the elimination of legal barriers to international trade and investment. Output of non-Communist countries, in real terms, probably more than trebled between 1950 and 1976, and the share of GNP exported increased from 3.9 to 6.4 percent in the United States and from 7.3 to 14.1 percent in the world as a whole between 1955 and 1977. Are the policies supporting these changes any more or less secure under a regime of managed floating exchange rates than they were under the Bretton Woods monetary rules? Are there new perils hinging on policy choices? And can one discern, even dimly, the outlines of a viable and attractive future monetary evolution? These difficult questions are the subject matter of this final chapter.

Fostering the Liberal Treatment of Trade and Investment

The goal of a high degree of freedom for private international trade and investment embedded in postwar international institutions such as the IMF and the GATT is worth defending. It leads to an efficient distribution of goods among people and to efficient production and consumption decisions for the interpersonal distribution of wealth and tastes that corresponds to the production taking place. It maximizes the harmony of interest among states and tends to minimize government-to-government conflicts. And, by broadening the geographic extent of markets and hence the domain of potential competition, free trade and investment among countries help police market effectiveness within countries by weakening the power of monopoly groups which would otherwise misallocate resources and aggravate the problems of maintaining the value of money. The fact that liberal approaches to international markets were being threatened in the twilight years of the Bretton Woods arrangements by exchange rate misalignments was a major cause for the move to greater exchange rate flexibility.

Protectionist pressures that have developed in many countries in the last half of the 1970s, however, indicate that the liberal trading system is not necessarily yet secure. Under- and overshooting of the exchange rates seem capable of creating sudden if temporary difficulties for particular producers and consumers. So, too, do government exchange market interventions and official measures to induce international capital flows when they cause the exchange rates to lag adjustments that are called for by divergent monetary policies. A danger in present arrangements is that countries with lower rates of inflation will protect their export and import competitive industries by resisting currency appreciation, while countries with higher rates of inflation will then turn, on balance of payments grounds, to import restrictions, export subsidies, and capital export controls.

The importance of maintaining a resolute defense of international commercial liberalism dictates certain constraints on decisions about economic policy in the years ahead. One is that there must be restraint in government measures to finance international payments imbalances, including avoidance of macroeconomic policies that induce capital flows. Another is that governments must resist the demands of pressure groups for relief from import competition and declining export markets, and that governments must especially seek to increase the lag in their response to such demands in order to give the exchange rates time to do their work. These constraints deserve elaboration.

Limiting Induced Capital Flows. The discussion of Chapter 7 emphasized the effects on inflation of the capital flows that were initiated or explicitly induced by governments for balance of payments reasons in the aftermath of the petroleum crisis. Our concern here is with the effects of such flows and of government interventions in the exchange markets on the structure of relative prices as a result of the influence of the flows on the exchange rates. In countries where currencies have been prevented from depreciating, officially induced capital flows have had the effect of taxing producers of exports and import substitutes and subsidizing users of such goods, and, in countries whose currencies have been prevented from appreciating, the flows have taxed users of traded goods and subsidized the producers, relative to what would have been the case had the exchange rates adjusted. On some occasions the policies stabilizing the exchange rates were part of a general policy to slow the pace at which a non-monetary disequilibrium or a long-standing monetary disequilibrium was removed, thereby mitigating the impact on domestic price relationships of an adjustment in process. In other cases the policies unsettled prices and production by denying exchange rates their role of compensating for divergent monetary developments among nations. In the latter circumstance, the policies surely fostered protectionist pressures in countries where the exchange rate was prevented from depreciating or made to appreciate.

One circumstance of this sort conducive to protectionism has no doubt arisen from time to time inadvertently, merely through failure of governments to synchronize the effects of their overall macroeconomic policies on credit conditions in their economies. Official discussions of policy coordination among governments till now seem to have been largely limited to the overall demand consequences of policy mixes and have not focused clearly on their potential to induce a capital flow and hence their exchange rate implications. The Keynesian orientation of policy discussions has led to a derogation of the consequences of monetary policy for national demand as a whole and to a simple association of each country's current balance of payments with its relative rate of GNP growth. The U.S. stance in the July 1978 summit meeting of heads of state and governments provides an example. The United States reportedly sought in this meeting, and indeed throughout 1977 and 1978, more rapid overall demand expansion in Germany and Japan in order to reduce the U.S. current international payments deficit. Little attention seems to have been given, however, to the balance of policy instruments by which the demand expansion might have been achieved, although the choice in that matter was in fact going to be critical to the outcome.[1]

[1] The dispute concerning the balance of payments weakness of the United States and the strength of Germany and Japan in 1977 and early 1978 seemed to reflect the strong past and weakly continuing attractiveness of the dollar as a haven for short- and long-term investments and the measures taken by Central European countries and Japan to limit changes in their exchange rates and to discourage capital inflows relative to outflows. In one view of this matter, there was in fact no problem: the current accounts were merely reflecting capital account decisions while overall balances of payments were equilibrated by the exchange rates. In another view, the 1977 U.S. current account deficit reflected an exchange rate pattern that temporarily overexposed U.S. producers to foreign competition. If one gives credence to the latter view, appropriate policy responses might have included considerably smaller U.S. government expenditures combined with

The simple Keynesian image of international economic relationships that still characterizes much consideration of policy issues has been made obsolete by the improvements in the international capital markets detailed in Chapter 7 and by the advent of flexible exchange rates. Inasmuch as changes in credit conditions among countries can influence capital flows and exchange rates and exchange rates can in turn alter international positions with respect to prices and competitiveness, disturbances to a country's credit conditions relative to conditions abroad should probably be thought of as importantly associated with changes in the country's surplus or deficit on current international account, while aggregate internal demand should be associated with the rate of domestic inflation. Of course the pseudovariables, "credit market conditions" and "aggregate demand," are interrelated, and these do not translate neatly into the traditional dichotomy of monetary and fiscal policy targets. Moreover, short-run aberrations cloud the relationships. But what must be clear is that the mix of policies, primarily monetary and fiscal, as long as interventions elsewhere in the economy are not changing rapidly, must be directed toward the mix of credit conditions and aggregate demand that will yield desired results simultaneously for the structure of the balance of payments (the current account net deficit and capital account net surplus) and the internal inflation rate.

As noted in Chapter 5, over any short to intermediate period a policy mix that gives rise to change in government debt and money in private hands in the proportion desired by residents would minimize the inducements that the monetary and fiscal policies provide for international capital flows. The exchange rate could then adapt so as to eliminate the tendency for any increased or decreased domestic

somewhat slowed monetary growth to achieve lowered inflation and smaller pressures on dollar interest rates, on the one hand, and reduced exchange market intervention, tax reduction, and lighter controls on capital imports in Europe and Japan, on the other. Of course, trade policy measures, including U.S. measures that would have reduced imports of petroleum, could have had a positive effect. But such measures should generally have been taken for their own virtues, not because of the state of the balance of payments. Attaching trade policy decisions to the state of the balance of payments risks opening a Pandora's box that will justify trade restrictions for any country experiencing a current balance of payments deficit. U.S. subsidies to domestic energy consumption and implicit taxes on domestic energy production are bad policies on their own, as are European and Japanese import restrictions and export subsidies and similar U.S. measures. Restraints on international capital movements have been freely employed by countries explicitly for balance of payments reasons in recent years and are in any case less subject to political pressures for establishment or continuation than are trade controls. It would have been appropriate to call for their removal on balance of payments grounds in 1978.

demand for goods to spill over into a changed international balance on goods and services. This argument is *ceteris paribus*. In the face of disturbances abroad, the strategy must be an adaptive one. The mix in the use of instruments of monetary and fiscal policy is vital to the outcome of the measures taken. And until governments give closer attention to the implications of their policy mixes for relative credit conditions among countries, their efforts at policy making risk substantial failure even when the governments agree on demand management goals.

While it is not easy to coordinate policies among governments responsive to national rather than international electorates, the level of coordination required under flexible rates is politically less demanding than that under fixed. Whereas fixed exchange rates require countries to adopt aggregate demand policies that are not too different from those chosen elsewhere, flexible exchange rates impose no such requirement on most countries. Under flexible rates governments may choose overall demand policies to meet the needs officials perceive. The international coordination required is no more than one of means—obtaining the mixture of monetary and fiscal policies that minimizes the effect of the mix on international capital movements. While these means of stabilization can hardly be considered unimportant—they involve distributive questions which are the essence of politics—a certain amount of coordination at this level may nonetheless be achievable.

Resisting Protectionist Pressures. The unit labor cost and exchange rate data of Figure 5, together with the record of current payments imbalances and intergovernmental policy disputes, tend to confirm that exchange rates have not always promptly and correctly reflected changing price and cost realities among countries. The exchange rates have sometimes lagged the adjustments that would give balance to international competitive positions, and they have sometimes overshot intermediate- to long-term requirements. While flexible exchange rates have almost certainly performed better in this regard than a system of adjustable pegs could have done, the rates have been affected by direct and indirect interventions in the exchange market by governments and by waves of capital movements that were in turn influenced by uncertainty. Protectionist pressures have generally been increased when exchange rates did not reflect changes in the relative internal purchasing powers of national moneys.

Even if governments succeed in the future in reducing the effects of their policies on capital movements, however, the nature of flexible exchange rates provides some stimulus to protectionism. Flexible rates shift some of the uncertainty of markets on to producers and consumers in a way that would not take place under officially fixed rates. Without official financing to buffer short-run disturbances, producers and consumers of traded goods now share with other managers of short-term money balances the task of assessing the meaning of momentary market pressures in a way they did not before. There is danger that producers of import substitutes and of exports will seek legislation that gives new and permanent protection to their market positions in order to restore the market security they have lost through the change in the exchange rate regime.

Fortunately, when capital flows induced by government policies are not sustained, exchange rate aberrations are also temporary. It seems important now that governments do not yield to protectionist pressures during temporary exchange rate displacements by making political concessions that cannot subsequently be retracted. Examples of government failure on this score appear to be the U.S. actions in 1976–1977 to negotiate controls on Japanese exports to the United States of steel, television sets, and textiles. Although subsequent appreciation of the yen removed much of the rationale for the controls, the regulations were not then promptly abandoned. The U.S. producers in the end got more protection than they bargained for.

As disequilibriums inherited from the fixed exchange rate era and the period of petroleum crisis disappear, and as understanding of the nature and inevitability of risk bearing in global markets grows, pressures on governments for protection from every adverse turn of the market may become more controllable. Governments can help enhance resource mobility through policies that provide training and job information, remove barriers to market entry, and eliminate price ceilings and floors. But the viability of a liberal international trading system in a world of flexible exchange rates is also going to depend heavily on (1) the willingness and ability of governments to delay their responses to protectionist pressures until exchange rates do what they can do to sustain the competitive position of traditional producers, and (2) the ability of governments to minimize the tendency of their own policies to misalign the short- to intermediate-term exchange rates. Countries whose currencies have tended to appreciate seem to have been the worst offenders with respect to misaligning the exchange rates, and this must be seen as the contemporary form of a beggar-my-neighbor policy.

Misalignment admittedly eludes definition. It is certainly proper that some countries be capital importers and others capital exporters, on a long- as well as short-term basis, and that the exchange rates between any such pair bring about a surplus in the current external account of the capital exporter. What is to be avoided is (1) government exchange market intervention on one side of the market for more than a quite short-run period or for repeated periods, (2) government borrowing or lending abroad for balance of payments reasons, (3) government steps to induce private individuals and firms to borrow or lend where the purpose is to influence the exchange rate, and (4) government failure to minimize the effects of macroeconomic policies on conditions in the international market for financial assets. If governments can avoid such measures, and if there is no substantial flight from the dollar to change the character of the system, the remaining international capital flows will be those arising from investment criteria and those which should be accommodated by the exchange rates.

The System and Inflation

It was popular among writers in the early 1960s to say that the international monetary system based on fixed exchange rates had a deflationary bias because surplus countries facing accumulation of reserves could resist inflation while deficit countries facing reserve exhaustion sooner or later had to deflate. There was some truth in the generalization, and the truth may help explain the weakness of generalized inflationary pressures in Europe and North America in the 1950s and early 1960s, although moderation in monetary policy in the United States where the bias was not applicable was no doubt more important. After having been drowned and largely forgotten in the global flood of monetary expansion and spending that followed abandonment of monetary restraint in the United States in the 1960s, the generalization is now worth recalling. Flexible exchange rates do imply an international sharing of the adjustment burden not present under fixed rates, and they consequently remove the bias that was implied when the deficit country was typically the one that had to adjust. Furthermore, since under flexible exchange rates adjustment is brought about through relative price changes and changes in the purchasing power of existing money balances rather than as a result of an increase or decrease in nominal money supplies anywhere, monetary deflation is no longer required. The removal of a rationale for deflation in deficit countries that these differences imply can be an inflationary factor in the system as a whole and sharpens the case that must be made now for monetary and fiscal discipline. However, flexible exchange rates do create some downward price pressures in countries that appreciate along with upward price pressures in countries that depreciate. In fact, flexible exchange rates generally deal evenhandedly with inflation and deflation. Except possibly in the case of the key currency in the system, flexible exchange rates leave to each government the determination of the inflation rate in its own currency.

The analysis in Chapter 5 emphasized that the central element in the inflation of the 1960s and 1970s was the pervasive intellectual tradition that put demand expansion in a hallowed position as the cure for every excess of measured unemployment over a historical standard and that directed attention away from the importance of monetary restraint. The tradition has led in many countries to abuse of the demand-creating potential of governmental borrowing and money creation, and the abuse has been especially notable when unemployment was enlarged from the supply side—restraints on production from nonlabor supply shortages, requirements for resource reallocation, disincentive effects of taxes and transfer payments, rapid and unbalanced changes in labor supply, and uncertainty stemming from the inflation itself. It can be said flatly and candidly that only when governments exercise restraint in the use of their power to print money and issue bonds will the purchasing power of money and bonds cease to fall.

While progress in this direction is not generally a matter of the international monetary arrangements, it is probably significant that all money is now credit money. Gold, the last survivor of the commodity moneys, has been dethroned and only partially replaced by a dollar that is itself neither well controlled nor essential in any country's inflationary-deflationary decisions. The restraints on inflation have been made entirely a matter of government choice.

When claims are highly mobile between countries and "money" is not, one country's excess fiscal deficits can match up with another's excessive monetary expansion to create inflationary forces that neither country would have expected from experience under fixed exchange rates. By excessively expanding its money supply, for example, a country may experience rapid inflation even while it has a current balance of payments surplus, and a country with profligate fiscal operations but modest monetary expansion may largely escape inflation although it experiences a balance of payments deficit. These processes through which international economic disturbances are propagated are not yet familiar, but they are implied by mobility of capital among countries with flexible exchange rates. They make each country's monetary policy especially critical for the inflation that the country will encounter.

Countries wishing to combat inflation can do so, however, even in an inflationary world, by restraining growth in their own money supplies and then ensuring that they themselves and other countries do not prevent their currencies from appreciating. Indeed, the capability of flexible exchange rates to confine inflation to the countries of its origin is perhaps the greatest present source of hope for inflation control. Possibly the intensity of inflation now experienced by countries engaging in excessive monetary expansion will induce those countries to draw back from inflationary policies earlier than they would otherwise have done. But unfortunately such an international control cannot yet be considered reliable. Germany and Switzerland, of course, illustrate the possibilities that countries have for evading inflation, even though these two countries have made significant efforts to inhibit their currencies' appreciations.

While international investors may occasionally tend to capitalize expected future appreciations by purchasing an appreciating currency until a once-for-all overvaluation at today's price levels is achieved, misalignments from this source should be temporary insofar as the investors hold interest-bearing deposits and securities. Since interest rates in an appreciating country come to reflect fully the rate of price change expected in that country by both internal and external observers, the real rate of return obtainable on assets denominated in that currency will come to be the same as the real return abroad without an overvaluation of the currency at present prices.[2] On this score, therefore, countries which resist appreciation need not fear that their prudence will in the long run overvalue their currencies.

On another score, however, discussed more fully below under consideration of the future role of the dollar, a tendency for sound currencies to be overvalued does exist. That arises because a share of the balances held in internationally acceptable currencies for transactions purposes is not held in interest-bearing form and will gravitate toward currencies expected to appreciate in value. Because of this pressure, major countries seeking to avoid inflation may find that a little prudence goes a long way.

The United States, in championing greater flexibility in exchange rates, has not escaped its responsibilities as the provider and regulator of the monetary system's key currency, even though it has gained a potential for international adjustment that was absent in the waning

---

[2] It is not inconceivable that the equilibrium nominal rate of interest in an appreciating country would be negative, although this would imply a price level that was *falling* (partly as a result of currency appreciation) at a greater rate than the historical real rate of return on loans, which is close to 3 percent.

years of the Bretton Woods arrangements. Indeed, the changes in the U.S. role in the system are primarily those that will turn the brunt of U.S. monetary policy failures back on the United States itself to a greater extent than before. Whereas overexpansions of Federal Reserve credit in the 1960s led to inflation abroad, excessive expansions now must be expected to accelerate inflation at home, possibly dangerously so. Excessive U.S. monetary growth now stimulates inflationary forces throughout the dollar bloc by processes familiar from the 1960s. But it also induces dollar depreciation against the currencies of other industrialized countries and places strains on the dollar-centered international system. If an atmosphere of dollar distrust should be permitted to develop, not only would international trade and investment be adversely affected by lack of a suitable value numeraire, but this country could find its internal inflation tragically accelerated.

Growth in Developed and Developing Countries

After declining in 1974 and 1975 and surging in 1976, the growth rate for GNP at constant dollar prices in the United States seemed to be returning in 1977 and 1978 to levels not lower than the 4.3 percent per annum compounded rate for the decade of the 1960s. On a per capita basis, the growth rate was higher, standing at 4.1 percent in 1977 against 3.0 percent for the 1960s. The growth was won, however, at the expense of accelerating inflation. In industrial countries fighting inflation with greater determination, growth rates were slightly lower. Total real GNP growth in seven large OECD members, including the United States, was only 4 percent in 1977 as compared with 5.3 percent on the average between 1959–1960 and 1970–1971. A substantial factor in the change abroad was, of course, the decline in the dramatic growth rate of Japan, from an earlier compounded annual rate of change of 11.1 percent to a still respectable 6 percent. But growth rates in Germany, France, Italy, the United Kingdom, and Canada also were off in 1977. Growth in these countries not only suffered from the transitional effects of anti-inflation measures, but it was no doubt continuing to be influenced by the dislocations and uncertainties arising from the change in oil prices, by the costs of measures to preserve the environment, and by fluctuations in exchange rates. In developing countries measured real growth rates were surprisingly well maintained. World Bank estimates put them at 6.2, 5.5, and 6.1 percent for 1974, 1975, and 1976, as compared with 5.5 for 1961–1965 and 6.3 for 1966–1972.[3]

[3] World Bank, *Annual Report, 1977*, Statistical Annex, table 1.

To the degree that societies have chosen to take some of the growth in their potential product in the form of a cleaner environment, greater job safety, and other "products" not normally captured in the measures of marketed national output, one must expect measured rates of growth to be biased unfavorably in future years compared with the past, even though suitable measures of welfare gains would not show such a change.

International monetary arrangements may affect growth rates in individual nations through the effects on employment levels, on the efficiency with which resources are employed, and on resource transfers among nations. There is some reason to believe that the move to exchange rate flexibility may have salutary consequences in each of these areas.

Flexible exchange rates permit countries individually to pursue overall demand management policies tailored to their structural requirements and to conditions in their labor markets. Diversity across countries in the disturbances encountered, and the absence of that international labor mobility that could help keep the diversity small, is a prime reason that fixed exchange rates have been abandoned. Opportunities now to pursue overall macroeconomic policies more closely tailored to national needs can make possible more sustained high levels of employment than would be possible under a regime requiring that fixed exchange rates be defended.

If governments will allow the exchange rates reasonably freely to reflect changing international conditions, the rates should also make possible an abatement in protectionism and in those distortions in resource allocation which have in the past been introduced by misaligned exchange rates. Therefore, by improving allocative efficiency, too, flexible rates may contribute to growth in individual countries and in the world as a whole.

Progress in poorer countries can be accelerated by achievements of the sort just mentioned. High employment levels and open markets in the more developed countries will help to provide strong and dependable markets for the exports of developing countries, and foreign aid programs can be abetted. Official resource transfers from rich to poor countries tend to be affected by the state of employment and the state of the balance of payments in the major aid-providing countries. To the extent, therefore, that flexible exchange rates contribute to balance of payments equilibrium and to high levels of output in critical industrialized countries—perhaps above all in the United States—they may help sustain those foreign aid programs which make possible a critical increment in developing country growth.

Private international investment need not be adversely affected by exchange rate flexibility and can be favorably affected insofar as flexibility contributes to open national markets for goods and capital. A global market for capital efficiently allocates this scarce resource, and the international elements of such a market are already in place. Improvement in the capital markets within developing countries may now be one of the institutional changes that can contribute most to successful progress in those nations.[4]

Cooperation for Collective Security

The perceived need for collective defense among the industrialized countries of Western Europe, North America, and Asia was for a time in the 1950s and early 1960s a powerful force favoring the quick resolution of differences in economic policy views among the non-Communist nations. In particular, the willingness of the United States to provide military and nonmilitary aid to its defense partners smoothed over incipient differences. But with the emergence of a protracted deficit in the U.S. balance of payments in the 1960s and the fading of U.S. economic hegemony, the NATO alliance became more turbulent. Disputes over trade policy and the sharing of defense burdens undermined U.S. relations with Europe and the U.S. ability to mediate intra-European differences.

If flexible exchange rates now can reduce the role that balance of payments disequilibriums play in such decisions, the vital objectives that the countries hold in common may once again be seen in their proper perspective. Clearly the balances of payments of nations ought to accommodate rather than thwart national purposes, as those purposes are expressed through markets and political decisions. Moreover, a nation's payments imbalance should not be construed as a measure of its ability to contribute to international programs. Its wealth (compared with the wealth of other nations at equilibrium exchange rates) is a superior measure. In the degree that flexible exchange rates can prevent the misassessment of priorities in these matters, they will contribute to collective security as well as to economic well-being in non-Communist countries.

The Future of the Monetary System

While hazardous, it is perhaps not useless to attempt to peer into the future of the monetary system. What is the outlook, for example, for

---

[4] See Ronald I. McKinnon, *Money and Capital in Economic Development* (Washington, D.C.: Brookings Institution, 1972).

the SDR? For the dollar? For monetary blocs? Some opportunities, some false hopes, and some perils seem to be visible.

The SDR. It is difficult to see an important role for the special drawing right in the years to the end of the century. As was pointed out in Chapter 6, official monetary reserves now change, and will no doubt continue to grow in the aggregate, as a result of government decisions to influence the exchange rates. The prophecy that reserves will continue to grow in the aggregate merely predicts that countries whose currencies are under pressure to appreciate will continue to intervene in the exchange markets more than countries whose currencies tend to depreciate. Foreign exchange reserves so acquired are not now convertible into SDRs, and governments have perhaps properly resisted a substitution facility that would replace foreign exchange reserves with new SDR allocations. As pointed out in Chapter 6, the superimposition of an effective SDR-centered system on a working dollar system would require further extensive international monetary regulation. National commitments would include mandatory substitution of SDRs for foreign exchange in reserve holdings, loss to countries of independence in the use of reserves in SDR form, loss of country freedom to balance official portfolios, requirements that countries stand ready to sell SDRs as well as to buy them, and restraints on some countries' acquisitions of additional reserves in the form of foreign exchange. In spite of these commitments, the system would continue to be dominated by U.S. monetary policy unless the use of international credit markets for financing balance of payments deficits were somehow debarred. If it were introduced as an asset to be publicly traded, the SDR would have a value determined by its open market demand and supply. Its supply as a liquid asset would almost unavoidably be influenced by bank willingness to engage in liquidity transformation in SDR denominated assets and liabilities so that control of an SDR contribution to inflationary forces would then be no different from control of any other currency. Regulation would have to be undertaken by national monetary authorities or by an IMF that was transformed into yet another of the world's array of monetary regulators. Dramatic changes in the form and role of the SDR seem in fact unlikely. If, indeed, they are not forthcoming, the significance of SDRs in monetary reserves, already small, will continue to dwindle.

A role for the SDR as a convenient unit of account for both official and private transactions, on the other hand, appears assured, and the use of the unit for that purpose is very likely to grow. An increasing number of countries prescribe their exchange market interventions in terms of their exchange rate against the SDR; and IMF accounts, a number of bond issues, a few short-term claims, and several prices of internationally traded goods and services are stated in terms of the SDR. Flexible exchange rates have emphasized monetary diversity, and further experimentation to adapt accounting units to changing problems will no doubt occur.

The Dollar. If the SDR's future as anything but a unit of account is not bright, is the same to be said of the dollar as an international money? This is a much larger and more important question, and the answer to it is favorable to the future of the dollar system if, but only if, U.S. authorities can be successful in limiting dollar supply. The dollar-centered monetary system has the strength of being a product of natural institutional evolution rather than design. But this system, like any monetary custom, can serve effectively and will be durable only if the monetary unit is kept scarce. It will not thrive and it will be an abomination to the United States if Federal Reserve credit is extended excessively.

This is not to say that the United States continues to serve as the monetary authority for the world in the degree that it did under the Bretton Woods rules. For the United States can no longer export its homemade inflations or recessions to other countries as it could under fixed exchange rates. Nevertheless, U.S. monetary policy will determine the characteristics of the system in a profound way.

Widespread use of the dollar outside the United States at present gives the world some of the virtues of a global money, and the value of this gain should not be discounted. Of the dollar's several external roles, the important ones at this time are its use as a transactions currency for traders and investors in various areas, and its use as a unit of account and a conveyor of information. Its official roles as a component of government monetary reserves and as an intervention currency are less important than the part it plays in the private sector, because official reserves and interventions are, or should be, relatively unimportant in the working of a system that is only lightly managed.

A common currency for private international transactions improves the efficiency of markets by conveying information at low cost and by permitting economies in the holding of cash balances. Market participants can consolidate their holdings into a single currency and are thus able to offset discrepancies in the time flow of payments and receipts in many directions.[5] A single world money, to be used within all countries as well as between them, would be optimum in this regard and for good reason is often mentioned in popular aspirations. But this idyllic arrangement does not itself meet the conditions for a social optimum so long as world factor markets and political institutions are poorly integrated; in the absence of such a system the second-best arrangement is one in which at least the *external* transactions of many traders and investors can be settled with the use of a common currency. This is the advantage that the system is obtaining, albeit not in the full degree possible, from its present dollar orientation. This advantage is revealed by the substantial private and official working balances of dollars that are held by non-U.S. residents out of free choice.

The forces that created the dollar-centered system are of course forces that tend to stabilize its continuance. Governments that have acquired dollar reserves by exchange market interventions aimed at preventing appreciation of their currencies will not lightly sell off those reserves for another asset. This action would worsen the competitive position of their residents as sellers, a situation the governments avoided in the past. Similarly, oil-exporting holders of dollars will hesitate to depreciate the value of their own outstanding dollar claims by any change in the share of their ongoing financial accumulation allotted to dollars. While all governments may therefore, from time to time, consider diversifying their foreign exchange holdings, they will contemplate the exchange rate cost of any move in that direction and set it against the gain expected from diversification. The importance of the United States as a trading nation and the magnitude of the dollar-denominated holdings of foreign governments constitute important sources of stability for present arrangements.

Private dollar holdings outside the United States, however, are less directed by concern for the effects of diversification decisions on the exchange rates. Since individual transactors are small with respect to the market, they disregard their individual market influences. In recent years private holdings have appeared to be a stable function of the level of trade, interest rates, and world wealth.[6] The continuance, however, of that relationship cannot be taken for granted.

[5] A. K. Swoboda, *The Euro-Dollar Market: An Interpretation*, Essays in International Finance, no. 64 (International Finance Section, Princeton University, February 1968).

[6] Peggy Swanson, "Foreign Holders of Short-term Dollar Assets," Ph.D. dissertation, Southern Methodist University, May 1978.

Private dollar balances invested in interest-bearing securities can be expected to be willingly held as long as the excess of dollar interest rates over interest obtainable on similar securities denominated in other money equals the expected rate of depreciation of the dollar against the other money. Inducements for such holders to exchange their dollars for other money will typically arise only when the rate of money growth and inflation in the United States accelerates relative to money growth rates elsewhere. In periods in which this occurs an accelerated rate of dollar depreciation may not initially be offset by an increase in money interest rates; sales of some foreign-held assets will then take place until U.S. interest rates are driven up. Meanwhile, the price of foreign currency will rise as well, and if this leads to expectations of a still higher dollar depreciation rate in the future, further liquidation of dollar assets could take place. The dynamics of these moves need not be stable, at least in the short run, and the events could give rise to chronically accelerating dollar depreciation. If, however, U.S. monetary authorities merely keep U.S. monetary growth rates from *accelerating* vis-à-vis foreign monetary growth rates, such disturbances will be largely avoidable and will be self-limiting when they occur.

But a substantial part of private dollar balances held for purposes of transactions is held in non-interest-bearing demand deposits. The value that the liquidity of the demand deposit form of asset gives to these holders offsets the interest they forgo on other dollar assets. Given a choice between dollar demand deposits and demand deposits in other currencies, however, holders choose dollars only because of their superior utility as a transactions medium. *This difference in utility between national currencies may be offset by any expected change in the value of the dollar relative to the alternative.* Therefore, for holders of non-interest-bearing dollar assets to be willing to continue their dollar preference, the dollar must at least hold its value vis-à-vis foreign currencies. This is the challenge to U.S. monetary authorities. If the United States does not succeed in limiting its rate of inflation to at least the average rate of inflation in other industrialized countries, the dollar will chronically depreciate in value relative to the currencies of the other countries, and the dollar's use for private purposes will be abandoned.

At this time there is admittedly no money asset which is a good alternative to the dollar in its use as a medium for private transactions. Currencies such as deutsche marks and Swiss francs are attractive as assets to holders of internationally liquid money balances, but the supplies of these currencies and the markets for them are small relative to world dollar holdings. Furthermore, to prevent values of the limited supplies of their home currencies from being bid up by demand, both the German and Swiss governments have at various times taken steps to prevent the development of markets that would serve external use of their currencies. Artificial (basket) units of account stand in the wings as possible international monetary mediums, but for now these can be considered only in terms of their potential. An impeccable principle of economics, nevertheless, is that supply has a way of responding to demand. If there is chronic attrition in the value of the dollar relative to the value of other major currencies, there will be attrition on the external demand for dollars to be held for purposes of transactions and chronic growth in demand for alternatives. In time, financial institutions will under these circumstances offer deposits denominated in a unit for which market participants express a preference.

The cost to the international economy of a shift away from a dollar orientation will be substantial if it materializes. In time, the financial market would supply an alternative global monetary medium, but meanwhile important economies in money usage could be lost. The transition period could last a decade or more, during which present holders of dollar balances could retreat to their own national currencies, the system of banks with Eurodollar liabilities could be put in difficulty, and exchange rates would be unsettled along with price levels and production.

Special and possibly tragic burdens would fall on the United States. The flight from the dollar would possibly begin slowly but then accelerate as more private holders of dollars and then governments joined the action, and it would enormously exaggerate the inflationary consequences of an undisciplined U.S. domestic monetary policy. In real terms, Americans would be required to repay the vast credits that accrued to this country in the 1960s and 1970s when foreigners accumulated liquid assets in the United States. Sharp rises in the prices of imports and exports and all domestically produced substitutes for those goods would give rise to an intensified inflation that could be reversed possibly only by a dramatic redistribution of income and wealth, and that might be associated with political upheaval and violence.

Another, and happier, course of events can be envisioned if U.S. monetary policy is restrained adequately to keep the dollar from depreciating against the currencies of most other major trading nations.[7] Such a development will enable a dollar-centered system to thrive and to serve important international monetary needs with ever-growing effectiveness. One can imagine that dollar deposit banking would over time be extended to more and more monetary centers throughout the world, coming to play a part in retail banking wherever dollars were found to serve local as well as international needs for transactions balances. A dollar expected to grow in value relative to other money, even if not in purchasing power, would be everywhere in strong demand. In the event of such an evolution, a central bank controlling the global dollar supply would eventually become a necessity. This path would then have led to great progress toward an efficient global monetary system. Weak currencies would have been replaced in many parts of the world by a strong one, and national monetary autonomy would have begun to wither. The stage would be set for further political integration among nations.

The two lines of evolution described are not mutually exclusive in the short run, although in the long run they may be simple alternatives. Economic policy-making machinery in the United States is not so ineffective as to establish and maintain a course of action leading to early disaster. But neither does it inspire confidence that opportunities for global monetary improvement and defeat of domestic inflation will be exploited. Rather a stop-go policy is likely, with growing inflation concerns leading to occasional spasms of monetary discipline, while increasing experimentation with nonmonetary inflation controls leads to worsening market performance. In the end, this course of action leads to the pessimistic evolutionary alternative but at an unsteady pace.

Americans are in danger of accepting inflation as a way of life, as many other people have come to do, especially in developing economies. But the United States is not a small nation, and the country's short-term liabilities to others of some $185 billion constitute a bomb which will be activated by lax monetary and fiscal policies. While the United States has gained a degree of balance of payments adjustment capability and hence a degree of monetary independence as a result of the move to more flexible exchange rates, it is in a unique position with regard to the cost it will incur if it

[7] The dollar need not hold its own or appreciate against all other currencies in order to continue to be willingly held since economies of scale in its usage are otherwise continuously working to increase its unique utility. But it probably cannot depreciate much in a given period in terms of the trade-weighted needs of any individual or firm holding the dollar for purposes of transactions without causing that holder to consider marginal asset exchanges.

abuses that independence. There is little evidence that this lesson has yet been learned.

Monetary Blocs. It must be expected that countries will continue to experiment with monetary blocs as they perceive changing needs. The arrangement for narrow exchange rate margins in Western Europe has proved durable for a small core of countries, albeit with numerous currency realignments. It may yet be revived on a broader scale if the objectives of stability in the EEC-wide purchasing power of national moneys and the resuscitation of programs which require greater intra-EEC exchange rate stability (such as the common agricultural policy) outweigh the costs countries are likely to encounter in their efforts to harmonize overall demand policies. In the summer of 1978 a proposal to centralize a substantial proportion of the international monetary reserves of EEC countries was announced with the objective of stabilizing exchange rates among participants and providing a European counterweight, which would presumably not fluctuate as much against the dollar as have individual European currencies. The plan is significant and is alleged to have the support of both the French and the German governments. In view of the frailty of past arrangements for fixed exchange rates in Europe, however, one cannot be sanguine that they are going to be durably established now. While the commitment of massive reserves to a common stabilization fund is a show of force, in the end reserves are not what count. It is the willingness of countries to endure over- or undervalued currencies, with consequences for the prosperity of important domestic interest groups, that determines the durability of such arrangements. Until the French and the Germans can agree to reasonably synchronous demand policies and can satisfy domestic political needs while doing so, they will not forge a durable exchange rate between their currencies.

In less developed countries, the approach to regional monetary blocs based on local currencies has generally been hesitant and seems likely to continue so. Currency arrangements are repeatedly put forward as means of accelerating economic growth in such countries and of enhancing regional solidarity. In fact they commonly contribute little to either. Of themselves, they do not facilitate efficient resource allocation and may impair it, if they have any effect at all, and they give rise to sources of friction that might have been avoided among neighbors. Arrangements in effect in the late 1970s range from simple clearing agreements to monetary unions with pooled international reserves. Most involve few commitments, however, that limit national monetary independence.

Since many developing countries are small, they have linked the external value of their respective currencies more or less loosely to the dollar, or to the currency of a country with which they have cultural and economic ties, or to the SDR or another basket accounting unit. The particular exchange rates at which the linkages are made are typically thought of as impermanent, and indeed the nature of the linkage itself is continuously open to review. The arrangements *de facto* define monetary blocs, but each country's adherence to the bloc is only as permanent as the arrangement is convenient to the adherent. The independence to proceed in this way is one of the few rewards of being economically small, and it is predictable that individual developing countries will continue carefully to guard that independence. In view of the advantages that flexible exchange rates have for even developing countries, where those countries exercise monetary independence, it seems likely that the loose bonds that now bind currencies into discernible blocs will become looser. In the event of a more sanguine evolution of the dollar-centered system, however, competition of the dollar for local usage would in many countries require a monetary policy closely allied to that for the dollar. The cement holding the dollar bloc together would then become harder.

Apart from the acceleration of worldwide inflation and the move to more flexible exchange rates, the dramatic development in the international economy of the 1960s and 1970s was the strengthening of market organization on a global scale for both short-term money and long-term capital. The institutional changes that have occurred are unlikely to be reversed. They imply an increased mobility of capital from country to country that sets the stage for more profound changes in world society that can only be imagined at present.

The multinationalization of production facilities, supported by multinational banking, has certainly created incentives for a parallel multinationalization of trade union activity as labor in one country finds itself increasingly a substitute for labor in other countries. In an effort to curb the ability of managements to shift production among nations to take advantage of labor cost differentials, the unions will make great efforts to bridge the gaps across countries that now separate them. If international confederation proves at all possible, internal pressures within the confederations could arise that would work toward reducing national barriers to labor mobility. Whatever materializes along these or other lines that has the effect of harmonizing labor market conditions across countries will make the international synchronization of demand policies less costly. With improved synchronization of national aggregate demand strategies would come smaller variation in the exchange rates.

The penetration of national boundaries by international investors, in countless repetition, will weave a pattern of common interest that can strengthen political ties among market-oriented economies. This closeness, however, may be in contrast with the development of ties between market-oriented and radical socialist regimes. For while trade and investment will cross the lines between the groups, the hesitant pace of East-West commercial contacts will be surpassed by the intensification of contacts within the groups. The prevention of situations that might build up to armed conflict could become more difficult in such a world.

Assuming the avoidance of nuclear war and other highly destructive forms of international conflict, the challenges to the non-Communist industrialized countries in the 1980s are to curb inflation, to improve economic efficiency and maintain technological progress, and to sustain those transfers within and between nations that are necessary to ensure widespread access to the opportunities for affluence.

The control of inflation in the United States is at the center of these challenges. Orderly movements of the exchange rates can help in the improvement of efficiency and in maintaining an international flow of development capital. But progress toward the reduction of inflation is in the hands of democratically responsible governments, and the position of the United States in a dollar-oriented system poses for its democratic institutions what could be a critical test. Indeed, monetary policy in the United States appears to occupy a position near the front of the stage in the drama of economic history about to be played.

Epilogue, August 1978–February 1979

Events of the fall and winter of 1978–1979 extended major trends surveyed in this book. The developments help sustain hope that some opportunities may be grasped, but they also reveal commitments by governments and international organizations to goals that are unwise. Major events of the period include a series of measures taken at the International Monetary Fund to extend that organization's balance of payments financing capability, the launching of the European Monetary System (EMS), and a very welcome reappraisal of monetary policy in the United States.

Changes at the International Monetary Fund

The seventh general review of IMF quotas, in progress since 1976, ended in December 1978 with adoption of an IMF Board of Governors resolution increasing members' quotas by 50 percent, from a total of SDR39 billion to SDR58.6 billion. Members having 75 percent of 1978 quotas must approve their respective quota changes and pay their additional subscriptions before November 1980 to make the new amounts effective. Governors also approved in December SDR12 billion of new special drawing rights allocations. These are to be carried out in installments totaling SDR4 billion each in 1979, 1980, and 1981. Further, in February 1979 the Fund's supplementary financing facility (at one time referred to as the Witteveen facility) became operational; this made another SDR7.75 billion of resources available for IMF lending. Through these several measures, therefore, the IMF has arranged for new official balance of payments financing power, amounting to SDR39.35 billion, to become available over the next three years. In addition to these steps, the governors agreed in

December to reduce from 30 to 15 percent the proportion of cumulative SDR allocations to which each member must reconstitute its SDR holdings over moving five-year periods. This action has the effect of releasing for long-term use some 1.5 billion SDRs heretofore tied up in required balances; it also, of course, extends the usability of future allocations.

The actions at the IMF unfortunately contrast with the recommendations in this study that the Fund focus for the time being on its surveillance responsibilities rather than on balance of payments financing. The chief results of the steps to increase the Fund's resources will be to prolong inflationary policies in some countries and to facilitate the transmission of the effects of those policies to the rest of the world. Some observers may argue that it is better to have conditional balance of payments financing available through the IMF than to have countries with deficits turn to the open market where loan conditions can be less strict. But clearly the imposition of IMF conditions is not as restraining to users as would be the unavailability of IMF credit, for otherwise countries would not accept the IMF terms. Those who favor more IMF conditional credit capability also argue that much financing is important to ensure that countries do not attempt to solve their balance of payments problems by trade restrictions. But relief from protectionist pressures can also be obtained through prompt and appropriate exchange rate changes, and in any case countries have commitments under the GATT to avoid illiberal policies. If global inflation is to be subdued, improved demand management techniques, exchange rate adjustments, and the GATT commitments, rather than a turn to new financing, must be relied on at this time as the international community's chief defense of an open trading system.

In summary, one cannot help but see the provision of new resources for balance of payments financing as evidence that political leaders continue to be excessively concerned for the possibility of deficient monetary demand in the world. Governments' willingness to mitigate some problems by widening the likelihood of an inflation problem has reached a stage that involves high risk to productivity and political stability in society.

The European Monetary System

Stemming from decisions taken in principle in July 1978, the European Monetary System was launched on March 13, 1979. Its objectives are the creation of a zone of monetary stability in Europe and greater convergence of economic policies among participating countries. The new system is, in essence, an extension and elaboration of the older narrow margins exchange rate arrangement (the snake) through which the currencies of a number of countries have been linked in more or less fixed relationships since 1972. A new currency, the European currency unit (ECU), with a value equal to a weighted average of the nine European Community member currencies, is given prominence as the exchange rate numeraire for the group and as the basis for official intermember financial settlements. Participating countries are initially to swap 20 percent of their gold and of their dollars with the European Monetary Cooperation Fund for ECUs and are to renew those swaps each six months. Existing short- and medium-term financial assistance programs for countries experiencing balance of payments difficulties are continued. With the withdrawal of Norway, the snake arrangement was reduced at the end of 1978 to four currencies—those of Germany, Belgium-Luxembourg, the Netherlands, and Denmark. The European Monetary System now reintroduces France, Italy, and Ireland to the scheme. Of the members of the European Economic Community, only the United Kingdom remains outside. Italy, however, has initially availed itself of the opportunity to maintain ± 6 percent exchange rate margins on the other currencies of the group instead of the margins of ± 2.25 percent which the other countries will maintain.

The grid of central exchange rates and the prescribed intervention intervals establish a pattern of exchange rates at which the central banks must intervene to restrain movements of the market rates. A divergence indicator reflects the degree to which each currency is moving away from the average for the others, and at a threshold level it is presumed that the government concerned will consider changes in its policies. Intervention at the obligatory intervention limits may apparently take place in any of the participating currencies or, alternatively, in the currency of an external country. Intervention may also take place when exchange rates are within the margins.

On the delicate but critical question of policy coordination, the European Council's December 5 resolution establishing the EMS is unfortunately not detailed. It declares, "We are firmly resolved to ensure the lasting success of the EMS by policies conducive to greater stability at home and abroad for both deficit and surplus countries," and it requests economic and finance ministers to strengthen "procedures for coordination" in order to improve convergence of policies. But there are no new formal obligations.

While some journalists have hailed the EMS as a step toward a common currency for Europe, there seems little in the experience since 1972, or in the commitments now undertaken, to support bold claims or hopes. Until labor and capital have sufficient mobility among EEC countries that the countries experience excess demands or supplies in the labor market at about the same time and governments can justify common monetary and fiscal policies, it will be difficult for nations to relinquish their independence to deal with pressing domestic problems. As long as European governments engage in divergent monetary and fiscal policies, the goal of maintaining fixed ratios in the values of their currencies will remain unrealistic. Policy coordination of the sort recommended in Chapter 5 would provide opportunities for European countries to satisfy the need for internal stabilization policies with minimal disturbance to international trading relationships under flexible exchange rates. In my view such an approach would be superior to the effort governments now make to maintain a fragile intra-EC exchange rate grid.

Monetary Policy in the United States

In a number of ways, in August and September 1978, prominent members of the executive branch of government in the United States made clear the administration's reluctance to incur any threat to its employment and growth targets in order to curb inflation. The President himself said in September, after another rise in the Federal Reserve discount rate in August, that he thought interest rates were too high and that "high interest rates hurt our country." Remarkably, that statement came at a time when the rate of expansion of Federal Reserve credit had been above its trend for months, when real interest rates, viewed in the light of inflation, were certainly very low, and when the dollar's foreign exchange value had been sliding for more than a year. Then, in October, the anti-inflation program announced by the administration focused only on voluntary public adherence to wage and price standards and slowly declining government budget deficits. It was conspicuously silent on the vital issue of monetary policy. The consequence of these misjudgments was a flight from the dollar in the final week of October and a critically sharp depreciation of the foreign exchange value of the currency. Then, on November 1, faced by the necessity to rescue the dollar internationally, the President himself announced a turnaround in Federal Reserve policy.

The discount rates at all the Federal Reserve Banks were raised a full percentage point, and reserve requirements on selected large-denomination time deposits were increased. To provide immediate support to the foreign exchange value of the dollar, the government assembled a package of up to $30 billion of foreign currencies to be used for exchange market intervention. The Treasury also announced an expansion in its program of gold sales.

This more restrictive monetary policy resulted in an actual decline of the narrowly defined U.S. money supply (M_1) between the end of October and the end of February and in a dramatic slowing of the growth of M_2—the money supply measure which includes time deposits. The growth of broader measures of money holdings, however, accelerated as households and firms continued to seek means of obtaining higher returns on reasonably liquid assets. The restraint in discretionary policy, nonetheless, was shown clearly by the fact that Federal Reserve credit outstanding not only ceased its growth but declined in the period.

In spite of the monetary restraint, the inflation of wholesale and consumer prices accelerated in the early months of 1979. The increased velocity of turnover of M_1 and M_2 during the 1978–1979 winter presumably represented in some degree a temporary public adaptation to declining real cash balances, in some degree a natural activation of balances created earlier, and in some degree an independent result of heightened inflationary expectations. The expansion of Federal Reserve credit that had taken place in mid-1978 apparently ensured that there was no shortage of liquidity in the economy in December and January, and this facilitated the continued expansion of spending. Efforts by sellers to hedge themselves against the new program of wage and price standards also added to the inflationary spurt. After announcement of the President's program in October, sellers had a strong economic incentive to press prices upward wherever they could before effective enforcement of the measures to avoid being caught later with too low a price or a record of low price increases. Restraint on growth of Federal Reserve credit could be expected to slow aggregate spending in due time if the restraint were maintained and if it were sufficiently tight, but a lag was inevitable before the effect of the policy would be visible.

The monetary actions of November did stop the long decline in the dollar's external value, at least temporarily. After appreciating 5.5 percent in November the dollar settled down in subsequent months to an average value some 3 percent above its low point. Proponents of exchange market intervention pointed to the use of approximately

$5 billion of the U.S. intervention arsenal as the cause of the dollar's new stability. But it seems likely that improved public confidence in U.S. policies and higher U.S. interest rates relative to those in Central Europe and Japan were more important.

The closing paragraph of Chapter 9 of this book suggests that monetary policy in the United States will be near the center of the stage in the economic history of the 1980s. The restrictive measures at last introduced in November 1978 are changes in the right direction. The fact that they did not come until there was a clear and present international danger, however, raises the question whether genuine restraint will be sustained through national elections in 1980 and beyond. The 1978–1979 program of wage and price standards does little more than obscure the true nature of the inflation problem in the United States. The standards will be either unnecessary or unenforceable, depending on the degree of monetary expansion finally decided upon. It is to be hoped that politicians do not yield to misguided advice to try to make wage and price controls mandatory if monetary policy makes the "voluntary" form of the controls unworkable. Mandatory controls would represent a long, and perhaps irreversible, further step by the United States into pressure group management of the national economy and toward a society in which goals of efficiency and justice would be subjugated to the struggle of groups for power and advantage. Especially if the step were accompanied by continued excessive monetary expansion, it would certainly erode hope for an orderly international monetary system in our time.